The New York Times
ESSENTIAL LIBRARY

Opera

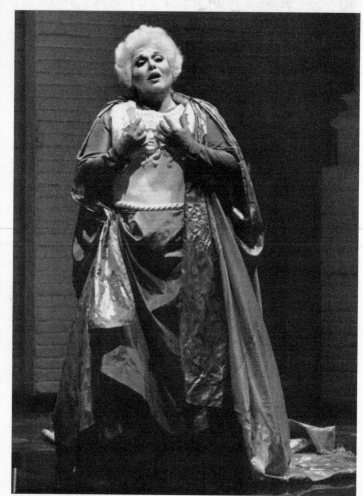

Mezzo-soprano Marilyn Horne as Arsace in Semiramide

The New York Times
ESSENTIAL LIBRARY

Opera

A Critic's Guide to the 100
Most Important Works
and the Best Recordings

ANTHONY TOMMASINI

TIMES BOOKS
Henry Holt and Company   New York

Times Books
Henry Holt and Company, LLC
Publishers since 1866
115 West 18th Street
New York, New York 10011

Library of Congress Cataloging-in-Publication Data
Tommasini, Anthony, date.
    Opera : a critic's guide to the 100 most important works and the best
recordings / Anthony Tommasini—1st ed.
    p. cm.—(The New York times essential library)
Includes bibliographical references (p.) and index.
ISBN 0-8050-7459-7
1. Operas—Discography. I. Title. II. Series.

ML156.4.O46T66 2004
782.1'0266—dc22   2004049846

First Edition 2004

Designed by Paula Russell Szafranski

Printed in the United States of America

1 3 5 7 9 10 8 6 4 2

Contents

Preface

Opera is a form of theater. Though this may seem obvious, it's too often forgotten. So, naturally, the best way to experience opera, the best way to learn about it, is by attending performances at the opera house. Even if you're new to the genre, take my advice and just go. Don't be hesitant to attend something cold. Ever since opera houses introduced supertitles and other systems of simultaneous translation, it hasn't even been essential to read a plot synopsis in advance. Suddenly, even neophytes are getting the point: "Ah, I'm at a show; I can just sit back and take it in."

Yet, opera is specifically a form of musical theater. The drama is inextricably bound to the music, and a great opera offers an abundance of great music. Hopefully, after going to your first *La Bohème,* you will want to immerse yourself in its music, to experience great singers past and present in these benchmark roles, to hear the score performed by artists with powerful connections to the work, like Arturo Toscanini, who conducted the 1896 premiere of *La Bohème,* then recorded it famously with the NBC Symphony and a memorable cast fifty years later.

This is why recordings of complete operas have long been cherished by opera buffs. I never heard Maria Callas perform live. Yet when I listen to her stunning 1954 recording of Bellini's *Norma,* I have a palpable sense of what it must have been like to experience her portrayal of this all-encompassing role in person. Then there are the many invaluable recordings of fascinating operas that, for whatever reasons, are not often performed, like Rimsky-Korsakov's enchanting *The Legend of the Invisible City of Kitezh,* a repertory work in St. Petersburg, Russia, but nowhere else.

Moreover, for all the excitement of attending an opera, there is something about hearing recordings at home, about getting away from the theatrical experience and focusing your full attention on music that actually enhances your feeling for the drama.

This book offers one hundred short essays on operas I consider essential, including recommendations of recordings. This is not a book of plot synopses. Though such books are immensely useful, there already are many of them. (Try John W. Freeman's two-volume *Stories of the Great Operas,* published jointly by the Metropolitan Opera Guild and W. W. Norton.) While summarizing story lines is not my primary goal, in discussing an opera, I inevitably delve into its characters and plot. My aim is to give an overall sense of the work—its place in the repertory, the achievement it represents, the challenges it poses, its historical context, the background of its composer, whatever seems most pertinent—and to suggest why a recording or two are the ones to own. I have tried to tuck overall comments about the backgrounds and creative approaches of the major opera composers into the essays on their works. Only in the case of Mozart have I prefaced my entries on the operas with a general introduction. It seemed to me that the crosscurrents of the international opera scene during the years of Mozart's life and his uncanny ability to sail through them required a larger context.

One problem: these days any book that recommends opera recordings is subject to being instantaneously obsolete. For a lot of complex reasons, including the economic slowdown and the proliferation of CDs, the classical music recording industry has been floundering for years. Instead of seeing the financial challenge as an opportunity to redefine their artistic missions, most recording companies responded by flooding the market with releases in hopes that a few would catch on. Important recordings have been blithely eliminated from the catalogs. By now the worst of the crisis is over, it would seem, and new means of distribution, especially through the Internet, are enabling companies to keep more of their products available.

Still, given the volatility of the market, I have tried as often as possible to recommend recordings that are so fixed in the discography that they seldom disappear from the stores, or are obtainable from on-line services like amazon.com and barnesandnoble.com. And in most cases I list a few choices, including more recent releases that are likely to be available.

A word about DVDs. Obviously, a DVD of a live opera performance offers visual as well as audio elements, which is quite an enticement. No previous technology has been taken up by the public so quickly. Still, as of this writing, most of the truly classic recordings of operas are only available on CDs. So I only recommend recordings.

Besides, call me retro, but for home enjoyment I still prefer opera recordings to DVDs. I never tire of listening to a great historic performance like the conductor Otto Klemperer's magisterial, exciting account of Beethoven's *Fidelio* starring the colossal tenor Jon Vickers and the incomparable mezzo-soprano Christa Ludwig. It offers the chance to get lost in the music without visual distraction.

So, for whom is this book intended? Though I hope what I have to say about these works and their composers will be of interest to all opera aficionados, I particularly want to reach newcomers. The book is not intended as an opera primer. Still, I'd like to offer some general remarks about a few crucial topics that can be confusing to inexperienced operagoers.

1. VOICE TYPES

In theory, this should not be a controversial subject. The five main vocal categories in opera, based on range and in descending order from high to low, are: soprano, mezzo-soprano, tenor, baritone, and bass. But there are subcategories in each type, more than you might imagine. A roomful of impassioned opera buffs thrashing out the true essence of Cecilia Bartoli's voice would make a roomful of baseball fanatics arguing over whether a Yankees pitcher is by natural endowment a starter or reliever look like rarified parliamentarians.

The main thing to know is that each voice category has lyric and dramatic branches. Lyric voices tend to be lighter, brighter, and more agile. Dramatic voices are heavier, darker, less agile, but more powerful. Ingenue roles, like Mozart's Pamina and Strauss's Sophie, call for lyric soprano voices. In contrast, Wagner's Brünnhilde is the textbook example of a dramatic soprano role.

Yet there are operatic roles that ideally require voices that can combine the floating highs and shimmer of a lyric voice with the thrust and weight of a dramatic voice. For sopranos, such roles include Verdi's two Leonoras (in *Il Trovatore* and *La Forza del Destino*) and Puccini's Cio-Cio San (in *Madama Butterfly*). Sopranos who specialize in these hybrid roles are called spintos, or, more specifically, lirico spintos.

These distinctions hold true for all voice types. For example, we need lyric tenors for roles like Donizetti's Nemorino, dramatic tenors for Wagner's Tristan, and the tenorial equivalent of spintos for Verdi's Manrico.

Many singers wind up hurting their voices by singing roles inappropriate to their voice type. Yet, a great operatic voice sometimes defies categorization. Callas's soprano voice was probably too dark and weighty for a role like Rosina in *The Barber of Seville,* but her recording of it is fascinating, a triumph of going against type. By nature, Luciano Pavarotti's voice was a classic lyric tenor. But his voice had far more sound and substance than a typical lyric's. This tempted Pavarotti into weightier roles, like Verdi's Radames, which in his prime he sang wonderfully, with an uncanny combination of fine-spun lyricism and heroic heft. But some opera purists argue that Pavarotti went against his vocal nature when he moved beyond the lyric repertory. In a way, he did. And I'd say, thank you, Luciano. What hurt him in the latter part of his career was not that he sang too many inappropriate roles, but that he rested on his renown and did not discipline himself.

Finally, a word on castrati. For those who may not know this, a castrato was a male singer who had had his testicles removed before puberty so that his voice retained a high register. These singers were the superstars of opera during most of the eighteenth century. Many castrati grew to be hulking adults with barrel chests and enormous vocal power. Their clarion voices must have been something to hear. But, for all sorts of reasons that anyone, certainly any man, could imagine, the practice lost favor. Today those roles are taken either by women costumed as men or by the new generation of skillful counter-tenors, David Daniels and Bejun Mehta among them.

2. RECITATIVE

All genres of musical drama need a way to advance the story quickly, convey background information to the audience, and allow for quick exchanges between the characters. The Broadway musical accomplishes this through spoken dialogue. Some operas have spoken dialogue as well, and not just frothy operettas like *Die Fledermaus,* but also gripping dramas like *Carmen.*

Still, most opera composers, from Monteverdi to Messiaen, have relied on recitative, or some kind of musical equivalent, to advance the plot. It's easiest to recognize recitative in its "secco" (or "dry") manifestation, as in the Mozart operas, when, for example, Figaro and Susanna banter in the first scene about the true intentions of Count Almaviva. Their vocal recitatives capture the natural flow and sputtering rhythms of speech and are accompanied only by a harpsichord.

Elsewhere in the Mozart operas, including whole stretches of *The Marriage of Figaro,* you encounter a heightened form of recitative called either "recitativo accompagnato" or sometimes "dramatic recitative." This style involves vocal lines that have more lyrical substance and are accompanied by larger groups of instruments or even the full orchestra. Arias, though often the most melodic and memorable moments of an opera, tend to be dramatically static.

As opera developed in the late eighteenth and nineteenth centuries, the distinctions between recitative and aria lessened. Verdi, especially in his early works, still clung to the convention of traditional, orchestra-accompanied recitative. But he blended it so deftly into his scores that you almost don't notice when the recitative stops and the aria begins.

Wagner was the master of the through-composed score, meaning a score in which the music seems to just ebb and flow and spin on and on without clear sectional divisions. But even Wagner gives his characters the Wagnerian equivalent of recitative. For example, in act 2 of *Die Walküre,* the progress of the opera essentially stops as Wotan slowly, haltingly, painfully, relates the whole sorry and secretive tale of his life to his beloved daughter Brünnhilde, the Valkyrie of the title. If performed with dramatic tautness by a powerful Wagnerian bass, like Hans Hotter in the golden age and James Morris more recently, this creepingly slow and seemingly inert scene can be intensely moving. Audience appreciation of "Wotan's Narrative," as it is called, has been boosted by the adoption of supertitles. What used to seem like snooze time now seems riveting when you can follow Wotan's every word.

3. BEL CANTO

Finally, I offer some points about bel canto, a basic but confusing aspect of opera. The confusion comes from the fact that "bel canto," which translates, literally, as "beautiful singing" or "beautiful song," applies both to a style of vocal writing and voice technique, and to a specific period in opera history that exemplified this style.

In its purest sense, bel canto refers to an esteemed tradition of Italian singing, dating from the seventeenth century, that values beautiful tone, evenness of sound throughout the range, proper breath support for the voice, elegant legato (meaning "connected") phrasing, and technical agility. As opera developed, these principles of singing remained. Even Wagner, who demanded unprecedented levels of stamina and power from singers, still espoused the bel canto approach to singing. The tradition and technique remain basic components of every singer's training.

But bel canto also refers to the era of opera in the late eighteenth and early nineteenth centuries that put these principles into practice. Rossini, Bellini, and Donizetti are considered the purest exponents of the bel canto operatic style. Their operas give enormous priority to the vocal line. Melodies are long-spun, rich with coloratura filigree, and highly ornamented (typically with embellishments of the singer's choice). These composers understood that singers would shape, float, animate, and embellish the melodic lines with considerable freedom. To their detractors, bel canto operas are musically thin. But the tradition is best considered a less-is-more art form. Harmonic and orchestral complexities are kept to a minimum in deference to rich, elegant melodic writing and the glorious human voice.

The point to remember is that while Verdi's turbulent *Otello*, a masterpiece of his late years, is hardly a bel canto opera, remnants of the tradition run through the score. Verdi fully expected singers taking on these roles to have been thoroughly trained in bel canto technique. He wanted a powerful tenor for Otello, but he intended the role to be sung, not shouted.

A WORD ON MY CHOICES

If you are new to the genre, one hundred operas may seem like a lot. Yet, Verdi alone wrote twenty-eight operas, of which at least ten are unassailable masterpieces. And if you count the *Ring* cycle as four operas, there are arguably ten Wagner operas essential to any list of one hundred. Trying to whittle my choices was not easy.

Some opera buffs may find certain of my inclusions and exclusions quirky. But opera is an ongoing art form and it was important to me to choose a sizeable number of twentieth-century works (and two very early twenty-first-century works). So, Busoni's *Doktor Faust* made my list but Gounod's *Faust* did not. If that seems heretical, my thinking was that the popular Gounod work has been vastly overpraised and does not need a boost from me, while Busoni's fascinating opera, still little-known, can use some help. And I wanted the book to reflect at least some of my more recent passions, like the operas of Prokofiev. I also wanted to include at least a few important chamber operas, like Britten's *The Turn of the Screw* and Judith

Weir's *A Night at the Chinese Opera.* This meant, here and there, leaving out major works like Wagner's *Lohengrin* and Strauss's *Arabella.* And, regrettably, some of the recent operas that have really excited me have not yet been recorded, like Kaija Saariaho's *L'Amour de Loin,* which I saw at the Salzburg Festival, and Thomas Adès's *The Tempest,* which had an acclaimed world premiere at London's Covent Garden in 2003.

Trust me. This book includes essays on almost all of the operas considered staples. As to my more personal choices, especially from the twentieth century, know that every unfamiliar opera I have included in this guide is a work I deeply admire and strongly recommend.

1. JOHN ADAMS (b. 1947)

Nixon in China

Alice Goodman, librettist

First performance: Houston Grand Opera, October 22, 1987

Countless operas have originated with a librettist proposing an idea to a composer. But *Nixon in China* has got to be one of few operas that began as the idea of a director. In 1983 Peter Sellars approached the composer John Adams with the notion of creating an opera about President Nixon's breakthrough visit to China in February 1972. Adams, who was reared in a liberal Democratic household in New Hampshire and remains proud to have cast his first vote for the anti Vietnam War candidate Eugene McCarthy in the Democratic primary of 1968, the year of Nixon's election, was resistant at first. By the early 1980s, Adams felt, Richard Nixon had become easy fodder for humorists and a focal point for legitimate national outrage.

But, as Adams has written, after the poet Alice Goodman signed on to the project, proposing to write a libretto in rhymed couplets, the opera took on a wonderfully complex guise, "part epic, part satire, part a parody of political posturing, and part serious examination of historical, philosophical and even gender issues."

The opera examines an event that was an audacious exercise in the manipulation of public opinion as practiced by two masters: Nixon and Chairman Mao. That the meeting took place at all was the point, and the opera reflects this. Not much else happens. It begins with the ceremonial arrival in Beijing of Air Force One, a "coup de theatre," as Adams puts it, "worthy of *Aida*," with pulsing, brassy music at once exultant and garish, complete with a sly quote of the magic sword motif from Wagner's *Ring*. As the scene continues, Adams and Goodman reveal the subtext of the encounter in ways that only opera can.

Next we witness the formal meeting of Nixon, Mao, Chou, and Henry Kissinger (the one portrayal that slips into oafish caricature, though many would say that Kissinger deserved it). That the Chinese are investing this encounter with a genuine philosophical import that eludes the Americans is palpably suggested by the awkward interchanges of views expressed and the contrasting takes on the concept of revolution and contemporary history. Act 1 ends with a grand banquet scene, though relentlessly insistent rhythm patterns in the orchestra and overly forced choral exhortations convey the personal tensions and political posturing that are really at play.

For many, the most crucial scene in the opera comes in act 2 when Pat Nixon is given a tour of a commune and the Summer Palace. She is presented as the embodiment of the political wife, who has embraced family values and her husband's causes, having long ago learned to shield her insecurity and depression behind a stoic smile. Yet in a long, affecting aria she conveys genuine fragility and essential decency. You identify with her bafflement about the world. "This is prophetic!" she sings as she pauses before the Gate of Longevity and Good Will. "I foresee a time will come when luxury dissolves into the atmosphere like a perfume, and ev'rywhere the simple virtues root and branch and leaf and flower."

At the end of the opera the five principals are seen in the loneliness of their separate beds, each confronting personal regrets and reflecting on opportunities lost. "How much of what we did was good?" asks Chou En-lai.

When *Nixon in China* received its 1987 premiere at the Houston Grand Opera, some critics and opera buffs found Adams's score, with its long stretches of repetitive riffs, lacking in purely musical interest. This was an opera conceived by a director. It seemed to some that music took a backseat, like a score to a film.

But beneath the rippling minimalist surface of Adams's music there are rhythmic and contrapuntal intricacies to savor, as well as wry and ingenious evocations of everything from Richard Wagner to Glenn Miller. And the penetrating characterizations stay with you, especially as performed by the original cast members, who recorded the work in 1990 with Edo de Waart conducting the Orchestra of St. Luke's. The baritone James Maddalena captures the jerky speech patterns and uptightness of Richard Nixon, while still managing to sing with robust vocalism. The baritone Sanford Sylvan as Chou En-lai, the bass-baritone Thomas Hammons as Henry Kissinger, tenor John Duykers as Mao, and the soprano Carolann Page as Pat Nixon are all excellent. You can tell how much they admire Adams's music and Goodman's words from the involvement they project and the clarity of their diction.

Nonesuch (three CDs) 79177
Edo de Waart (conductor), Orchestra of St. Luke's; Maddalena, Page, Sylvan, Hammons, Duykers

2. BÉLA BARTÓK (1881–1945)
Bluebeard's Castle

Béla Balázs, librettist

First performance: Budapest Opera, May 24, 1918

Bartók was nearing thirty in 1911 when he wrote his only opera, *Bluebeard's Castle,* a grim and unconventional one-act work. Bartók's collaborator was the writer Béla Balázs, a contemporary who, like Bartók, was interested in creating something both idiomatically Hungarian and bracingly modern. The fairy tale by Charles Perrault that they settled on as a subject had been told before with different slants. As is explained in a spoken prologue to the opera, often omitted in performance, this operatic version is meant as an interior drama, a reflection of action that ideally will take place within the mind of each spectator.

In legendary times, Duke Bluebeard brings his new young wife, Judith, to his bleak and Gothic castle. Judith has heard the rumors that Bluebeard murdered his previous wives but she refuses to believe them, convinced that her love can bring peace of mind to her husband's world. The central hall of the castle is a vast circular room with seven massive doors. Judith is intensely curious to know what lies behind them. Husband and wife must have no secrets from one another, she says. Frightened but determined, she tells Bluebeard that she can hear the walls weeping and wants to warm and dry them. Symbolically, as many commentators have noted, the walls represent Bluebeard's head, long grown numb to feeling and pain.

Those who know Bartók's later work, which incorporates elements of eastern European folk music into an unhinged harmonic idiom, will not likely recognize the ethnic music influences in this score, which are much more subtle. Bartók draws from ancient modes, prevalent in the folk music of his region, to inflect the opera with a plaintive earthiness. There are scant moments of real lyricism. Most of the vocal writing conforms closely to the contours of the Hungarian words. In contrast to Bluebeard's stolid and chilling vocal lines, Judith's are more varied, skittish, and animated, to suggest the ways she tries to loosen the rigid confines of her husband's world.

Bluebeard refuses to give Judith the keys to the doors. But in beguilingly romantic music she wears him down. The first door flies open to reveal a hideous torture chamber. Judith must know more, so she extracts a second key. This door contains a chamber of armaments. Together these two rooms represent the means by which Bluebeard wields his fearsome power. Having let Judith go this far, Bluebeard seems to want his wife to delve more. So in turn he relinquishes three more keys, whose doors reveal a radiant jewel house (conveyed by a riot of harps and celesta in the orchestra), a leafy garden, and, to the pealing tones of an organ and a brass choir, a vista of Bluebeard's domain.

Judith sees blood again. But her husband seems overcome. Could this young woman actually bring light to his life? The next door reveals a lake of tears. The light fades, the music deflates, and bleakness returns. Judith questions Bluebeard about his previous wives. Perhaps the rumors are true. Sure enough, through the final door emerge three silent and vacant-eyed women, Bluebeard's previous wives. They are, he explains, the loves of his dawns, noons, and evenings. Judith, the most beautiful of all, is to be the love of his nights. Taking her place, Judith enters the door with the other three wives and Bluebeard is left alone in his dank and forbidding castle.

Béla Bartók

If this opera is not often staged, one reason is that it calls for a huge orchestra, among the largest of any Bartók work. Also, it's hard to find something to pair with this overwhelming yet unconventional sixty-minute opera to make a full evening. Yet, as many critics have pointed out, because *Bluebeard's Castle* is such an interior drama, its impact comes through on a recording, none more so than the 1988 account with Adam Fischer conducting the Hungarian State Orchestra. The gleaming-voiced Hungarian soprano Eva Marton captures both the vulnerability and plucky determination of Judith, and sings the text with stylistic command. Samuel Ramey brings his stentorian bass to his gripping portrayal of Bluebeard. Fischer conducts an urgent and vibrantly colored performance.

If you have trouble finding this Sony Classical recording, another excellent version, reissued in 1998 on Decca's Legends series and surely available, offers István Kertész conducting the London Symphony Orchestra in a 1965 performance with the great mezzo-soprano Christa Ludwig as Judith and the bass-baritone Walter Berry as Bluebeard.

Bluebeard's Castle shocked Bartók's contemporaries. The Budapest Opera was reluctant to present it until, six years after its composition, Bartók and Balázs had a success with their ballet *The Wooden Prince*. The opera had its premiere in a double bill with the ballet in 1918.

Sony Classical (one CD) MK 4452
Adam Fischer (conductor), Hungarian State Orchestra; Marton, Ramey

Decca (one CD) 466377
István Kertész (conductor), London Symphony Orchestra; Ludwig, Berry

3. LUDWIG VAN BEETHOVEN (1770–1827)

Fidelio

Joseph von Sonnleithner (original 1805 version), librettist, with later revisions by others for the productions of 1806 and 1814, the final version

First performance: Vienna, Theater an der Wien, November 20, 1805 (original version); Kärntnertortheater, May 23, 1814 (final version)

Beethoven's instrumental music abounds with endless subtleties and ambiguities of expression. Yet in his personal life, despite his volatile mood swings, chronic irritability, and bouts of sentimentality (as H. L. Mencken put it, Beethoven managed his household servants by alternately overpaying them and heaving crockery at them), he was rigid and moralistic and evinced little sympathy for human frailties. It's not surprising that he had scant feeling for musical drama. When he finally determined to write an opera, with a commission from the Theater an der Wien in Vienna, he chose a somewhat two-dimensional subject whose themes of unjust suffering and heroic determination resonated with him: at the time, in 1804, he was anguished by the tragic deterioration of his hearing.

It took Beethoven ten years and three different versions of this opera (with four different overtures) before the work we know today as *Fidelio* was finally produced in 1814. Yet the result, however clunky and implausible a drama, succeeds despite itself. On page after page of the score you encounter Beethoven the musical colossus. The music flattens you into emotional submission, forcing you to put aside any quibbles with the story. In a great performance, something that does not come along too often since the music is so challenging, few operas move me more.

The plot is constructed from two overlapping strands. There is a lighter domestic drama involving Rocco, a jailor at a prison in Seville, and his comely daughter, Marzelline, who has grown infatuated with Fidelio, a young man who has recently become Rocco's assistant, though Jaquino, another prison assistant, pines for her.

But Fidelio is actually Leonore, the courageous wife of a Spanish nobleman, Florestan, a champion of some liberation cause alluded to only vaguely. Leonore has disguised herself as a young man and comes to work at the prison in hopes of rescuing her husband, held captive there in a secret subterranean cell by order of Don Pizarro, a corrupt governor.

The music for the lighter domestic scenes is sometimes awkwardly comic, as in Rocco's blustery aria admonishing Fidelio to appreciate the value of money. Sometimes the music overwhelms the situation, as in the justly renowned act 1 quartet. During this static ensemble, Leonore, Marzelline, Rocco, and Jaquino merely reflect to themselves on their individual situations. Yet, this quartet, written in an elaborate theme and variations form, could not be more stunning. As it begins, a choir of strings and winds in the middle registers sustains the melting harmonies supported by a bare pizzicato bass line. The slow movements of several Mahler symphonies come right out of this music's sound world. The ensemble exemplifies the paradox of *Fidelio*. It doesn't matter what the characters are saying or how little is going on. This divinely mysterious music convinces you that they are ruminating on the most profound matters of life.

And at times Beethoven nails the dramatic moment. We don't meet the imprisoned Florestan until the opening of act 2 when, in most productions, we see him only dimly in his cell and hear the rattling chains. The heavy, halting orchestral introduction is music of abject misery. Yet a quality of restraint ennobles the character's suffering, until, out of nowhere, we hear a cry of "Gott! welch' Dunkel hier!" (God, what darkness here!). With a powerful dramatic tenor in the role, the moment is shattering.

One tenor seemed born to the role: Jon Vickers. I heard him perform it live only once, with the Opera Company of Boston, a high point of my operagoing life. Thankfully Vickers sings the role on a renowned 1962 EMI recording conducted by the great Otto Klemperer with the distinguished mezzo-soprano Christa Ludwig as Leonore. For all the power of Vickers's force-of-nature voice there was a quality of poignant sadness embedded in his sound, which ideally suited him to suffering young heroic roles like Siegmund, Tristan, and Florestan. Ludwig's Leonore, a role written for a dramatic soprano, is also a classic. She sings with intensity and fervor. Yet her vocal elegance, along with her keen musicianship and intelligence, lends dignity to her portrayal. When, in the penultimate scene after Leonore liberates her husband, Ludwig and Vickers break into the exultant duet, "O namenlose Freude" (Oh nameless joy), their singing is so exuberant they make you forget that the jittery vocal lines with their regular leaps up to punishing high notes are almost impossible to execute. Walter Berry makes a robustly menacing Pizarro.

For this project the enlightened record producer Walter Legge recruited other excellent singers who were steeped in the German repertory, including the gravelly bass Gottlob Frick as Rocco, the soprano Ingeborg Hallstein as Marzelline, and the tenor Gerhard Unger as Jaquino. Klemperer draws luminous and vibrant work from the Philharmonia Orchestra and Chorus. In the final celebratory scene, when the townspeople sing breathless praises to the valiant Leonore and the steadfast Florestan, the joyous energy of Klemperer's performance makes the rousing finale of Beethoven's Ninth seem tame by comparison. EMI will never let this recording slip from its catalog. I envy those who are about to hear it for the first time.

EMI Classics (two CDs) 5 56211 2
Otto Klemperer (conductor), Philharmonia Orchestra and Chorus; Ludwig, Vickers, Frick, Berry, Hallstein, Unger

4. VINCENZO BELLINI (1801–1835)

Norma

Felice Romani, librettist

First performance: Milan, Teatro alla Scala, December 26, 1831

Richard Wagner was an enormous admirer of Vincenzo Bellini. But perceptive as he was, Wagner was mistaken in thinking of Bellini as "the gentle Sicilian," in Wagner's words, and a "delicate soul," whose operas are elegant confections of long-spun melodies that waft atop simple and unobtrusive orchestral accompaniments.

Bellini was a highly skilled and comprehensive musician, a precocious talent who played the piano nimbly at five, studied modern languages and philosophy at seven, and composed elegant sacred works in his early adolescence. Later in his short life (he died of gastroenteritis at thirty-three) he spent long periods in London and especially Paris, moving in highly cultured social circles. Moreover, Bellini could be a real tough guy. He publicly put down his fellow composer Donizetti and carried on some shameless affairs with smitten married women.

Still, for me the utter eloquence of his music makes Bellini the purest master of the bel canto idiom. "Opera, through singing, must make one weep, shudder, die," Bellini wrote in an 1834 letter, a phrase that pretty well sums up his aesthetic approach.

He was enormously influenced by Rossini, who though just nine years older became a mentor and friend. From Rossini's example he acquired the essence of the bel canto style, which involved trusting, emboldening, and honoring the singing voice and the lyrical line. Flowing, curvaceous, and, when called for, highly charged melody should be the hallmark of opera, giving maximum potential to singers to make audiences weep, shudder, and die. Of course, Rossini filled his vocal lines with long flourishes of virtuosic coloratura as well, something that went against the simplicity-above-all credo of bel canto, another facet of the style that Bellini incorporated.

Yet, Bellini's melodic writing was also influenced by his love of Sicilian folk music, with its long-lined melodies that move by small steps and hew closely to the often irregular poetic phrases. Bellini carried these characteristics into his lyrical writing for the stage, which lent his long-spun lines a wondrously elusive quality: Where is this melody leading to? Why does it keep shifting phrase lengths?

"Bellini's music comes from the heart and is intimately bound up with the text," Wagner observed. While true, Bellini's musical dramas do lack psychological sophistication. As the scholar Friedrich Lippmann has observed in the *New Grove Dictionary of Opera,* in Bellini a love aria is a love aria, no matter who sings it. The same exquisitely lyrical style serves hateful and noble characters alike.

And yet, there are few characters in all of opera more complex and fascinating than Norma. Set in a sacred forest and temple in Gaul during the Roman occupation, the story centers on the illicit and secret love affair between Norma, a high priestess of the Druids, and Pollione, the Roman proconsul. Norma is the daughter of Oroveso, the head of the Druids, but from the moment we meet her it's clear that she commands the loyalty of her people, who turn to her for guidance about whether to organize a revolt against the Romans.

Norma counsels against rebellion. What the Druids don't know is that she has secretly borne two children to Pollione. Just how she kept her pregnancies hidden is never explained. Presumably a high priestess could disappear for a few months into her quarters to pray without arousing suspicion. But the character of Norma touches on timeless issues of being a woman. Norma, a religious leader who has violated a vow of chastity, is also a pragmatic political operator who understands the need to come to terms with the occupiers. She has a sisterly bond with Adalgisa, a young priestess in the temple, but attacks her with invective when she learns that Pollione has also been secretly romancing Adalgisa. Norma adores her children, but is ready to murder them rather than see them raised by Pollione and Adalgisa.

Is it any wonder that Norma became a career-defining role for the fiery Maria Callas, who almost single-handedly brought new appreciation to the works of Bellini and Donizetti after bel canto had fallen into neglect during the first half of the twentieth century? (Joan Sutherland, it must be said, followed closely on Callas's heels as a champion of bel canto.)

Listen to Callas lash out at Pollione and Adalgisa in the confrontational act 1 trio, leaping from high to low and back with a chilling ferocity, and you won't think of Bellini as a delicate soul. Yet listen to Callas plead with her people for peace in the exquisite "Casta Diva" (chaste goddess), an aria with choral refrains, and you will be disarmed both by Norma's vulnerable tenderness and Bellini's boldly long-spun melody.

But, ah, which Callas recording to own? There are three choices, now all available as part of the EMI Classics Callas Edition. The consensus choice is probably the 1954 studio recording, made in Milan with the forces of La Scala (the company that presented the opera's 1831 premiere). Some Callas fans find her singing too forceful and hard-edged here. This is Norma the menacing warrior more than Norma the suffering woman. Still, Callas's anguished singing in the despondent act 2 scene with her children moves me every time I hear it. This is a classic recording with the great mezzo-soprano Ebe Stignani as Adalgisa, the ardent tenor Mario Filippeschi as Pollione, and the stylistically authoritative conductor Tullio Serafin.

By 1960 Callas's voice was growing less reliable. Still, many Callas fans, including the expert John Ardoin, prefer the studio *Norma* Callas recorded that year, again with the forces of La Scala conducted by Serafin, but this time with the heroic tenor Franco Corelli as Pollione and the rich-voiced mezzo-soprano Christa Ludwig as Adalgisa. There is a breathy quality in Callas's singing at times, but overall this is a warmer, more pliant account of the role.

A live 1952 performance from Covent Garden in London (once available only as a pirated recording) offers Stignani again as Adalgisa, the honorable tenor Mirto Picchi as Pollione, and Vittorio Gui conducting. Though she starts out a little tremulously, Callas's performance is charged with intensity and wonderfully spontaneous. And, in a historic note, the small role of Clotilde, Norma's servant, is sung by a young soprano named Joan Sutherland.

Get Callas crazoids in a room comparing these three versions and the specificity of their opinions and passions will either amaze or baffle you. The live 1952 version has attained a cult status. I'd probably recommend the 1954 recording. But you can't go wrong with any one. Callas owned the role of Norma.

EMI Classics (three CDs) 5 56271 2 (recorded in 1954)
Tullio Serafin (conductor), Orchestra and Chorus of Teatro alla Scala, Milan; Callas, Stignani, Filippeschi

EMI Classics (three CDs) 5 66428 2 (recorded in 1960)
Tullio Serafin (conductor), Orchestra and Chorus of Teatro alla Scala, Milan; Callas, Ludwig, Corelli

EMI Classics (three CDs) 5 62668 2 (recorded live in 1952)
Vittorio Gui (conductor), Orchestra and Chorus of the Royal Opera House, Covent Garden; Callas, Stignani, Picchi

5. VINCENZO BELLINI (1801–1835)

I Puritani

Carlo Pepoli, librettist

First performance: Paris, Théâtre Italien, January 24, 1835

I Puritani, Bellini's final opera and his most sophisticated work, was written for a production at the Italian opera theater in Paris, which perhaps explains why he so labored over the score. Though already hugely popular in Paris, he was determined to wow the discerning Parisian audiences. And wow them he did. When the original Paris cast, headed by the acclaimed prima donna Giulia Grisi and the sensational tenor Giovanni Battista Rubini (famous for his gleaming voice, wide range, and distinctive expressive sob), performed the opera in an 1835 production at the King's Theatre in London, the city was overcome with *"Puritani* fever," the English critic Henry Fothergill Chorley wrote: "Errand boys whistled it, barrel-organs ground it." At

La Fenice in Venice the next year the leading soprano role was sung by Giuseppina Strepponi, who would become Verdi's lover and eventually his wife. The influence of *I Puritani* on Verdi's work is unmistakable.

The story offered Bellini the typical dilemmas and fraught situations that bel canto opera composers required, including a mad scene for a prima donna. The libretto by Carlo Pepoli (Bellini had had a falling-out with his regular librettist, Felice Romani) sets the story at a fortress near Plymouth during the English civil war in about 1650. Hostilities have been raging between Protestant forces, mostly Puritans, who have set up a radical government under Cromwell, and the besieged Stuart dynasty. Elvira, the daughter of Lord Walton, the governor-general of the fortress, is eager to marry Lord Arturo Talbot, her father's approved choice, a cavalier and, unbeknownst to Elvira and her family, a Stuart sympathizer. Talbot's true loyalties are suspected by Sir Riccardo Forth, a Puritan officer who pines for Elvira from afar and wishes he could marry her. Arturo is exposed by his principled but risky attempt to aid a mysterious female prisoner at the fortress who turns out to be Enrichetta, the hated, French-born Catholic widow of England's Charles I, who had been beheaded.

More than in any other opera Bellini was concerned here with the organic and dramatic shape of the score. Though the pace is often boldly spacious, there are no dead spots in the narrative flow. Choral outbursts and stirring marches emerge naturally from the overall structure. Yet, Bellini subtly blurs the demarcations between recitative, arioso, and aria. Arturo's tender act 1 cavatina, "A te, o cara, amor talora," in which he greets his bride with beautifully subdued longing, grows voice by voice into an elaborate and impressive quartet, a technique Verdi would later borrow. Bellini's harmonic language is richer and more intriguingly elusive than in any previous opera. Elvira's mad scene is a remarkable achievement, not a typically pathological display of soaring melodic lines and virtuoso roulades, but a subtle and insightful depiction of an emotionally unhinged yet touchingly fragile woman. *I Puritani* ends happily, by the way. A message from Cromwell confirms that the Stuarts have been routed, so Arturo's execution is halted and he is reconciled with Elvira's father, just as Elvira regains her reason and looks forward to wedded bliss.

I Puritani had fallen into obsolescence when Maria Callas sang

Soprano Joan Sutherland in I Puritani

Elvira in a Venice revival in 1949. Joan Sutherland gave landmark performances of the role in 1960 at the Glyndebourne Festival in England and in 1964 at the Royal Opera, Covent Garden—the first time the work had been heard there in seventy-seven years. She recorded it with the forces of Covent Garden, conducted with stylish sensitivity by her husband, Richard Bonynge, a bel canto expert, in 1973 for Decca, and that recording is the one I recommend.

The perception persists that Callas and Sutherland were artistic opposites: Callas intensely dramatic yet vocally imperfect; Sutherland vocally glorious, technically flawless, but emotionally bland. Actually, Callas was capable of exquisite and technically formidable singing. And Sutherland, as this recording vividly demonstrates, could take dramatic risks and convey real temperament and spontaneity.

The recording offers quite the cast, starting with Luciano Pavarotti as Arturo. Though in his later career Pavarotti grew shamelessly lazy, here he is captured in prime condition, focused, intense, and clearly exhilarated by the example of Sutherland, whom he held in awe. It's thrilling to hear Bellini's elegantly long-spun melodies sung by a tenor who adds such exciting vocal heft to his lyrical grace. The baritone Piero Cappuccilli brings his hardy voice and sure sense of Italianate style to his portrayal of Riccardo. The bass Nicolai Ghiaurov makes a stentorian and consoling Giorgio, Elvira's uncle who has been like a second father to her.

Callas's historic 1953 EMI recording is also splendid. This was the first complete recording of the opera. The vocally charismatic tenor Giuseppe di Stefano sings Arturo compellingly, though his voice is somewhat tight in the upper range, and Tullio Serafin conducts a stylish and surely paced account. But the Sutherland recording offers essentially a complete version of the opera, while the Callas account takes some cuts.

Decca (three CDs) 417588-2
Richard Bonynge (conductor), Chorus and Orchestra of the Royal Opera, Covent Garden; Sutherland, Pavarotti, Cappuccilli, Ghiaurov

EMI Classics (two CDs) 5 56275 2
Tullio Serafin (conductor), Orchestra and Chorus of Teatro alla Scala, Milan; Callas, di Stefano, Panerai, Rossi-Lemeni

6. ALBAN BERG (1885–1935)

Wozzeck

Alban Berg, librettist

First performance: Berlin, Staatsoper, December 14, 1925

Newcomers to twentieth-century music may wince at the prospect of an atonal opera. Atonal music? You mean that dissonance-saturated, angst-ridden, awful stuff that disdains the system of major and minor keys and makes no harmonic sense? Alban Berg's *Wozzeck* will shatter such preconceptions. It's hard to resist the powerful sway of this musically arresting, emotionally brutal, and, in the end, humanely tragic opera.

Given his early career, Berg may have seemed an unlikely candidate to create the greatest opera of the first half of the twentieth century. Born in Vienna, Berg was a largely self-trained composer when in 1904 at nineteen he began composition lessons with Arnold Schoenberg. It's a testimony to both the young man's talent and his teacher's excellence that seven years later Berg emerged from Schoenberg's studio as one of the most skilled, astute, and mature composers of his generation. In 1913, the premiere performance in Vienna of sections from Berg's first large-scale work, five songs for soprano and orchestra on poems by Peter Altenberg, incited a scandal over its radical harmonic language. But soon Berg won a coterie of admirers.

In 1914 he attended the Vienna stage premiere of Georg Büchner's play, *Woyzeck,* and found an idea for his first opera. The author, who died at twenty-three in 1837, had left the play in rough sketches. (The Vienna producers misread the title as *Wozzeck* and the error made it into Berg's libretto.) Büchner's play shocked audiences not just for its story of a delusional and oppressed soldier who supplements his meager pay by performing menial tasks for an overbearing captain and offering himself as a subject for crackpot medical experiments, but also for its daring structure, with twenty-five short scenes barely connected by any form of narrative continuity. As many critics have pointed out, the play's construction anticipated the techniques of film editing, especially rapid cutting and flashbacks.

Berg seized on the subject as ideally suited to his harmonically unhinged music. Atonality seemed to him the native tongue of the unconscious. And Berg's music does tap into the inner demons and unspoken yearnings of his lowlife characters. He also embraced the story as an indictment of society. In a world of predatory people who ruthlessly wield power over the oppressed, the subservient soldier Wozzeck and his common-law wife, Marie, are the only characters who evince some humanity.

Moreover, Berg identified with Wozzeck. In 1915, while working on the opera, he was ordered to report for infantry training. Though he served during the war without seeing combat, the grueling rituals of military life made a lasting impression. He later wrote to a friend that there was a bit of himself in Wozzeck, that he too spent the war years dependent on people he hated, and felt just as sick, captive, and humiliated.

Berg was also inspired to imitate the play's bold structure in his ninety-minute opera, which is organized in a series of fifteen short scenes grouped into three acts meant to be performed without break. In a fascinating stroke, Berg married his turbulent, harmonically ungrounded music to a series of precisely structured musical forms: suite, rhapsody, military march, sonata movement, a series of inventions, and such. Few listeners will consciously detect these structures during a performance. But your subconscious detects them, which makes Berg's score seem at once bristling with untamed emotion yet organic and inexorable.

For all its bleakness, Berg's music humanizes the central characters. Marie poignantly emerges as a beleaguered woman bound by the impulsive acts of her early adulthood. Clutching the young son she has borne Wozzeck, she sings a wistful yet unsettling lullaby in act 1. Though she is trying to be a loving mother, she is despondent over her powerless family's future. No wonder she can't resist the strapping

Drum Major who flirts with her. It's not just that he's handsome; it's that he's so refreshingly uncomplicated. When Wozzeck discovers her infidelity, his spiral into madness and tragedy begins. The only shred of manhood in his life has come from his relationship with Marie. In a fit he stabs her to death. In the penultimate scene, searching for the murder weapon by a forest pond, he deliriously imagines himself covered in blood and wanders into the water, where he drowns.

Naturally the opera was decried by conservative critics at its 1925 premiere at the Berlin Opera, conducted by Erich Kleiber, who took much heat for scheduling the work. One critic called Berg's score a "capital offense." But *Wozzeck* immediately won defenders. The two recordings I cherish are conducted by major musicians who were early advocates.

Dimitri Mitropoulos conducted a historic live concert performance with the New York Philharmonic at Carnegie Hall in 1951 that became the first commercial recording of the complete opera. This dynamic, vivid, and probing account features the husky-voiced baritone Mack Harrell as a volatile Wozzeck and the radiant soprano Eileen Farrell as an anguished and vulnerable Marie. The heroic tenor Frederick Jagel makes a dashingly manipulative Drum Major. A sense of discovery comes through in this great recording, now available on a remastered Sony Classical release.

The first studio recording of *Wozzeck* was conducted by Karl Böhm in 1965. It remains, overall, the recording of choice. The cast is superb, with Dietrich Fischer-Dieskau in the title role, Evelyn Lear as Marie, Gerhard Stolze as a sneering and aptly buffo Captain, and the sweet-toned lyric tenor Fritz Wunderlich as Andres, Wozzeck's one honorable friend. Böhm conducts the Orchestra of the German Opera, Berlin, in a confidently expansive performance that treats the score as an extension of Wagner. The recording is now available on a three-CD set that also includes Böhm's account of Berg's second and final opera, *Lulu*. But that's the next story.

Sony Classical (two CDs) MH2K 62759
Dimitri Mitropoulos (conductor), New York Philharmonic; Harrell, Farrell, Jagel, Mordino (includes performances of Schoenberg's Erwartung *and Krenek's* Symphonic Elegy for String Orchestra)

Deutsche Grammophon (three CDs) 435 705-2

Karl Böhm (conductor), Orchestra of the German Opera, Berlin; Fischer-Dieskau, Lear, Stolze, Wunderlich (includes Böhm's performance of Berg's Lulu)

7. ALBAN BERG (1885–1935)
Lulu

Alban Berg, librettist

First performance: Zurich, Stadttheater, June 2, 1937 (acts 1 and 2); Paris, Opéra, February 24, 1979 (three-act version, completed by Friedrich Cerha)

Among its many amazing qualities, Alban Berg's first opera, *Wozzeck*, is a marvel of dramatic concision. Georg Büchner's story about the downfall of an oppressed, impoverished, and delusional soldier is told in ninety minutes of intensely expressive music. I've always felt that with this opera Berg was announcing to the twentieth century that dramatic works had to adjust to modern sensibilities, get to the point, and not ruminate like nineteenth-century operas and plays.

But Berg veered from his precedent in his second opera, *Lulu*, left incomplete at his death due to septicemia in 1935. For all its glories, *Lulu*, when performed in the version completed by the composer Friedrich Cerha, is a four-hour evening at the opera (with two inter-missions).

For forty years after its premiere *Lulu* was presented only in its aborted two-act version. Berg left behind a complete three-act piano-vocal score, but, except for one passage, the final act was not orches-trated. After much wrangling with the Berg estate, Cerha was able to orchestrate the final act in the late 1970s and now it's impossible to imagine the opera performed without it.

Wozzeck was based on a dramatic fragment of Büchner's play. But Berg drew on two tragic plays by Frank Wedekind when he wrote the text for *Lulu*. The compressed story is still a sprawling tale of an alluring young actress and dancer in late-nineteenth-century Germany whose only power in a patriarchal society comes from her desirability to men. "I have never pretended to be anything but what men see in me," she says in a moment of chilling self-awareness. Lulu goes through three husbands in two acts: an elderly professor of medicine, who dies of a heart attack when he sees her being painted by a leering artist; then that artist, who kills himself in a fit of jealousy and humiliation; and then Dr. Schön, Lulu's Svengali-like protector, whom she shoots to death during a pointless quarrel he provokes.

Yet, it's hard not to wonder whether Berg, had he lived, would have tightened up the score. The stretches of spoken dialogue seem less like bold theatrical strokes than Berg's way of getting through some of the dialogue faster. But if *Lulu* can seem overly long, in a sensitive performance this darkly shimmering atonal score comes across as the most dramatically incisive and pungently lyrical music imaginable. By this point in his career Berg had incorporated Schoenberg's technique of twelve-tone composition. (To help those baffled by this concept, Schoenberg's technique of twelve-tone composition replaced the system of diatonic, or major and minor, keys, in which certain notes in the scale have more prominence, with a method where all twelve notes in the octave are treated as "equal," and placed in an ordered relationship called a row. If this procedure sounds absurdly intellectual, trust me: the technique generated some of the most brilliant and expressive music of the mid-twentieth century.) But Berg uses it with far greater freedom. Passage after passage in the score radiates with Wagnerian harmonic richness.

The first performance of *Lulu* using Cerha's completion of act 3 took place at the Paris Opera in 1979 with Pierre Boulez conducting and Teresa Stratas in the title role. A Deutsche Grammophon studio recording was made in conjunction with that performance, and it's the one to have. Boulez draws lucid textures and piercingly beautiful colorings from the orchestra and makes the music seem at once an outgrowth of late German romanticism and a pathbreaking venture in modernism.

Berg intended the title role for a high, light soprano. The episodes of coloratura writing are meant to be unsettling, not frilly. Stratas may not have quite the requisite coloratura agility, but she certainly captures the tremulous anxiety in the music in this emotionally bare and vocally courageous performance. The resounding baritone Franz Mazura is brilliant in the double role of Dr. Schön and, in a biting twist, Jack the Ripper, who appears in act 3, set in London, and murders Lulu, who has been forced into prostitution to support two pathetically dependent men: Alwa, Dr. Schön's composer son, here the compelling tenor Kenneth Riegel; and old Schigolch, who may be Lulu's father, it is suggested, here sung by the bass Toni Blankenheim. The mezzo-soprano Yvonne Minton gives a complex and vocally rich portrayal as the lesbian Countess Geschwitz, whose love for Lulu in many ways is the most undemanding and pure.

The other recording to consider offers the conductor Karl Böhm in a live 1968 performance at the German Opera, Berlin. Böhm inflects the score with the same sumptuous colorings and post-Romantic sensibility he brings to his recording of *Wozzeck*. The cast is admirable, with Evelyn Lear as Lulu, Dietrich Fischer-Dieskau as Dr. Schön, and Patricia Johnson as the Countess Geschwitz. But this performance predates Cerha's completion of act 3. Still, this two-act version offers significant insights into the score and, coupled with *Wozzeck* in a three-CD Deutsche Grammophon set, it's a bargain.

Deutsche Grammophon (three CDs) 463 617-2
Pierre Boulez (conductor), Orchestra of the Paris Opera; Stratas, Minton, Mazura, Riegel, Blankenheim, Schwarz

Deutsche Grammophon (three CDs) 435 705-2
Karl Böhm (conductor), Orchestra of the German Opera, Berlin; Lear, Fischer-Dieskau, Johnson (includes Böhm's performance of Berg's Wozzeck*)*

8. HECTOR BERLIOZ (1803–1869)

Les Troyens

Hector Berlioz, librettist, after Virgil

First performance: Paris, Théâtre Lyrique, November 4, 1863 (acts 3–5 only); Karlsruhe, Grossherzogliches Hoftheater, December 6, 1890 (complete)

On the fourth page of Hector Berlioz's astute and compulsively readable memoirs he recalls the efforts of his father, a culturally minded doctor, to introduce him to the Greek classics. At first young Hector resisted. But by the time he was ten he was enthralled with Virgil's *Aeneid,* especially the account of Dido's sacrificial death in the throes of fateful passion for Aeneas. Berlioz describes the evening when he read this chapter aloud to his father and, overwhelmed, broke down and cried. His father closed the book and said, calmly, "That will do, my boy, I am tired." Berlioz adds: "I was intensely grateful to him for taking no notice of my emotion, and rushed away to vent my Virgilian grief in solitude."

Over forty years later Berlioz found another way to vent his Virgilian grief: by writing the libretto and music to his epic opera *Les Troyens*. He worked in a frenzy of inspiration as his health and emotional state declined. By 1858 the opera was essentially completed. But he spent the next five years trying to secure a production and was urged to divide the lengthy work—some four hours of music—in two. In 1863 he managed to have part two, *Les Troyens à Carthage,* produced at the Théâtre Lyrique, though after the first night the score was brutally cut. The idea that *Les Troyens* was too long and unwieldy persisted for decades after Berlioz's death. Indeed, it took until 1890 for the opera to be performed more or less complete, and until 1969 for a scholarly and definitive edition to be presented finally by the Royal Opera House at Covent Garden in London.

Though *Les Troyens* may be cumbersome and imperfect, it is also one of the supreme achievements in opera. Here all the contrary strands of Berlioz's art come together miraculously: Romantic fervor, sumptuous colors, and the sheer din of massed choral and orchestral forces are leavened by French elegance and delicacy. Cinematic battle scenes are contrasted with up-close soliloquies. The music looks forward with its wayward harmonic language, but also backward to the austere classicism of Gluck, Berlioz's idol. Berlioz manages to blend the mystical, historical, sensual, atmospheric, and psychological elements of the opera into a ravishing score that achieves coherence despite its length and hovers in some transcendent place beyond historical period.

Both leading female roles—Cassandra and Dido—are given to mezzo-sopranos, whose earthy, grounded voices are meant to contrast with the heroic tenor of Aeneas, the dreamer, though an ideal Aeneas must also have a refined sense of French lyricism.

Here and there the opera replaces traditional arias with urgent yet subtly structured monologues that in a good performance can sound almost improvised. Yet there are set-piece arias as well, like the forlornly beautiful song sung by the Phrygian youth Hylas aboard a warship as he thinks of his far-off homeland. And the blissfully subdued and soothingly undulant septet in act 4 seems more glorious every time I hear it.

For me there are only two recordings to consider, both conducted by Colin Davis. When Davis first came to attention in the late 1950s he was something of a firebrand. Yet his intensity was balanced by a quality of British restraint. The balance sometimes went off in certain repertory, but never in Berlioz. *Les Troyens* especially has been a lifelong passion for Davis. He is rightly proud of his second account of the opera, a Grammy Award–winning recording with the London Symphony Orchestra and a splendid cast, taken from live performances in December 2000 at the Barbican Hall and released on the orchestra's own label, LSO Live. The performance captures the rhapsodic sweep and radiant colorings of the score. The orchestra sounds glorious and the cast inspired, especially the clarion-voiced dramatic tenor Ben Heppner as Aeneas, the dusky-toned mezzo-soprano Michelle DeYoung as Dido, and the plaintive mezzo-soprano Petra Lang as Cassandra.

My preference, though, is for Davis's revelatory recording from

Tenor Jon Vickers in Les Troyens

1969, the centenary of Berlioz's death, made with the chorus and orchestra of Covent Garden. The performance commemorates the historic production in London that Davis presided over and which finally revealed the true achievement of this work to the public. The colossal tenor Jon Vickers brings heroic vocal heft to the role of Aeneas

Hector Berlioz

while also conveying the torment and insecurity of the character, so torn between helpless love for Dido and steadfast obligation to his country. Josephine Veasey is a rich, commanding, and articulate Dido and Berit Lindholm a molten Cassandra, terrifying in the certainty of her bleak predictions.

You can't go wrong with either recording. And hearing a recording provides the most effective entry into this sprawling and elusive opera.

LSO Live LSO 0010 (four CDs)
Sir Colin Davis (conductor), London Symphony Orchestra and the London Symphony Chorus; Heppner, DeYoung, Lang, Mingardo, Mattei

Philips 416 432-2 (four CDs)
Sir Colin Davis (conductor), Chorus and Orchestra of the Royal Opera House, Covent Garden; Vickers, Veasey, Lindholm, Glossop, Begg

9. GEORGES BIZET (1838–1875)

Carmen

Henri Meilhac and Ludovic Halévy, librettists

First performance: Paris, Opéra-Comique, March 3, 1875

Georges Bizet died at thirty-six, just three months after the contentious premiere of *Carmen*, having no hint that his final work would become one of the most respected and popular of all operas. From the start his career had been fraught with frustration.

Born in Paris in 1838, Bizet was a precociously gifted and prize-winning student at the conservatory who could have moved in several musical directions. But his only ambition was to be a successful composer for the theater. All told he worked on some thirty operatic projects, the scholar Winton Dean estimates, leaving most of them incomplete, some of them mere sketches. For several years prior to the composition of *Carmen* he was creatively aimless and had no steady source of income.

Even so, the managers of the Opéra-Comique, impressed by Bizet's one-act *Djamileh*, which had failed with critics and the public, invited him to compose a three-act work. His chosen subject, a Prosper Mérimée novel about a willful and sexually liberated gypsy woman, excited his librettists but scandalized De Leuven, the codirector of the company. That the heroine would be murdered onstage in the final scene was too much for a family theater, which is what De Leuven considered the Opéra-Comique to be.

At the time opéra-comique was a genre in crisis. Its defining element was that spoken dialogue took the place of sung recitative. The typical opéra-comique of the mid-nineteenth century was frothy entertainment with agreeable music. But a movement to make the genre more formidable had been gaining ground and Bizet seized on *Carmen* as an opportunity to lead the way.

In keeping with tradition *Carmen* would provide entertainment, he promised. There would be spirited choruses for impish urchins and rowdy gypsies, some comic characters, and many catchy tunes (the famous "Toreador Song"). But the opera would have unflinchingly serious elements as well. Bizet embraced the concept of spoken dialogue as a way to lessen the artificiality of opera and tell true-to-life stories, however tragic.

Bizet's score, which teems with fetching melodies and colorful crowd scenes, is so immediately appealing it's easy to overlook its ingenious subtleties. In the opening scene outside a tobacco factory in Seville, some soldiers assigned to the weary detail of keeping order in the public square sing a lilting, breezy chorus. The music perfectly captures the feel of this hot and lazy day. Yet with its restless harmonies and teasing tune, this chorus also conveys the curiosity of the soldiers as they watch the people come and go and await the midday break of the women who work in the factory, especially Carmen.

One short scene that never fails to impress me comes in act 3, set in a rocky place near Seville at night. The gypsy smugglers, laden with stolen goods, are warily climbing some bluffs. Danger lies below, as they convey in steadily treading music, meaning not just that one foot-slip could be fatal but that a slipup in their thievery could bring the law upon them. This warning is illustrated by a sudden outburst from the chorus and orchestra: a pungently chromatic series of descending chords as harmonically daring as anything in Wagner.

But the glory of the opera comes from Bizet's ability to depict character through music. Though Carmen is willful and contemptuous of convention, she is one cool operator. When she turns her attention to the strapping, uptight young corporal Don José during the famous "Habanera," the sinuous melody expresses her brazen seductiveness, but the restrained and steady dance rhythm reins her in, suggesting that here is a woman in command of the situation, careful not to get ahead of herself.

In lesser hands the contrast between the voluptuous Carmen and the virginal Micaëla, the seventeen-year-old orphan who has been taken in and raised by Don José's widowed mother, could have seemed terribly melodramatic. But Bizet gives Micaëla poignantly elegant music—soaring phrases full of goodness and touched with longing for Don José.

It also makes sense that when Escamillo, the toreador, arrives on the scene, Carmen sees him as an antidote to Don José, who has become annoyingly possessive. Carmen and Escamillo are two of a kind. Like her, he values freedom above all and faces life (and the bull) with swagger and flair. Carmen intuitively knows that if she were to take another lover Escamillo would probably chuckle wryly and move on to someone new himself.

After the premiere of Carmen, Bizet was pressured by the company directors to set the spoken dialogue to music. The opéra-comique style was just wrong, many people thought, for a shocking opera in which rowdy gypsy women smoke cigarettes and pick fights with each other onstage! Bizet agreed to set the spoken dialogue to recitative for a proposed production in Vienna, but died before doing so. The task fell to Ernest Guiraud, a solidly professional but uninspired composer. For the next seventy-five years the version of Carmen with Guiraud's recitatives became standard. The original version with the spoken dialogue has been by far the preferred choice since at least the 1970s. So though I grew up with the old Risë Stevens recording, which I love, I can no longer listen to Guiraud's bloated and ponderous recitatives.

An excellent recording of the original version is the 1977 account with Teresa Berganza in the title role, the young Plácido Domingo as Don José, the almost-as-young Sherrill Milnes as Escamillo, and Claudio Abbado conducting a typically insightful and lucid performance. Though Berganza's rich mezzo-soprano voice may lack a little weight for the role, she compensates with her subtle and nuanced singing, refreshingly free of vulgarity. Her Carmen is the eerily calm epicenter of a tempestuous operatic storm.

My favorite *Carmen* recording has many debunkers: the 1973 account with Marilyn Horne in the title role and Leonard Bernstein conducting, which documents a Metropolitan Opera production. Many of Bernstein's tempos are daringly, provocatively slow. Some find his work mannered; I find it revelatory. The orchestral prelude to *Carmen* begins with a march that reappears in the final act before the bullfight. Most conductors really whip it up. Bernstein's performance reminds you that this music is a march. How fast can a march realistically be? You have to be able to march to it. At Bernstein's steady and emphatic tempo, the music gains gravity and richness and anticipates the sudden burst of terror when the ominous curse motif intrudes. And Bernstein's held-back tempos in the "Habanera" compel Horne to spin out Bizet's long sultry phrases with haunting restraint (not to mention impressive breath control). This is a take-charge Carmen. James McCracken impressively scales down his powerhouse tenor voice to the refined French contours of Don José's music. The radiant soprano Adriana Maliponte as Micaëla and the virile baritone Tom Krause as Escamillo are also excellent.

A myth has arisen that *Carmen* was a terrible failure at its premiere. Actually, it was presented at the Opéra-Comique forty-nine times in the space of a year, a quite decent run. Though many uncomprehending critics denounced the opera, it soon won powerful advocates, including Saint-Saëns, Tchaikovsky, Brahms, and Wagner.

Still, Bizet died thinking *Carmen* a bust. Few premature deaths in music history rival the loss of Bizet. He was just getting going.

Deutsche Grammophon (three CDs) 41936

Claudio Abbado (conductor), The Ambrosian Singers and the London Symphony Orchestra; Berganza, Domingo, Cotrubas, Milnes

Deutsche Grammophon (three CDs) 427 440-2

Leonard Bernstein (conductor), Metropolitan Opera Orchestra and the Manhattan Opera Chorus; Horne, McCracken, Maliponte, Krause

10. BENJAMIN BRITTEN (1913–1976)

Peter Grimes

Montagu Slater, librettist, after George Crabbe's poem "The Borough" (1810)

First performance: London, Sadler's Wells, June 7, 1945

Following the discouraging reception to the premiere in May 1941 at Columbia University of his first dramatic work, *Paul Bunyan,* an operetta, Benjamin Britten officially withdrew the score from his catalog. Yet just two months later, while traveling in California with his lover and colleague, the tenor Peter Pears, Britten plunged to work on an opera that would become one of the central masterpieces of the twentieth century.

During their travels Pears had found a copy of a book by the early-nineteenth-century British poet George Crabbe, and seized on "The Borough," a long poetic narrative, as a subject for an opera. Crabbe, who had recently been championed in an article by E. M. Forster, was born in Aldeburgh and his poems vividly evoked the people and landscape of England's southeastern coast, a region Britten was drawn to. The mournful birdcalls, the briny mists, the relentless swells of the sea, the well-meaning but suspicious people, so wary of outsiders—all this came to life in Crabbe's verse.

The character Pears and Britten fixed on was Peter Grimes, the abused son of a God-fearing fisherman. In Crabbe's telling, after Peter's father dies, the young man sinks into a twisted state, fishing, stealing, and cheating to pay for his liquor. Living out the sins of his father, Grimes acquires a poor boy as an apprentice whom he can bully and beat. The boy eventually dies from the ordeal of his life with

Grimes. The fisherman acquires another, who falls to his death from the mast of a boat, and another still, who dies at sea. Ostracized by the townspeople and forbidden by the local court to have another apprentice, Grimes loses all reason and dies in the presence of the villagers.

Pears and Britten had devised a complete scenario for the opera by the time they turned to the poet and dramatist Montagu Slater as a librettist. It is often forgotten that after settling in London in 1933 at the age of nineteen, Britten earned most of his living for the next decade as a composer of incidental music for theater, film, and radio—ideal preparation for an opera composer. But he also brought to his dramatic works an astute sensitivity to the psychological ambiguities of human nature, insights fueled by his own conflicted feelings about being homosexual and, consequently, an outsider. He and Pears felt sympathy for Peter Grimes, though the character they created with Slater is more tragically flawed and ambiguous. The operatic Grimes can seem as much victim as victimizer.

Yes, Grimes is a brutish man, a recluse with thwarted sexual yearnings. But in Britten's imagining Grimes is also a dreamer, a clueless and hurt soul with a faint vision of what life could be. In a critical departure from Crabbe, the opera ends with Grimes's one remaining friend, old Captain Balstrode, telling him to sail out to sea and sink his boat, rather than face the murderous fury of The Borough, the small coastal town in 1830s England where the story is set.

Britten's attitude toward Grimes and his uncanny ability to evoke character in a few musical strokes come through from the opening pages of the prologue. Grimes is the reluctant key witness at a coroner's inquest into the death of his apprentice. As Swallow, the lawyer, conceived for a sturdy bass, questions Grimes, the music is a web of officious and slightly bungling counterpoint. With Grimes's first response, "I swear by Almighty God," Britten envelops the fisherman's answers in a consoling choir of low-pitched strings that seems to sanctify his words.

Following the prologue, in the midst of a rowdy choral scene at The Boar, an inn, the music builds with a bustle of strophic drinking songs (given an extra pointed edge with Britten's spiky harmony) and chaotic overlapping conversations, as Grimes bursts in expecting to pick up his new apprentice. But his wild-eyed look silences the crowd, who deeply distrust him. Oblivious, Grimes breaks into the elegiac aria "Now the Great Bear and Pleiades," in which we see his dreamy inner nature, entranced by the constellations in the evening sky, and his contrasting defensiveness and paranoia ("Who can turn skies back and begin again," he sings).

Britten conceived the title role for Pears, who recorded it definitively in 1958 with Britten conducting the forces of the Royal Opera, Covent Garden. Pears conveys Grimes's intemperate anger but also shows his dreamy nature, the side that Ellen Orford, the trusting schoolteacher (here the tender-voiced Claire Watson), sees in him, or tries to, until his dangerous streak cannot be denied. In this classic performance *Peter Grimes* comes across as an utter and avoidable tragedy. Every community, the opera suggests, has a tendency to isolate a culprit, an "other." Grimes is an easy target. But if only he could have been less defensive and the uncomprehending townspeople more insightful, this whole downwardly spiraling cycle might have been avoided.

In 1967 the tenor Jon Vickers sang the role for the first time in a production at the Metropolitan Opera and completely altered the perception of the work. Vickers's heldentenor was the diametric opposite of Pears's light and plaintive lyric voice. Vickers emphasized the menacing anger and inner torment of Grimes in this impassioned and fitful performance. Speaking of his interpretation, Vickers said that he wanted to "suck the public" into being sympathetic with the condemning crowd, and lay bare Grimes's universal sense of otherness so that the public would see just how rash they were.

Britten and Pears were taken aback with this take on the role. But Vickers had a powerful ally in the conductor Colin Davis. Their 1978 recording of the work, also with the forces of Covent Garden, and the sublime soprano Heather Harper as Ellen, is indispensable. (One caution: Philips rereleased it in 1999 as a two-disc Duo budget set, but with no libretto.) Davis dares to convey the terrifying hostility of the crowd in act 3 when the avenging townspeople invoke the name of Peter Grimes in a steely and shattering chorus. Ultimately the title role is as complex, ambiguous, and open to interpretation as Shakespeare's Othello or, another Vickers specialty, Verdi's Otello.

Composer Benjamin Britten

Decca (three CDs) 414 577-2
Benjamin Britten (conductor), Orchestra and Chorus of the Royal Opera, Covent Garden; Pears, Watson, Pease

Philips (two CDs) 289 462 847-2
Colin Davis (conductor), Orchestra and Chorus of the Royal Opera, Covent Garden; Vickers, Harper, Summers

11. BENJAMIN BRITTEN (1913–1976)

The Rape of Lucretia

Ronald Duncan, librettist, after a play by André Obey

First performance: Glyndebourne, England, July 12, 1946

Shortly after the 1945 premiere of *Peter Grimes,* Benjamin Britten set to work on a chamber opera, a commission from the Glyndebourne Festival. The challenging experience of getting *Peter Grimes* written and produced had led him to question the efficacy of traditional full-fledged opera. So he readily turned his attention to *The Rape of Lucretia,* scored for an instrumental ensemble of just thirteen players, featuring a cast of eight and starring a female singer in the title role, a rarity in Britten's work.

The libretto by Ronald Duncan, based on a play by André Obey, curiously drenches the pagan story in Christian moralizing, which just enhances the compelling strangeness of the work. The story, set in ancient Rome (the year is 509 B.C.), concerns the occupying Etruscan prince Tarquinius, a tyrant who treats the cowering city like the whores he nightly frequents. In homage to Greek tragedy the opera presents two solo singers, called Male Chorus and Female Chorus, who relate and comment upon the story as it progresses. Much of the opera's grisly action and emotional ambiguity are conveyed in Britten's pungent and unconventional writing for the chamber orchestra. Whole stretches of the dialogue are set in a haunting quasi-recitative minimally accompanied only by a piano, a choir of wind instruments, or a scraggly harp.

After the Male Chorus and Female Chorus set the opening scene, we see Tarquinius and two other generals, Junius and Collatinus, drinking on a hot summer's night in a camp on the outskirts of Rome and bemoaning the inconstancy of women. The previous night some Roman officers had paid a surprise visit to the city and caught their spouses cheating. Only Lucretia, the noble wife of Collatinus, was faithful, something that rouses Tarquinius to fits of envy and jealousy.

A composer with lesser dramatic instincts would have turned this drinking scene boisterous. Britten writes music of lulling ambiguity. There is a slowly rocking figuration in the orchestra as the generals erupt with inebriated outbursts. The hazy humid evening air, like the hazy state of their thinking, permeates this weirdly subdued music.

Later that night, as the Male Chorus describes Tarquinius impulsively rushing to Rome to demand lodging from the unsuspecting Lucretia, you hear the galloping of his horse in Britten's rhythmically charged, harmonically grating instrumental music. When, having warily welcomed the prince into her home, Lucretia is lulled to sleep by her nurse and her maid, there is an element of foreboding in this deceptively tranquil music. It could be some pastoral lullaby with an unsettling undercurrent.

Tarquinius steals into the sleeping Lucretia's room. He furtively kisses her. Startled, she awakes, and he violently rapes her. But the horror and brutality in the music suddenly dissipates into a strangely calming interlude for the Choruses, a chorale in which they describe the sorrow of Christ when virtue is assailed by sin; they proclaim that "nothing impure survives, all passion perishes" and promise consolation through "Mary most chaste and pure."

The next morning, as Lucretia's attendants breezily greet the day, their lady appears, eerily controlled yet obviously shaken. In an ingenious stroke Britten gives Lucretia a poignantly simple aria in which she confesses her abject shame to Collatinus, who had suspected the worst. In a moment when Collatinus is consumed by his own anger and impotence Lucretia stabs herself to death. There is a funereal ensemble for all eight singers, who ask, "Is this it all?" Is inconsolable grief for the survivors the end result of a good woman's life?

In a perplexing epilogue the Choruses answer in what seems at first glance pious Christian platitudes about repentance and eternal life. Britten insisted that Duncan add this epilogue because he did not want to end the opera with a dirge. However convoluted as theology, this wistful and harmonically intricate epilogue does provide a sense of musical and emotional resolution, which matters more.

The great British contralto Kathleen Ferrier created the role of Lucretia, but you could not ask for a better portrayal than Janet Baker's on the definitive 1970 recording, with Britten conducting the English Chamber Orchestra. The all-British cast is matchless. The tenor Peter Pears sings the Male Chorus with a haunting ambiguity, at once cool and poignant. The elegant soprano Heather Harper brings sweet-toned sadness to the Female Chorus. The baritone Benjamin Luxon makes a volatile Tarquinius. The baritone John Shirley-Quirk is the other standout, as the honorable and finally helpless Collatinus.

The recording includes a performance of Britten's *Phaedra* for mezzo-soprano and chamber ensemble, with Janet Baker singing and Steuart Bedford conducting the English Chamber Orchestra.

Decca (two CDs) 425 666-2

Benjamin Britten (conductor), English Chamber Orchestra; Baker, Pears, Harper, Luxon, Shirley-Quirk, Drake

12. BENJAMIN BRITTEN (1913–1976)
Billy Budd

E. M. Forster and Eric Crozier, librettists, after Herman Melville's story

First performance: London, Royal Opera, Covent Garden, December 1, 1951 (original four-act version)

There are two contrasting dimensions to *Billy Budd* that might have proven incompatible had not Britten by this point in his career found a commanding way to adapt the genre of opera to his own ends. On one level *Billy Budd*, which mostly takes place aboard the HMS *Indomitable* during the French Wars of 1797 as the ship nears enemy waters, is opera in the grand manner, a pulsing, sweeping story with massed choral scenes, elaborate ensembles, outbursts of individual emotion, and lush music for the orchestra, one of the largest in the Britten canon.

On another level *Billy Budd* is a penetrating psychological exploration of innocence and twisted envy. In choosing Herman Melville's story as a subject, Britten, abetted by his like-minded librettists, E. M. Forster and Eric Crozier, drew out the tale's homoerotic subtext, as he had in *Peter Grimes*. Rather than diminishing the story with a personal agenda, Britten created a powerfully ambiguous work.

The all-male opera is framed by two scenes with Edward Fairfax Vere, the retired captain of the *Indomitable,* who in old age ruefully recounts the events of 1797 and his misguided treatment of the young sailor, Billy Budd. So the main body of the work is a sprawling flashback.

Like most of the sailors on the *Indomitable,* Billy has been taken from a merchant ship and pressed into naval service. Unlike the others, though, Billy, a foundling, a sturdy, boyishly handsome and simple-minded youth with a troublesome stammer, is pleased to have been chosen. Finally he is wanted somewhere. A king's warship no less.

In the libretto Billy is continually described as a beauty. To most of the men his looks go hand in hand with his innocence. They rib him and treat him like a mascot. But the malevolent John Claggart, the ship's feared master-at-arms, seethes with envy and repressed desire for Billy. The only way to conquer his feelings is to impugn and destroy the lad.

The opera begins with a haunting motif, a slowly undulant figure that oscillates between a major and minor third, creating a subdued conflict of intervals. That seemingly simple idea becomes a gnashing and pervasive theme threading through the entire score. In the boisterous scenes when the sailors sing shanties, drink rum, and pick fights, and in the near encounter with a French ship that is chased off by cannon fire, the music builds with frenzied intensity. But it's the searching, elusive, and internalized scenes that claim you and that make the title role for a strong baritone with a lyrical bent so rewarding.

In the climactic scene, Billy, falsely accused of inciting mutiny by Claggart, is overcome with anguish and anger. He tries to speak but can only stammer. Impotent, he strikes at Claggart, who collapses, hitting his head fatally on the floor. Paradoxically, in the next scene when Billy, about to be hanged for his unintended offense, sadly ponders his life, the wistful music and poetic verse endow him with an articulate elegance that is of course out of character. Yet, for that moment, Billy transcends himself, becoming the Christlike figure Britten imagined him.

That is certainly true of the hardy and sensitive baritone Peter Glossop's Billy, who can be heard on the classic 1967 recording with Britten conducting the London Symphony Orchestra. This account also offers Peter Pears as Vere, the role he created, an ethereal and multilayered performance. Vere's regard for Billy was clearly tinged with unexpressed desire. Was the captain's unwillingness to counter naval law and reprieve Billy a way of punishing himself? The recording also boasts the chilling Claggart of the bass Michael Langdon.

The cast of a more recent version, a 2000 Chandos recording, is headed by the charismatic baritone Simon Keenlyside as Billy, with the veteran and probing tenor Philip Langridge as Vere and the powerful bass John Tomlinson as Claggart. Richard Hickox conducts the London Symphony Orchestra in a dynamic performance.

A live recording of the work's 1951 premiere at Covent Garden, now available on a VAI Audio release, offers the original version of the opera, structured in four acts. For a 1961 radio broadcast, Britten trimmed some scenes, cut one out, and fashioned the opera into two acts. And that version has become standard (Britten conducts it on his own recording). But besides providing a document of the opera in its original conception, the recording features the disarming portrayal of Billy by the vibrant tenor Theodor Uppman in a role he was rightly proud of having created.

Decca (three CDs) 417 428-2
Benjamin Britten (conductor), London Symphony Orchestra, Ambrosian Opera Chorus; Glossop, Pears, Langdon, Shirley-Quirk (includes recordings of "The Holy Sonnets of John Donne" with Pears singing and "The Songs and Proverbs of William Blake" with Dietrich Fischer-Dieskau singing; Britten accompanied both artists)

Chandos (three CDs) 9826(3)
Richard Hickox (conductor), London Symphony Orchestra and Chorus; Keenlyside, Langridge, Tomlinson, Opie

VAI Audio (three CDs) 10343

Benjamin Britten (conductor), Orchestra and Chorus of the Royal Opera, Covent Garden; Uppman, Pears, Dalberg, Alan

13. BENJAMIN BRITTEN (1913–1976)

The Turn of the Screw

Myfanwy Piper, librettist, after Henry James's novella (1898)

First performance: Venice, La Fenice, September 14, 1954

Benjamin Britten had ambiguous attitudes toward just about everything and everyone. So it's not surprising that he had ambiguous attitudes toward opera, especially the operatic establishment with its wariness of contemporary music and its penchant for grandiosity. With *The Turn of the Screw,* commissioned for the Venice Biennale and premiered there in 1954, Britten made a decisive move away from large-scale opera and toward more intimate concepts of musical drama. He had enjoyed working with smaller, flexible companies. Reducing the scale of his works allowed him to better tackle one of his main aims in writing opera, as he once put it, namely, "to try to restore to the musical setting of the English language a brilliance, freedom and vitality that have been curiously rare since Purcell."

Though a model chamber opera with a cast of six and an orchestra of just thirteen instruments, *The Turn of the Screw* is challenging to stage. The story, adapted from the Henry James novella by the librettist Myfanwy Piper, is intricately bound to its setting, a rural country house in Victorian England. Yet this tale of two children, their absentee guardian, the governess and housekeeper who raise them, and the dead manservant and schoolmistress who come back to lure them into wickedness is atmospheric and profoundly ambiguous. Britten's music quivers with murkiness. But staging the opera poses some critical choices. Do you, for example, make Peter Quint, the deceased manservant, who, it is suggested, may have abused the two children, an apparition veiled behind a scrim? Or a flesh-and-blood incarnation?

Of course, these issues can be readily disregarded by those who listen to Britten's transfixing opera on a recording. The score daringly juxtaposes music of contrasting styles: skittish twelve-tone motifs are anchored by tonally clear but shifting harmonies; outpourings of plaintive vocal arioso are interrupted by eerie, almost minimalistic repetitions of simple accompaniment patterns.

The Turn of the Screw is a tightly structured and compact work. Britten presents the tale in a prologue and two acts with sixteen scenes. But he subtitles act 1, scene 1 a "Theme," and the subsequent scenes are a series of numbered variations. Each scene is related to its predecessor by a restatement or a variation of a twelve-note theme that runs through the entire score. Some critics have found this formal layout, along with Britten's concern with thematic development of motifs and figurations, overly intellectual or inhibited. The opera has been faulted as lacking an intensity of expression its subject warrants.

Its champions, I among them, admire the opera for its cool reticence. Arnold Whittall in his insightful entry on the work in the *New Grove Dictionary of Opera* puts it well when he writes that Britten's music "reveals its absolute rightness in the way it brings to convincing life the extraordinary Jamesian blend of starchy social conventions and turbulent emotional forces which those conventions promote, while seeking their suppression." Dramatically the opera quickly becomes a battle of wills between the ominous Peter Quint and the stalwart and good-hearted but naive Governess over the welfare of the children. And Quint wins.

Vocally, Britten demands a lot from the singers portraying the two youngsters. Flora can be sung by a young adult soprano. But Miles, the boy, must be a treble (a boy soprano), and the role is long and musically involved.

The Turn of the Screw was the first Britten opera to be recorded complete, the same year as its premiere, with Britten conducting the English Opera Group Orchestra and the original cast. Peter Pears effectively adapts his tremulous lyric tenor voice to the double role of

The Prologue and Peter Quint; the lustrous soprano Jennifer Vyvyan sings the Governess; Olive Dyer is a sadly subdued Flora. And fans of the 1966 Antonioni film *Blow-Up* will enjoy hearing its leading man, David Hemmings, as a thirteen-year-old treble in the role of Miles.

The other recording to consider is a 2002 Virgin Classics release with the brilliant young British conductor Daniel Harding leading the impressive Mahler Chamber Orchestra in a taut and articulate performance that may have a more inexorable sweep than Britten's account. Of special interest is the Quint of the tenor Ian Bostridge, who brings ethereal sound and chilling restraint to his work in an aptly Jamesian portrayal.

Decca (two CDs) 425 672-2
Benjamin Britten (conductor), English Opera Group Orchestra; Pears, Vyvyan, Hemmings, Dyer

Virgin Classics (two CDs) 5 45521 2
Daniel Harding (conductor), Mahler Chamber Orchestra; Bostridge, Rodgers, Leang, Wise

14. BENJAMIN BRITTEN (1913–1976)
A Midsummer Night's Dream

Benjamin Britten and Peter Pears, librettists, after Shakespeare

First performance: Jubilee Hall, Aldeburgh, England, June 11, 1960

One could argue that the impact of Shakespeare's *A Midsummer Night's Dream* has been undermined over many years by productions that treat it merely as a fantastical comedy. Benjamin Britten's great 1960 operatic version of the play, with a libretto adapted from Shakespeare by the composer and his lifelong partner, the tenor Peter Pears, brings out the disturbing subtext to this whimsical tale.

Britten thrusts at you all the twisted conflicts that drive this strange and resonant story. The plot turns on a battle between Oberon, the tyrannical and coolly seductive king of the fairies, and his headstrong wife, Tytania, over an orphaned boy to whom she has become a surrogate mother. Oberon wants the boy to serve as his henchman. Tytania will not give him up, and with good reason, for she senses that Oberon's feelings for the boy are muddled with desire. Moreover, she has seen all too often the brutal way Oberon gets the impish sprite Puck to do his bidding.

As a tactic in their domestic battle, Tytania has refused to share her husband's bed, which doesn't seem to bother him all that much, but badly upsets the natural order. It is partly Oberon's desire to right that imbalance that tempts him into intervening, through the help of a magic love herb, in the romantic entanglements of two Athenian couples who inhabit the other major strand of the story.

Britten enhanced the unearthliness of Oberon by assigning the role to a countertenor, whose music mingles archaic baroque-tinged melodies and spiky modern harmonies. In another effective dramatic stroke, Puck is made a speaking role for a nimble young actor whose words are accompanied by restless volleys of percussion and brass.

Though the opera was a rush job, written in just eight months, the score represents Britten at his most masterful. Sometimes I wish I had never heard it, just so I could experience afresh the revelation of the opening orchestral music: eerie string glissandi wheeze slowly up and down through a succession of all twelve major triads, to uncannily suggest the breathing of an agitated dreamer. The frantic scenes for the mismatched pairs of Athenian lovers are too disturbing to be funny. With their passions enhanced by the magic herb, the young adults express themselves over and over in intentionally high-flown and elaborate lyrical outpourings.

In stagings of the Shakespeare play, the episodes with the rustics, the six tradesmen who think themselves great tragedians, can be problematic. Unless acted with effortless comic verve, the scene when the rustics perform their own version of *Pyramus and Thisbe* as a wedding present for Theseus, the duke of Athens, and Hippolyta, the queen of the Amazons, often seems just stock humor. But the endearingly bumptious music Britten devised for the rustics makes them haplessly and hilariously human.

Britten ends this extraordinary work with a final chorus for a children's choir of fairies as well as Oberon and Tytania, now uneasily reconciled, who greet the night with a transfixing hymnal anthem, wonderfully ambivalent music that mingles beguiling modal harmony with a restrained yet jerky dotted-rhythm gait, like some fractured version of a slow baroque court dance.

The nearly perfect 1966 recording of the work for Decca, conducted with keen imagination and calm authority by Britten, is the one to have. The London Symphony Orchestra plays vibrantly for the composer. With a single exception the cast, several of whom are re-creating roles they originated, is superb. It reads like a list of the finest British singers of the day: Elizabeth Harwood as Tytania, John Shirley-Quirk as Theseus, Helen Watts as Hippolyta, Peter Pears as Lysander, Thomas Hemsley as Demetrius, Josephine Veasey as Hermia, with the exquisite Irish soprano Heather Harper as Helena. The weak link, sadly, is Alfred Deller as Oberon. The role was written for Deller, a distinguished and pioneering artist. But countertenors were rare birds back then and standards were not what they are today. Deller's vocal imperfections are too prevalent to be ignored.

An alternative choice is the excellent 1995 recording on Philips with Colin Davis conducting the London Symphony Orchestra. A solid cast is headed by the fine countertenor Brian Asawa as Oberon. Still, the performers under Britten clearly knew they were involved in a historic project, and that excitement and sense of event comes through.

Decca 425 663-2 (two CDs)
Benjamin Britten (conductor), London Symphony Orchestra; Deller, Harwood, Pears, Watts, Veasey, Harper

Philips 454 122-2 (two CDs)
Colin Davis (conductor), London Symphony Orchestra; Asawa, McNair, Lloyd, Ainsley, Watson

15. BENJAMIN BRITTEN (1913–1976)

Death in Venice

Myfanwy Piper, librettist, after the Thomas Mann novella

First performance: Snape, the Maltings, England, June 16, 1973

Benjamin Britten was twenty-three when he met the tenor Peter Pears at a luncheon with a mutual friend in 1937. Within a year they were sharing a London flat. They would remain together until Britten's death in 1976.

It took personal bravery for Britten and Pears to live openly as a devoted couple at a time when legal prohibitions against homosexual behavior still existed. Yet, Britten had tormented feelings about his sexuality, never alluded to it directly in public, and was continually smitten by adolescent boys and young men drawn to his circle.

Though most of his operas have either overt or oblique homo-erotic themes, none delves into the subject more than *Death in Venice,* Britten's last opera and an underappreciated masterpiece, adapted from Thomas Mann's 1912 novella. Pears created the role of Gustav von Aschenbach, and no role in the Britten operas was more dependent upon the intimate, intensely subdued, and plaintive quali-ties of Pears's voice. Though *Death in Venice* was well received at its 1973 premiere, many critics shared the reactions of Peter Heyworth, who wrote in the *Observer* that "Britten does not penetrate far into the dark side of the subject matter," adding that, unlike Mann, he "seems to flinch before the abyss" he evokes. I could not disagree more.

Perhaps audiences expected Aschenbach's longings to be conveyed with lush and emotional music, like the Adagietto from Mahler's Fifth Symphony, which recurs throughout the Luchino Visconti film version of *Death in Venice* that had appeared just two years prior to the opera. In his spare, refined, and precise score, Britten demon-strated that he could hold his own with the more radical (meaning, atonal) composers of the new generation. His musical language deftly incorporates elements of twelve-tone writing into the pungently diatonic harmonic idiom he never abandoned. For me, the incisiveness of the opera's curiously haunting music slices right to the core of Aschenbach's subliminal emotions. In many scenes the orchestral scoring has the delicacy of chamber music. Long stretches of Aschenbach's soliloquies are accompanied only by piano.

Though Myfanwy Piper's libretto follows the events of the novella, the opera is structured as a series of scenes in which Aschenbach both recounts and enacts the story. A master writer in Munich, Aschenbach is creatively spent, weary, and sick at heart. So he travels to Venice for a dose of replenishing sun and sea and the pleasures of the Lido hotel. There he observes a vacationing Polish family with an adolescent boy, Tadzio, who becomes the unwitting object of Aschenbach's consuming desire.

For me the most overwhelming moment of the opera comes at the end of act 1. In an aching soliloquy, no longer able to convince himself that he is drawn to Tadzio as an idealization of natural beauty, Aschenbach is shaken when the boy passes by and smiles at him. "Ah, don't smile like that!" he says to himself. "No one should be smiled at like that." Then, in a rare moment of vulnerable lyricism, he sings, "I—love you."

Baffled at first over how to depict Tadzio, whose conversation Mann's Aschenbach only overhears now and then, Britten and Piper came up with a choreographic solution. Tadzio, his mother and two younger sisters, and all his vacationing playmates are portrayed by dancers. So the opera is half ballet. At the premiere the role was danced by a teenage member of the Royal Ballet whom Pears, true to the character of Aschenbach, became infatuated with. In most productions, Tadzio is a strapping young dancer who wears only a loincloth for the scenes on the beach, where he leaps and spins and is tossed about by his adoring playmates. This solution certainly puts Britten's own twist on the novella. Mann's Tadzio is a lovely but everyday and imperfect boy. When Aschenbach chances upon him in an elevator he notices the boy's poor teeth. But to the repressed writer, Tadzio is a bewitching Greek Adonis. The dancer playing Tadzio in the opera usually looks like a genuine Adonis, and the Dionysian undercurrents are enhanced by a small battery of percus-

Tenor Peter Pears

sion instruments in the dance music, which evokes the sound of Indonesian gamelans. Paradoxically, those listening to the work on a recording, undistracted by the ballet, may more immediately sense the emotional impact and astringent allure of Britten's score.

Another unconventional yet effective idea was Britten's decision to have a whole series of characters that Aschenbach encounters portrayed by the same bass-baritone: The Elder Fop, The Old Gondolier, The Hotel Manager, The Hotel Barber, The Leader of the Players, the Voice of Dionysus. (At the premiere the roles were sung by John Shirley-Quirk.) This casting stroke conveys the sense that Aschenbach is being followed by some phantomlike, all-knowing figure who understands the disturbing truth of the writer's feelings.

The recording to have, of course, is the 1974 Decca release offering the original cast with Steuart Bedford conducting the English Chamber Orchestra. Shirley-Quirk's multirole performance is a tour de force. And through the eerie beauty of his singing and the tension between his refinement and anguish, Pears simply becomes Aschenbach. In his early sixties, Pears enjoyed a career milestone with this role.

Decca (two CDs) 425 669-2
Steuart Bedford (conductor), Members of the English Opera Group, the English Chamber Orchestra; Pears, Shirley-Quirk, Bowman, Bowen

16. FERRUCCIO BUSONI (1866–1924)
Doktor Faust

Ferruccio Busoni, librettist

First performance: Dresden, Sächsisches Staatstheater, May 21, 1925

The German-Italian pianist, composer, editor, essayist, and educator Ferruccio Busoni, who died in 1924, was one of music's great visionaries. In his writings, his teaching, and his music he anticipated the coming of pantonality, atonality, microtonal scales, and even electronic music. Culturally he straddled the north-south European divide, which could have proved confusing to his work. Instead, his experience simply convinced him that internationalism would increasingly characterize music in the twentieth century, which is essentially what happened.

Yet Busoni never codified his thinking into a cogent aesthetic belief system. His essays are fascinating but full of contradictions. And his music, strikingly original and stylistically all over the place, reflects those contradictions.

There is no better illustration than his ambitious, jumbled, and engrossing opera *Doktor Faust,* which he worked on from 1910 until his death, leaving two scenes unfinished, notably the final segment of the last scene. So freely did he borrow music from earlier compositions that you could say that the score to *Doktor Faust* was assembled as much as it was composed.

Busoni, who also wrote his own libretto, believed that opera had stifled itself by adhering to conventional narrative structures. Opera, he thought, better than any other type of theater, could depict states of mind, could embrace the "incredible, unreal and improbable" through music. No story invited such treatment more than Faust.

Busoni used sixteenth-century puppet plays as theatrical models for his opera. His tragic hero is the rector magnificus at a university in Wittenberg, where the opera is set, except for one crucial episode in Italy, where the wandering Faust, egged on by Mephistopheles, steals away the Duchess of Parma on her wedding day to the duke.

Busoni lived through the early-twentieth-century revolutions in atonality (the breakdown of the major and minor scale system) that he had anticipated. Yet, he never really embraced these challenges to harmony. So his musical language is like Alban Berg's but with more tonal grounding, or like some spacey, far-out modern version of Liszt. The inimitable quality of the score is announced in the orchestral prelude, during which the music sways between quietly ominous surgings of richly chromatic, almost unhinged harmony and celestial shimmerings from an eerie offstage choir. Busoni wrote that he shaped each scene of the opera into an organic if unorthodox symphonic form. So the wedding festivities at Parma are in the form of a dance suite, and the tavern scene with the students in Wittenberg has a Bach-inspired prelude, chorale, and fugue. The role of Faust requires a heavyset, weighty baritone voice with power, stamina, and the ability to bring lyrical shape to the sometimes tortured vocal lines. The tenor role of Mephistopheles sits high in the voice and requires a singer who can convey the oily, needling malevolence of the character. The orchestral score teems with thick harmonies, multilayered textures, fitful counterpoint, gnashing dissonance, and sudden stretches of airy impressionistic colorings.

Staging this fantastical opera is a daunting task. It may be easier to appreciate the music from a recording, at least if you listen to the Erato recording made in 1997 and 1998 by the conductor Kent Nagano with forces of the Opéra National de Lyon—a landmark achievement. Nagano conveys the sweep, strangeness, and inexorable power of the work, more than three hours of music, eliciting an assured and arrestingly colored performance from the orchestra and the robust chorus. The large cast is excellent, topped by the robust baritone Dietrich Henschel as Doktor Faust and the bright-voiced tenor Kim Begley as Mephistopheles. Nagano conducts the version of the score completed by Busoni's student Philipp Jarnach. In extra tracks at the end of the recording Nagano includes a newer version of the missing scenes prepared from Busoni's sketches by Antony Beaumont. The entire project is a labor of love from Nagano, the Lyon Opera, and Erato. May it long stay in the catalog.

Erato (three CDs) 3984-25501-2
Kent Nagano (conductor), Orchestra and Chorus of the Opéra National de Lyon; Henschel, Begley, Hollop, Jenis, Roth

17. AARON COPLAND (1900–1990)

The Tender Land

Horace Everett (Erik Johns), librettist

First performance: New York, City Center Theater, April 1, 1954

Aaron Copland used to say that composers were either hopelessly drawn to opera or chronically ambivalent about the genre. "For me," he wrote, "opera was really a very problematic form—la forme fatale—as I called it after my experience with *The Tender Land*."

That experience was certainly discouraging. *The Tender Land*, Copland's second venture into the genre, was his only full-length opera. It was intended for performance by college students and opera workshops. Commissioned as an opera for television, NBC rejected it. The New York City Opera gave the 1954 premiere, which received an underwhelming reception. Talking about the opera in later years, Copland was self-effacing to the point of being defensive. He wanted "simple rhetoric and a musical style to match," Copland wrote; the music was "very plain, with a colloquial flavor," closer to "musical comedy than to grand opera," and so on.

Copland underestimated *The Tender Land*. It may not be a great opera, but it's essential to me—an affecting, musically elegant, and pointedly honest work, especially in the revised, slightly expanded three-act version that Copland composed for a 1955 production at Oberlin College in Ohio.

His librettist was Erik Johns, a dancer, painter, and, at that time, Copland's lover, who for the purposes of this project took the pen name Horace Everett. The opera's seemingly simple story, set in the rural American Midwest during the 1930s at harvest time, is an insightful take on an archetypal American saga. Laurie Moss, a vibrant and restless young woman about to graduate from high school, lives on a farm with her mother, Ma Moss, her grandfather, Grandpa Moss, and her kid sister, Beth. Two drifters, Martin and Top, show up looking for odd jobs. Grandpa and Ma Moss are wary, since there have been stories of two strangers molesting young girls in the area. But at Laurie's urging the young men are hired.

Word spreads and Martin and Top are charged with being the molesters. Though the charges are proven baseless, the men are still forced to leave town. But not before Laurie and Martin, in a beguiling love scene, fall for each other and decide to leave together. That night the well-intentioned Top persuades Martin that it would be foolhardy to take a young girl on the road. In the morning when Laurie discovers that Martin has left without her, though shattered, she decides to leave home on her own, not sure of what will come. The stoic Ma Moss must now put her hopes on Beth to continue the family legacy, such as it is.

The story touches on a recurring American theme: the tension between identifying with your roots and feeling compelled to venture off and leave those roots behind. In addition, the idea of a community of people who seek comfort in sameness and are quick to demonize outsiders is something that was much on Copland's mind at the time. *A Lincoln Portrait*, Copland's work for narrator and orchestra, scheduled for performance at the inaugural concert of President Eisenhower in 1953, was hastily pulled from the program at the behest of congressmen who were suspicious of the composer's left-wing associations during the 1930s. Copland was later brought before the House Un-American Affairs Committee for questioning, though not much came of his appearance.

The score to *The Tender Land,* soothingly rooted in tonality and mostly free of angst and dissonance, represents Copland in his Americana mode. Elements of folk songs, country dances, and hymn tunes are mingled into stretches of conversational recitative and plaintively lyrical arias. But Copland's ear was too keen for his harmonic language to be as bland as he suggested it was. The music continually hooks you with its jabs of intense chromaticism and its lucid instrumental writing. And I defy anyone to listen to the act 1 finale, a quintet, "The Promise of Living," with its sturdy hymnal harmonies, and not get misty-eyed.

Though the revised three-act version of the opera is seldom performed, fortunately there is a lovely recording with Philip Brunelle conducting soloists, chorus, and orchestra of the Plymouth Music Series, an organization he founded in 1969 in Minnesota to present performances of newly composed and rarely heard American works. The cast is winning, headed by the sensitive lyric soprano Elisabeth Comeaux as Laurie, the ardent tenor Dan Dressen as Martin, and the dusky mezzo-soprano Janis Hardy as Ma Moss. Brunelle conducts a supply paced account of an opera that he clearly loves.

Virgin Classics (two CDs) 91113-2
Philip Brunelle (conductor), Soloists, Chorus, and Orchestra of the Plymouth Music Series, Minnesota; Comeaux, Hardy, Dressen, Bohn, Lehr

18. CLAUDE DEBUSSY (1862–1918)

Pelléas et Mélisande

Claude Debussy, librettist, abridgement of play by Maurice Maeterlinck

First performance: Paris, Opéra-Comique, April 30, 1902

In Paris in May 1893 Claude Debussy attended the first performance of Maurice Maeterlinck's *Pelléas et Mélisande,* a groundbreaking play of symbolist theater. He had already read the published script and was interested in adapting the play as an opera. Despite its dreamlike atmosphere, as Debussy wrote in an article at the time, the play contained "far more humanity than those so-called 'real-life documents.'" In it, he added, "there is an evocative language whose sensitivity can be extended into music and into the orchestral *décor.*"

And Debussy's impressionistic music, with its veiled harmonic language, blurry colorings, and ambiguous emotional character, was ideally suited to the subject. Maeterlinck shrouds his story, set in the kingdom of Allemonde in some unspecified but presumably medieval time, in mystery and indirection. One day Golaud, a sullen widower, the son of the aged King Arkel, chances upon Mélisande, a frightened, evasive, and lovely young woman who is lost, alone, and weeping by a well. Almost passively she follows Golaud and, later, joylessly marries him, never revealing anything about her true past. She soon finds her emotional barricade threatened by Golaud's handsome young half brother, Pelléas.

By the summer of 1895 Debussy had essentially finished composing *Pelléas et Mélisande,* his only completed opera, though in the process of preparing the work for its eventual 1902 premiere Debussy revised the score repeatedly and extensively. His music taps into the resonant undercurrents of Maeterlinck's play, into the subliminal feelings that stir beneath the often inconsequential dialogue. In some ways *Pelléas* is an antiopera. The music avoids explicit or overtly dramatic flourishes and moves at a deliberate, spacious pace. Yet, in another way *Pelléas* marks a triumph of opera. Debussy's music illuminates the unconscious in a way that spoken drama seldom matches.

Debussy had a love/hate attitude toward Wagner, mostly hate, though, if you take his writings at face value. But you cannot mistake Debussy's debt to Wagner, especially *Parsifal*. The radically static pace of *Parsifal* emboldened Debussy to compose music that was ever more timeless and still. And Wagner's radically chromatic harmony, often free from tonal moorings, also left its mark on Debussy, provoking him to explore even more far-reaching departures from the diatonic (major and minor scale) idiom.

Many Debussy devotees revere the historic recording of *Pelléas et Mélisande* conducted by Roger Desormiere from a live 1941 performance at the Paris Conservatoire (available on the EMI Classics label). But two more recent versions with excellent recorded sound are my favorites.

In late 1969 and early 1970 the modernist composer and exacting conductor Pierre Boulez recorded the work with the orchestra of the Royal Opera House at Covent Garden in London, a landmark achievement. Reacting to a performance tradition that had increasingly emphasized the amorphous impressionism of the music, Boulez brings out the rhythmic detail and inner textures of the score, without any loss of mystery and radiance. His Mélisande is the exquisite soprano Elisabeth Söderström, who sings with alluring beauty yet an expressive fragility that is just right. George Shirley sings Pelléas, and Boulez draws from this underappreciated American tenor perhaps the most subtle, intelligent, and stylish singing of his career. The baritone Donald McIntyre as Golaud, the bass David Ward as Arkel, and the contralto Yvonne Minton as the worrisome Queen Genevieve are all splendid.

If Boulez makes *Pelléas* sound like a pathbreaking work of early-twentieth-century modernism, Herbert von Karajan on his 1978 recording with the Berlin Philharmonic and a superb cast emphasized the opera's Wagnerian resonances. For all the roomy stillness of this performance, every moment of the nearly three-hour score pulses with subdued intensity. Two excellent American singers in their primes sing the title roles: the rich-voiced mezzo-soprano Frederica von Stade as Mélisande and the elegant baritone Richard Stilwell as Pelléas (a role that falls awkwardly on the divide between tenor and baritone and has been sung by both). José van Dam brings his distinguished artistry and plangent bass-baritone voice to the role of Golaud. EMI Classics has issued this release on its Great Recordings of the Century series, where it belongs. But I can't imagine not owning the Boulez account as well.

Sony Classical (three CDs) SM3K 47265
Pierre Boulez (conductor), Royal Opera Chorus and the Orchestra of the Royal Opera House, Covent Garden; Shirley, Söderström, McIntyre, Ward

EMI Classics (three CDs) 5 67168 2
Herbert von Karajan (conductor), Chorus of the Deutschen Oper Berlin, Berlin Philharmonic; Stilwell, von Stade, van Dam, Raimondi

19. GAETANO DONIZETTI (1797–1848)

L'Elisir d'Amore

Felice Romani, librettist

First performance: Milan, Teatro Cannobiana, May 12, 1832

In making a case for Gaetano Donizetti as an opera composer you have to account for his suspiciously prolific output: though he died at fifty he wrote some seventy stage works. Naturally, he took shortcuts, relied on formulas, and recycled music. Such practices were as common in the theater of Donizetti's day as they were in, say, Broadway of the 1920s when the Gershwin brothers churned out scores for musicals, sometimes two or three per season.

But Donizetti was a craftsman with a striking gift for melody and a savvy sense of what worked on the stage. Though many of his operas are negligible, many more are memorable, and more than a few are masterworks. He was the dominant Italian opera composer before the emergence of Verdi.

What's surprising, though, is that a composer mostly drawn to serious fare brought such a deft hand to comedy, for example, his charming *L'Elisir d'Amore*. It's easy to bask in the musical bounty of this score, with its tuneful arias and ebullient choral ensembles. But it's Donizetti's affection for his characters that lends the music its richness and makes the comedy so beguiling.

The Donizetti scholar William Ashbrook aptly calls the opera a "bucolic variant of the 'male Cinderella' myth." One of the most prosperous farms in a rural Italian village of the early nineteenth century is owned and run by Adina, a plucky and wealthy young woman. Adina is loved from afar by the simple, hamstrung, and smitten peasant Nemorino, who can hardly work up the courage to talk with her let alone confess his feelings.

Adina is no romantic. When we meet her she is engrossed in a book about the Tristan and Iseult myth. She starts to cackle with laughter, arousing the curiosity of the townsfolk, including Nemorino. In a deceptively lyrical and slyly debunking aria (Donizetti's fresh twist on the standard slow cavatina) Adina reads aloud the turn in the story when Iseult slips Tristan a potion that makes him want to stay with her forever. Wouldn't we women like to have such a potion, Adina says as she mocks the absurdity of the saga. But Nemorino is hooked by the idea that maybe this potion actually exists. In this inspired little scene Donizetti contrasts Adina's worldly skepticism with Nemorino's good-hearted gullibility and nimbly sets the plot in motion.

Sergeant Belcore, a role for a robust baritone, arrives on the scene to court Adina, quickly becoming a dramatic and musical foil to Nemorino. The sergeant is confident, articulate, a snap-to-it kind of guy with direct and hardy music to match. Nemorino's music, though full of rhapsodic ardor, is halting and circuitous. It's a lovely touch that when Nemorino beseeches Dr. Dulcamara, an itinerant quack who shows up in town, for a love potion, Dulcamara produces a secret elixir with a proven history of loosening inhibitions and making its drinker lively and irresistible: a bottle of Bordeaux.

Many fine tenors have excelled as Nemorino, but none more so

Tenor Luciano Pavarotti

than Luciano Pavarotti. This was a signature role for the superstar tenor. The combination of his husky, awkward physique and his tenderly lyrical singing made him a poignantly believable peasant. Yet, just as with Nemorino, within that hulk was a powerhouse voice waiting to be unleashed, which Pavarotti was all too happy to do.

He recorded the role twice with sopranos who could not have been more different. A 1985 Decca recording offers Joan Sutherland as Adina. Pavarotti sings incomparably, especially his matchless account of "Una furtiva lagrima," the opera's most famous aria, with its ambiguous mingling of major and minor modes and forlorn bassoon solo. Nemorino has seen Adina shed a "furtive tear" of sympathy, he says in this aria; suddenly he realizes that, amazing as it seems, he has won her love. Sutherland sings with exquisite style, flawless technique, and grace. Richard Bonynge, with his masterly knowledge of the bel canto style, conducts a shapely and buoyant performance.

Some listeners may find Sutherland's Adina lacking in charm and spontaneity. For a much more impish and coy Adina, sung with sweet tone and agility, there is Kathleen Battle's 1989 recording, also with Pavarotti. James Levine conducts the Chorus and Orchestra of the Metropolitan Opera. I find Levine's pliant way with the score more rewarding than Bonynge's. And both the baritone Leo Nucci as Belcore and the bass Enzo Dara as Dulcamara are stronger than their counterparts on the Decca recording, Dominic Cossa and Spiro Malas. But either recording will bring you pleasure.

Decca (two CDs) 414461
Richard Bonynge (conductor), Ambrosian Opera Chorus and the English Chamber Orchestra; Pavarotti, Sutherland, Cossa, Malas

Deutsche Grammophon (two CDs) 429 744-2
James Levine (conductor), Metropolitan Opera Orchestra and Chorus; Pavarotti, Battle, Nucci, Dara

20. GAETANO DONIZETTI (1797–1848)
Lucia di Lammermoor

Salvatore Cammarano, librettist, after Walter Scott's novel

First performance: Naples, Teatro San Carlo, September 26, 1835

My introduction to *Lucia di Lammermoor* came courtesy of Looney Tunes. In "Back Alley Oproar" Elmer Fudd is being kept up all night by Sylvester who is singing opera arias in the alley, especially a hypercharged performance of Figaro's "Largo al factotum" from *The Barber of Seville*. At his wit's end, Elmer takes care of the problem. Or so he thinks. All nine of Sylvester's pussy lives appear in the alley and start to sing the famous sextet from *Lucia di Lammermoor*.

As a kid I thought the cartoon was hilarious. Yet, I remember being curiously stirred by the music, even in that comic performance. Much later, after finding out what the music was and where it came from, I realized why it had so affected me.

That sextet demonstrates something opera can do that spoken theater can't. The story stops for a few minutes while the six main characters stand frozen in place and voice their internal feelings simultaneously in ennobled melodic outpourings prodded along by a graceful accompaniment pattern (imagine a dance rhythm strummed on an orchestral guitar). It's at once an artificial theatrical convention and a moment of exhilarating musical drama.

Lucia di Lammermoor is deservedly Gaetano Donizetti's best-known work. This abundantly tuneful score is also a psychologically insightful drama, an adaptation of Sir Walter Scott's novel *The Bride of Lammermoor*. Set in late-seventeenth-century Scotland during the reign of William and Mary, it concerns two neighboring families—the Lammermoors and the Ravenswoods—who have a long legacy of mutual hatred. Young Lucia of Lammermoor, whose parents have died, is duty bound to her stern brother Enrico Ashton, who has arranged for her marriage to Lord Arturo Bucklaw. The Lammermoors have come on hard times that a union with the wealthy Arturo would alleviate. But Lucia has secretly been meeting the dashing Edgardo, the Laird of Ravenswood.

We first meet Lucia at night near a fountain in a great park on the Lammermoor estate where she awaits a tryst with Edgardo. In the elegiac and restrained aria "Regnava nel silenzio" ("Enveloped in Silence") she tells her companion Alisa the story of a Ravenswood ancestor who cruelly abandoned the body of a Lammermoor girl he killed in a fit of jealousy. Lucia has seen visions of the girl near the fountain, which appeared to have water red with blood. When Alisa urges her to give up Edgardo, Lucia affirms her lover's faithfulness in the ecstatic aria "Quando rapito in estaci." But the ecstatic mood seems forced. So, two full acts before the famous "Mad Scene," Lucia already appears to be mentally unsound.

Through forged letters her brother tries to convince Lucia that Edgardo is false, and then forces her to sign a marriage contract with Arturo. On the wedding night guests are partying in the dilapidated main hall of the Lammermoor castle. To grim and shattered dramatic recitative, Enrico enters and tells the guests that Lucia has stabbed her new spouse to death.

The young woman comes down the stairway in a bloodstained white nightgown, transfixed by the sounds of a distant flute that no one else (except the audience) can hear. She is now ready to marry Edgardo, she says. The "Mad Scene" is an ingeniously structured tour de force. Dramatic recitative and partial quotes from melodies heard earlier are folded deftly into two elaborate arias. But the music seems to flow with a stream-of-consciousness inevitability. The florid coloratura passagework of the music is meant as an expression of Lucia's distraught mental state. It's as if she has entered some flighty and unearthly realm within her own mind.

Some great prima donnas sang the title role in the early decades of the twentieth century, including Amelita Galli-Curci and Luisa Tetrazzini. But Maria Callas can be credited with making the general public understand what a profound and arresting opera *Lucia di Lammermoor* really was. Her 1953 recording, which began her association with the EMI label, is not just Callas's best account of the role but is widely acknowledged as a milestone in the discography of opera. Callas brings utterly commanding technique, a sure sense of bel canto style, and probing emotional insight to her portrayal. The dazed, sometimes pale, and somnolent sound quality with which she begins the "Mad Scene" is hauntingly right. Tullio Serafin conducts a calmly authoritative performance. The tenor Giuseppe di Stefano is in virile voice as Edgardo, and the great baritone Tito Gobbi makes a formidable Enrico.

The other distinguished recording is a 1971 Decca release with Joan Sutherland in the title role and Luciano Pavarotti as Edgardo. Richard Bonynge conducts a surely paced performance with the forces of the Royal Opera, Covent Garden, and admirably includes sections of the opera that had become customary to omit. Some Sutherland fans prefer her first Lucia recording from 1961 for the youthful bloom in her voice. But the later performance is more incisive, dramatically charged, and mature. Pavarotti is in his glory here. You also get the he-man Enrico of the baritone Sherrill Milnes and the chilling Raimondo of the bass Nicolai Ghiaurov. Has that famous sextet ever been sung with more splendor? Even Elmer Fudd would stay up and listen to this performance.

EMI (two CDs) 5 66438 2

Tullio Serafin (conductor), Orchestra and Chorus of Maggio Musicale Fiorentino; Callas, di Stefano, Gobbi

Decca (three CDs) 410 193-2

Richard Bonynge (conductor), Chorus and Orchestra of the Royal Opera, Covent Garden; Sutherland, Pavarotti, Milnes, Ghiaurov

21. ANTONÍN DVOŘÁK (1841–1904)
Rusalka

Jaroslav Kvapil, librettist, after a tale by Friedrich Heinrich Karl de la Motte Fouqué

First performance: Prague, National Theatre, March 31, 1901

Though by far best known for his symphonies and chamber works, Antonín Dvořák wrote eleven operas that exist in performable versions. Most of these works have been thought of as contributions to the Czech nationalist movement in the arts in the late nineteenth and early twentieth centuries. *Rusalka*, which received its premiere in Prague in 1901, is the only Dvořák opera to have attained a canonical place in the repertory, and rightly so.

This lyric fairy tale of a water nymph who falls for a handsome prince and persuades a forest witch to turn her into a mortal fired Dvořák's imagination and inspired his most beguiling and accomplished music. Wagner's influence can be detected in the through-composed structure of the score, which stops only infrequently for set-piece arias and dances. Dvořák's use of recurring thematic motifs linked to characters and situations is another nod to Wagner. But the rustling evocations of Bohemian forests, the gossamer delicacy of the music for the water nymphs, the profusion of soulful melodies touched with the plaintive harmonies of eastern European folk music—all of these elements are distinctively Dvořák.

And yet, for all its beauties, *Rusalka* is a difficult opera to put across in production. Dvořák seems not to have been able to make up his mind whether he was writing a true fairy tale like *The Magic Flute* or a morality play like *Tannhäuser*. Rusalka learns too late to be careful of what you wish for. Mortals have souls and passions. But they are "outcasts of nature," as her father warns her, which means there is no constancy to their actions.

Dvořák's music is continually inventive, with haunting melodies of folkloric simplicity and lilting dances, all linked by a flowing current of subtly scored orchestra music. Yet the opera seldom comes together as a dramatic whole. It's as if Dvořák had been hesitant to tap too deeply into the implications of the story.

The remarkable soprano Renée Fleming, who adores the role of Rusalka, has no such hesitancy, which is why I so admire her 1998 recording with Sir Charles Mackerras conducting the Czech Philharmonic Orchestra. Fleming respects the opera enough to be willing to search out its ominous subtext and sadness. She sings the lyrical passages with poignant sound and unmannered phrasing, especially the bittersweet "Song to the Moon," in which Rusalka calls upon the moon to tell her beloved prince that she awaits him by the lake. Fleming has called this the most beautiful of all arias in opera, and hearing her luminous performance you may just agree.

Yet, she also brings darker hues and volatility to Rusalka's moments of torment, confusion, and jealousy. Her portrayal is abetted by a like-minded and excellent cast. With his heroic tenor voice, Ben Heppner makes the Prince intriguingly complex, romantic one moment, blustery the next. He is enchanted by Rusalka's beauty but threatened by her silence and frigidity. Does he love her? Or is he just bewitched? Heppner brings out the Prince's understandable confusions, though at the end he dissolves into misery and brings about his own death when he kisses Rusalka before she returns to her water world, as she must. The powerhouse mezzo-soprano Dolora Zajick is at once chilling and delightful as the all-knowing witch Ježibaba, and the bass Franz Hawlata makes a bellowing Vodnik, the Water Goblin. Mackerras draws crisp, colorful, and undulant playing from the Czech Philharmonic.

I'm not one to assess the Czech diction of this mostly American cast, though it sounds pretty convincing. But for an excellent version with a mostly Czech cast try the 1982 Supraphon import recording starring the distinguished soprano Gabriela Beňačková as Rusalka. Richard Novak as Vodnik, Vera Soukupova as Ježibaba, and Wieslaw Ochman as the Prince also bring stylistic authority and appealing vocal artistry to their performances. Vaclav Neumann conducts an insightful and lithe performance. The orchestra is again the Czech Philharmonic. You could say these players own this work.

Decca (three CDs) 289 460 568-2
Sir Charles Mackerras (conductor), The Kühn Mixed Choir and the Czech Philharmonic Orchestra; Fleming, Heppner, Hawlata, Zajick

Supraphon (three CDs) 10 3641-2
Vaclav Neumann (conductor), Czech Philharmonic Chorus and Orchestra; Beňačková, Ochman, Drobkova, Novak, Soukupova

22. CARLISLE FLOYD (b. 1926)

Susannah

Carlisle Floyd, librettist

First performance: Tallahassee, Florida State University, February 24, 1955

When Carlisle Floyd wrote *Susannah,* his first opera, he was a twenty-eight-year-old junior faculty member at Florida State University in Tallahassee. The 1955 premiere took place there under his supervision. The next year it was produced at the New York City Opera, conducted by Erich Leinsdorf. Since then it has had about eight hundred performances worldwide, Floyd estimates.

It's hard to argue with such success. Yet, *Susannah,* which transplants the biblical story of Susanna and the elders to a mountain village in Tennessee in the 1950s, has always drawn criticism from opera connoisseurs who deem it a regional work by a regional composer. True, the music eschews the modernistic language of complex composers who claimed the intellectual high ground during the mid-twentieth century. Its harmonic language, though sometimes touched by anguished dissonance, is unabashedly tonal; its melodic content is beguilingly lyrical and strewn with tunes that suggest Appalachia. Floyd evokes square dances, country fiddling, revival meetings, and Southern hymns.

But if *Susannah* is not a breakthrough opera, it is affectingly genuine. Floyd, born in South Carolina, the son of an itinerant minister, grew up with judgmental southerners like the characters in his opera. "These are the folks I went to school with and caught the itch from," he told me in a 1998 interview. Through his direct and guileless music and his naturalistic dialogue (Floyd always writes his own librettos), he does not look down on these characters and conveys the tragic loss that results from their small-mindedness.

Susannah Polk, a naturally sensual and hearty nineteen-year-old who dreams of far-off towns and exotic adventures, lives with her older brother, Sam, a hapless trapper with a drinking problem. Sam has raised Susannah, their parents having died. While the men of the town are aroused by Susannah's robust beauty, their wives don't trust her a bit. One day the elders of the town come upon Susannah bathing naked in a creek near her home, which for them is proof of her wantonness. Not content with shunning her, some elders pressure Little Bat, an impish and malleable young man who likes to hang out at the Polk house, into saying that Susannah forced him to "love her up."

The stern town minister, Olin Blitch, decides to confront her at her home. In a powerfully insightful scene, Blitch's moral indignation dissolves in the face of Susannah's vulnerability. "I'm a lonely man, Susannah," he sings, in a two-minute aria, a model of concision and character depiction. He forces himself upon her. Sick at heart and exhausted by the accusations, Susannah gives in. But Blitch soon realizes that Susannah is a virgin. He tries to dissuade the elders from exiling her, but is afraid to reveal his own guilt. Sam, who knows the truth, murders Blitch and escapes into the hills. Will Susannah flee the village? Or defy the town and live alone, ostracized and feared, and spend the rest of her days feeding her chickens? We never learn.

The title role was originated by the distinguished American soprano Phyllis Curtin, who would sing it in another thirty productions. A fine spinto soprano with a vibrant and penetrating voice, and a West Virginia native, Curtin was an ideal Susannah. She never recorded the role in a studio, but a live recording of a 1962 performance at the New Orleans Opera was released in 1998. Curtin had mixed feelings about the release since she and the cast had had problems with the conductor, Knud Andersson. But with the heroic tenor Richard Cassilly as Sam and the elegant bass-baritone Norman Treigle as Olin Blitch, the cast could not have been better. It's a fine and historic account of the work.

In 1995 the brilliant American conductor Kent Nagano led the forces of the Orchestre de l'Opéra de Lyon in a dynamic studio recording of the opera starring the soprano Cheryl Studer in the title role, the resounding bass Samuel Ramey as Blitch, and the bright-voiced tenor Jerry Hadley as Sam. Studer brings near-Wagnerian vocal richness to her singing, an effective approach, since Susannah is a larger-than-life character in New Hope Valley. It would be hard to choose between these recordings. I admire each.

Countless operas are more musically elaborate than *Susannah,* but few have such authenticity. Floyd received a tumultuous and grateful ovation from a full house at the Metropolitan Opera when the work was presented there in 1998 with Renée Fleming in the title role. The head of the public relations office, a sophisticated and multilingual gentleman with a vast knowledge of opera, was overcome by the performance. "The opera is so honest," he told me afterward. "It makes the characters in *Tosca* look phony."

VAI Audio (two CDs) VAIA 1115-2
Knud Andersson (conductor), New Orleans Opera Orchestra and Chorus; Curtin, Treigle, Cassilly

Virgin Classics (two CDs) 45039-2
Kent Nagano (conductor), Orchestre de l'Opéra de Lyon; Studer, Ramey, Hadley

---

23. GEORGE GERSHWIN (1898–1937)

Porgy and Bess

DuBose Heyward, librettist, after his novel *Porgy* (1925), with lyrics by DuBose Heyward and Ira Gershwin

First performance: New York, Alvin Theatre, October 10, 1935

In general I've found that Stephen Sondheim's musicals lose something when they are performed by opera singers in opera houses. The scores were written with musical theater voices in mind—singing actors who can project words with clarity and punch.

But I feel the opposite about George Gershwin's *Porgy and Bess*. The work has thrived in the opera house when singers with cultivated operatic voices send Gershwin's melodic lines soaring, when full-fledged orchestras play Gershwin's bright and deft orchestrations, when a robust opera chorus sings the ensemble numbers that run through the work, and especially when the score is performed complete. It took until 1976 for that complete performance to occur, an acclaimed production at the Houston Grand Opera, which was a turning point in the critical perception of the opera.

And *Porgy and Bess* is an opera, a sweeping, original, and ambitious opera, not just the "folk opera" that Gershwin, wary of being viewed as an interloper from Tin Pan Alley elbowing his way into the opera house, called the work. It took nine years to reach the stage, from the moment in 1926 when Gershwin had an epiphany reading DuBose Heyward's novel *Porgy* to the 1935 premiere at the Alvin Theatre on Broadway. Though the son of Russian Jewish immigrants, Gershwin was instinctively drawn to African-American music, from piano rags to blues, West Indian dances, and jazz, all of which permeated his songs and concert works. As has often been pointed out, at a time when Gershwin was the most sought-after and well-paid American songwriter, he devoted two full years to the composition of this work.

Naturally, from the beginning *Porgy and Bess* was vulnerable to critics who challenged its operatic pedigree and the authenticity of its subject matter. This folk opera was "a tale about Southern blacks by a white novelist, set to music by a New York–based Jewish songwriter-lyricist team and played on the Broadway stage," as Richard Crawford puts it in his entry in the *New Grove Dictionary of Opera*. And the story perpetuated racial stereotypes. The people of Catfish Row, a black neighborhood in Charlestown, South Carolina, in the 1920s, can be seen, as Crawford rightly adds, as feckless, prone to violence, and given to singing their sorrows away.

Opinion against the work was epitomized by the composer and critic Virgil Thomson in a 1935 article for *Modern Music*, a perceptive but opinionated and overly tough analysis. Though Thomson faults both the hokum of the opera's subject matter and Gershwin's music for "falling between two stools" stylistically, he begrudgingly—and patronizingly—admits to its emotional impact and musical distinction: "With a libretto that should never have been accepted on a subject that should never have been chosen, a man who should never have attempted it has written a work that has considerable power."

Of course, Thomson's comments came from having seen the original Broadway production, for which Gershwin was forced by his producers to cut the score severely. Today no professional opera house would present it other than complete. Some critics still view the work as a series of immortal arias, songs, and duets ("Summertime," "I Got Plenty o' Nuttin'," "Bess, You Is My Woman Now") connected by awkward stretches of arioso and recitative. Only a sensitive and complete performance can convey the engrossing narrative urgency and musical integrity of Gershwin's vision. And, showing respect for the African-American musical tradition, instead of quoting spirituals Gershwin composed his own, like the extraordinary choral lament "Gone, Gone, Gone."

The characters may trade in stereotypes, but Gershwin's music ennobles them. The glamorous Bess, whose willpower is undercut by a drug habit, is torn between her lust for her surly and hotheaded lover, Crown, a hunky stevedore, and her respect for the decent Porgy, a crippled beggar, who takes Bess in when Crown is forced to flee after killing a neighbor in a drunken brawl during a craps game.

But the authenticity of *Porgy and Bess* comes through best in a complete performance, and, to my own surprise, my favorite recording these days was drawn from a production at the Glyndebourne Festival in England, recorded in 1988. Sir Simon Rattle conducts the London Philharmonic, the Glyndebourne Festival Chorus, and a splendid cast. In keeping with the stipulation of the Gershwin estate, the major roles are taken by African-American artists (though I think the time may have arrived to end this de facto racial ban on casting).

While Rattle's feeling for blues and jazz is palpable in his conducting, what I admire is that he treats the score like a teeming, complex, and visionary contemporary opera. His performance has bracing energy, architectonic structure, and articulate phrasing. Willard White as Porgy, Cynthia Haymon as Bess, Harolyn Blackwell as Clara, Cynthia Clarey as Serena, and Damon Evans as Sportin' Life all give vibrant and affecting performances.

I must confess that after all my talk, another favorite recording, from 1963, offers only excerpts from the opera. The selling point here is the singing of the eloquent baritone William Warfield and, especially, the amazing Leontyne Price. It was as Bess in an international tour of *Porgy and Bess* in the mid-1950s that the young Price came to attention. This album of excerpts, though, allows her to sing not just Bess's music, but Clara's "Summertime" and Serena's "My Man's Gone Now," both of which are among the most extraordinary, radiant, and moving performances Price ever recorded.

But this opera, and it is an essential *opera,* must be heard complete to get the point.

EMI (three CDs) 5 56220 2
Simon Rattle (conductor), London Philharmonic, Glyndebourne Festival Chorus; White, Haymon, Clarey, Blackwell, Evans

RCA Victor Gold Seal (one CD) 5234-2-RG—excerpts
Skitch Henderson (conductor), RCA Victor Orchestra and Chorus; Price, Warfield, Boatwright, Bubbles

24. UMBERTO GIORDANO (1867–1948)

Andrea Chénier

Luigi Illica, librettist

First performance: Milan, Teatro alla Scala, March 28, 1896

An opera company does not decide to mount a production of Umberto Giordano's *Andrea Chénier* and only then contract a tenor to sing the title role. If any opera is a star vehicle, it's this 1896 verismo melodrama set in and around Paris during the French Revolution. Giordano's hero bears only scant resemblance to the historical Chénier, a high-born Parisian poet who championed the downtrodden but denounced their violent excesses and was executed on trumped-up charges of treason in 1794. No matter. In the opera house, this swashbuckling role has provided some powerhouse tenors with a chance for virile lyricism and dramatic impetuosity.

The success of this opera shot Giordano to the front rank of the *giovane scuola*, the new generation of Italian opera composers who looked to France (especially Massenet) and Germany (especially Wagner) for innovative approaches to musical drama. The winter of 1896 also saw the premiere in Turin of Puccini's *Bohème*, whose co-librettist, Luigi Illica, was the sole librettist of *Andrea Chénier*. But the two works take strikingly different approaches to opera.

Puccini's score is an intricate fabric of motifs and themes that keep getting recalled and transformed for dramatic effect. Giordano's score, in contrast, is as rhapsodic and sweeping as the events it describes. The title character dominates the work from the start. Arriving at a party of snobbish aristocrats in the posh salon of the Countess of Coigny in Paris, Chénier is coquettishly challenged by Maddalena, the countess's daughter, to improvise a poem about love. But he takes the challenge seriously, giving vent to his radical convictions about freedom and love in the scene-stealing aria "Un di all'azzurro spazio."

His love, he says, is the revered land of France whose oppressed peasants are suffering. The aria is deftly constructed to sound like a spontaneous and impassioned improvisation. The guests are outraged, all except for Maddalena, whose complacency is shaken by Chénier's grand and dangerous outpouring. The opera follows the story of Chénier and Maddalena over the next four years, as the poet falls into disrepute with the revolutionaries.

With his heroic Italian tenor voice, natural gravitas, and idiomatic feel for the Italian language (so important to this character, a poet who reveres the power of words), Mario Del Monaco was a charismatic Chénier and his 1957 Decca recording is splendid. More recently Plácido Domingo was a compelling Chénier, and he sounds youthful, rash, and fervent on his 1976 RCA Victor recording. A 1963 EMI recording offers Franco Corelli's Chénier. No tenor brought more vocal magnetism and swagger to the role and his full-voiced top notes have a thrilling ping. For me, though, Corelli's Chénier is too much the hothead. The character is a thinker as well as a radical. Still, all three tenors are spellbinding.

Del Monaco's Maddalena is Renata Tebaldi, who, though not at her best, still sings with sumptuous sound and radiance, especially in the ecstatic final duet when Chénier and Maddalena stride hand in hand to the guillotine. Corelli's Maddalena is the undervalued and elegant soprano Antonietta Stella, who sings beautifully.

But the Domingo recording, besides being the most readily available, may be the best overall choice. Conducting the National Philharmonic Orchestra, James Levine treats the score with musicianly respect while fully conveying its dramatic verve. The baritone Sherrill Milnes gives a smoldering performance as Gerard, a disloyal servant at the countess's home who becomes a key activist in the revolution. The soprano Renata Scotto's involving portrayal of Maddalena is capped by a riveting account of "La mamma morta," the aria that attained wide public attention in the 1993 film *Philadelphia*. In an Oscar-winning portrayal as a gay lawyer dying of AIDS, Tom Hanks, on the night before his employment discrimination suit, puts on a CD of Callas singing "La mamma morta" for the edification of the homophobic and opera-ignorant lawyer (Denzel Washington) who is representing him. In this abjectly sad and volatile aria Maddalena

Tenor Plácido Domingo

describes how her mother was burned to death when a revolutionary mob set fire to her house. By the end of the aria, though, Maddalena has a transcendent vision of life and love, and Hanks's character, teary, sweating, and overcome, shouts the lines as Callas sings them: "I am divine! I am oblivion! . . . I am love." No one can touch Callas's shattering account of "La mamma morta" on a 1955 EMI recording of arias. But the entire opera is very much worth knowing. If you can have only one recording, try Domingo's.

Decca (two CDs) 425407
Gianandrea Gavazzeni (conductor), Orchestra and Chorus of the Academy of Saint Cecilia; Del Monaco, Tebaldi, Corena

RCA Victor (two CDs) 2046-2-RG
James Levine (conductor), John Alldis Choir and the National Philharmonic Orchestra; Domingo, Scotto, Milnes

EMI Classics (two CDs) 65287

Gabriele Santini (conductor), Orchestra of the Rome Opera; Corelli, Stella, Sereni

25. CHRISTOPH WILLIBALD GLUCK

(1714–1787)

Orfeo ed Euridice

Ranieri de' Calzabigi, librettist

First performance: Vienna, Burgtheater, October 5, 1762

In a contest to name the most self-made of all the great composers my vote would go to Christoph Willibald Gluck. As a young boy in Bohemia, Gluck learned to sing and to play the violin and cello. But his father was set on directing his son into the family business: forestry. So Gluck ran away from home in his early adolescence and went to Prague, where he became a street musician who sang songs and played the Jew's harp. Eventually he got a job as a church organist and made formative but infrequent trips to the city's opera house, since he seldom had extra money. From all evidence, though, he seems to have been largely self-taught.

As a young adult Gluck became a resourceful itinerant musician, taking jobs as a string player in court chamber ensembles and orchestras, first in Vienna, then in Milan, where he played and heard works by the leading composers of the day. At the age of twenty-seven in 1741 his first opera, *Artaserse*, was presented with great success in Milan. Further trips to London and Paris enhanced his musical sophistication. Then in 1752 he made two life-altering decisions: he moved to the cosmopolitan city of Vienna, and he married the daughter of a wealthy merchant with a convenient connection to the imperial court.

Gluck's other fortuitous encounter came in 1761 when, already respected throughout Europe for his operas and ballets, he met the Italian poet, librettist, and theatrical entrepreneur Ranieri de' Calzabigi. Though Gluck is credited with instituting some long-overdue reforms of the existing postbaroque operatic style, Calzabigi was the force behind the campaign. Their first collaboration embodied their credo: *Orfeo ed Euridice,* an opera seria introduced in Vienna in 1762.

Italian opera seria had become prey to abuses and excess, Gluck felt. There was too much ostentatious vocal writing, too much automatic reliance on standard aria forms. Most operas were musically showy and dramatically absurd, Gluck believed. His preface to the published score of *Alceste,* a later collaboration with Calzabigi, can be read as a manifesto of the reformist agenda. "I have striven," Gluck wrote, "to restrict music to its true office of serving poetry by means of expression and by following the situations of the story, without interrupting the action or stifling it with a useless superfluity of ornaments."* Gluck was not willing to arrest a heated exchange of dialogue in order to fulfill some dated expectation for an orchestra ritornello, or such. Above all he aimed for a "beautiful simplicity" and avoided musical displays at the expense of clearness.

Beautiful simplicity is the hallmark of *Orfeo ed Euridice.* Gone is the standard alteration of elaborate arias with recitative. There is no secco recitative, the recitative accompanied only by harpsichord, at all. The orchestra accompanies arias and dialogue alike. The dramatic pacing is sufficiently flexible to incorporate emotional outbursts and drastic shifts of scene and tone while still seeming natural and elegant. The chorus, which variously depicts nymphs, demons, Furies, spirits, and heroes, has a greatly expanded role from what had been the norm in serious Italian opera.

The opera is also a model of dramatic concision. Gluck and Calzabigi get right to the kernel of the story. After a stirring overture, we come upon a funeral scene. Euridice, Orfeo's new bride, has already died. Gluck conjures real terror when Orfeo, determined to retrieve his beloved from death, descends into Hades. After winning permission to reclaim her, the scene changes to the Elysian Fields. Orfeo

*Translated by Eric Blom in Alfred Einstein, *Gluck* (London, 1936).

sings one of Gluck's most ingenious arias, "Che puro ciel," as he marvels at the splendors of the realm. The orchestra quivers with wondrous colors and tremulous harmonies. It's so blissful you begin to wonder whether Euridice will really want to leave.

The opera is all the more moving for its understatement, especially in the score's most famous aria, "Che farò senza Euridice?" Gluck ennobles Orfeo's despondent lament through his choice of a soothingly calm pacing and a major mode key scheme. Having broken the command of the Furies not to look back as he escorted Euridice back to the world, Orfeo has lost his beloved wife a second time. Of course, given Gluck's lofty aim and sympathy for the Age of Reason in which he lived, the opera ends happily. Cupid takes pity on the bereaved Orfeo and restores Euridice to life as a chorus of blissful shepherds and shepherdesses celebrate.

A lovely recording was made by the British conductor and early music expert John Eliot Gardiner in 1991. The winning cast is headed by the countertenor Derek Lee Ragin as Orfeo, a role conceived for a castrato, and the soprano Sylvia McNair as Euridice. Gardiner conducts the estimable Monteverdi Choir and the English Baroque Soloists in an undulant, lucid, and radiant performance. A strong selling point of the recording is the scholarship that was put into determining the performing edition used. In his liner notes Gardiner writes that no opera of the eighteenth century has been more dramatically bowdlerized. I'll leave it to scholars to say how closely Gardiner's version of the opera resembles Gluck's original, but as performed the work comes across as a seamless and inspired masterpiece.

Of course, the idea that any of his operas existed in an authentic original state probably would have struck Gluck as curious, for he constantly adapted them to the demands of new productions. Indeed, in 1764 he fashioned a French-text version of this opera for a production in Paris, called *Orphée et Euridice,* adding and removing arias and choruses and incorporating more dance music to please the ballet-mad French audiences. Donald Runnicles and the forces of the San Francisco Opera made an affecting recording of the French version in 1996 with the mezzo-soprano Jennifer Larmore and the soprano Dawn Upshaw as Orphée and Euridice. Both sing splendidly.

Philips (two CDs) 434 093-2

John Eliot Gardiner (conductor), Monteverdi Choir and English Baroque Soloists; McNair, Ragin, Sieden

Teldec (two CDs) 4509-98418-2

Donald Runnicles (conductor), Chorus and Orchestra of the San Francisco Opera; Larmore, Upshaw, Hagley

26. CHRISTOPH WILLIBALD GLUCK

(1714–1787)

Iphigénie en Tauride (Iphigénie in Tauris)

Nicolas-François Guillard, librettist

First performance: Paris, Académie Royale de Musique (Opéra), May 18, 1779

Having significantly reformed serious Italian opera, Christoph Willibald Gluck turned his attention to serious French opera, the *tragédie*. For the last part of his career Gluck continued to reside in Vienna but wrote operas for performance in Paris, traveling there to supervise productions. His crowning achievement, one of the greatest of all operas, was *Iphigénie en Tauride,* which had a celebrated premiere at the Paris Opera in 1779 when Gluck was nearly sixty-six.

A compelling, concise, and literate libretto by Nicolas-François Guillard, based on a French play that was itself modeled on Euripides, inspired Gluck to write music of unparalleled boldness. There is, essentially, no division between recitative and aria in this work. Dialogue is set in elegant arioso, by turns lyrically high-flown and, when the action demands it, snappy and incisive. The many arresting arias in the work are seamlessly folded into the overall musical and narrative structure.

Iphigénie en Tauride has one of the most original openings in the opera repertory. The story takes place in Tauris (the modern Crimean peninsula) five years after the Trojan War. Iphigénie, the daughter of King Agamemnon, having been rescued from a sacrificial death by the goddess Diana, is now the head priestess of a temple to Diana in Tauris, which is ruled by the brutal King Thoas, who lives in fear of the Greeks.

As the opera begins the orchestra plays a deceptively gentle minuet until a tempest breaks out in the orchestra, depicting turmoil within Iphigénie's mind as well as a storm battering the coast. Suddenly, Iphigénie breaks into the scene. You would think she had interrupted an overture. Iphigénie describes a dream she has just had so frantically that her priestess attendants are terrified.

In the dream she has envisioned her father running away from Clytemnestra, his wife, his murderer, and Iphigénie's vicious mother. Then an image appears of her beloved brother, Oreste, the young King of Argos and Mycenae, she says. But some ominous force is compelling her to kill him. The priestesses sing a serenely forlorn lament that serves to calm Iphigénie, who expresses her anguish in a beguilingly understated aria. Please, Diana, she pleads, relieve me of life.

King Thoas rushes in. Dismayed and shaken by the storm, the king has sought counsel from the oracles, who decree that the gods must be appeased with another sacrifice. Fortuitously, two young Greeks were cast up on shore during the storm, Oreste and his friend Pylade. The brother and sister, Iphigénie and Oreste, who have been separated for years, do not recognize each other. Equally oblivious, Thoas orders Iphigénie to choose and put to death one of these young men.

Iphigénie en Tauride is often described as a magisterial tragedy that, for once in opera, is without an element of romantic love. While technically true, the subtext of the music says otherwise. In act 2, Oreste, consumed by guilt over having killed his mother (in retribution for her murder of Agamemnon, of course, but still an act of murder), tells Iphigénie that young King Oreste has died. Lost in grief over her noble brother's death, she sings, "O malheureuse Iphigénie," an aria that in its anguished beauty rivals any ardent expression of romantic love in the operatic repertory. This is another one of

Gluck's inspired laments in a major key. The affirming quality of the major-mode harmonies lends Iphigénie's despair a dignity that makes it all the more heartbreaking.

The other element of abject love in the opera comes from the friendship between Oreste and Pylade. My understanding of their relationship was transformed by a revelatory production at the Glimmerglass Opera in 1997 directed by Francesca Zambello. The two men were portrayed by strikingly handsome and quite fine young singers: the baritone Nathan Gunn as Oreste and the tenor William Burden as Pylade. Often these captives are presented as fine Greeks in togas. Zambello made clear that they had been beaten and stripped by their captors. For most of the opera they looked grimy and sweaty, were chained together, and wore nothing but loincloths. The physical affection they tendered each other reminded you that theirs was a classic Greek friendship, no doubt physical as well as brotherly. For me, Zambello's conception of the characters stemmed from an insightful and sensitive reading of the opera. These two brave singers gave poignantly vulnerable performances. Still, in a good production, even one that lacks such a vividly realistic staging concept, the nature of the devotion between Oreste and Pylade should come through in Gluck's refined yet impassioned music.

The opera ends in wistful joy. Just as Iphigénie is about to sacrifice her brother, they recognize each other and embrace. Pylade, who had been ordered back to Greece, returns with an army he has raised and liberates the place. The goddess Diana herself appears to tell Oreste that the suffering he has endured for having killed his mother has expiated his crime. A sublime chorus of departure salutes the siblings and the heroic Pylade as they all set sail for the homeland.

The Glimmerglass production featured the excellent young American soprano Christine Goerke as Iphigénie and she sings the role on an impressive 1999 recording with Martin Pearlman conducting Boston Baroque, a period instrument orchestra. The winning cast includes the hardy baritone Rodney Gilfry as Oreste and the bright-voiced tenor Vinson Cole as Pylade. Pearlman's lithe and supply shaped performance captures both the impetuous sweep and classical grandeur of the work. Goerke's luminous voice and Apollonian expressivity are ideal for the title role.

Another choice is the fine 1985 recording with John Eliot Gardiner conducting the orchestra of the Lyon Opera and the Monteverdi Choir, a typically insightful and dynamic performance from a major musician. The orchestra plays on modern instruments, but with an informed sense of eighteenth-century style. Diana Montague, a mezzo-soprano, brings a dusky-toned beauty to her account of Iphigénie. The distinguished baritone Thomas Allen and the ardent tenor John Aler sing Oreste and Pylade.

You can't go wrong with either recording of this extraordinary opera. Berlioz and Wagner may seem worlds apart, but they shared a profound admiration for Gluck.

Telarc (two CDs) CD-80546
Martin Pearlman (conductor), Boston Baroque; Goerke, Gilfry, Cole, Salters

Philips (two CDs) 416 148-2
John Eliot Gardiner (conductor), Monteverdi Choir and Orchestre de l'Opéra de Lyon; Montague, Aler, Allen, Massis

27. CHARLES GOUNOD (1818–1893)

Roméo et Juliette

Jules Barbier and Michel Carré, librettists, after Shakespeare's play

First performance: Paris, Théâtre Lyrique, April 27, 1867

For most of his career Charles Gounod's operas were widely admired and influential. But by the 1880s, when in old age he ceased composing, Gounod's reputation was already in decline. What had once been embraced as rich and elegant musical drama started to seem artificial and ponderous alongside the radical experiments of the late nineteenth century. Gounod wrote twelve operas and all but two have been sidelined for the most part. Those two, however, remain enduring staples.

I must confess I'm not much of a *Faust* fan. Gounod was a beguiling melodist and the opera abounds with catchy tunes. I love Marguerite's soulful "Ballade of the King of Thule," with its hints of ancient modal harmonies. And her vivacious "Jewel Song" is always fun if you have a soprano in the role with agile coloratura technique. The character of Mephistopheles is a chortling villain right out of the opéra comique tradition. But in a way that's the problem. Gounod's score doesn't rise to the level of Goethe's epic play. He was too bent on entertaining audiences and inserting the requisite arias and ballet music. The seams show in the opera's structure. Too often a quality of placid beauty and efficient rather than urgent narrative pacing prevails.

But something about Shakespeare's star-crossed young lovers must have shaken up Gounod when he wrote *Roméo et Juliette,* his most impassioned opera. It begins with a stormy orchestral prologue depicting the ongoing hostility between the Capulets and the Montagues. At a feverish climax the music boldly breaks into a somber and sturdy fugue: Is the piling on of contrapuntal voices in the orchestra meant to suggest the stacking up of grudges over decades between the warring families? In any event, Gounod wisely cuts the fugue short and the orchestra segues deftly into a choral ensemble in which the voices, like some chorus from Greek tragedy, intone the background story and reveal the tragic end that awaits the young lovers.

The opera continues on this inspired level. Gounod was more willing here than in any other opera to discombobulate expectations, to meld his melodically enriched recitatives into arias and ensembles that shift in sync with the twists in the drama. There are four love duets for the adolescent hero and heroine, yet each one seems musically fresh and compelled by the plot.

The starry roster of great singers who for decades have found the title roles irresistible offer persuasive testimony that *Roméo et Juliette* is Gounod's most compelling opera. Of the many fine recordings two are standouts for me, though some Gounod buffs may quibble with my choices.

A classic 1968 recording offers Franco Corelli and Mirella Freni in the title roles. Obviously, you do not turn to Corelli, a powerhouse Italian tenor, for idiomatically French singing. Refinement is a hallmark

Soprano Mirella Freni

of French style, and with his huge and burnished voice Corelli was often a shameless showoff. But you cannot listen to his Roméo and say that this exciting artist did not understand stylish phrasing, vocal nuance, and elegance. In the fervently romantic passages he really lets his heroic voice soar. Yet you will not believe how tenderly he can sing pianissimo. This recording also captures Freni in her youthful glory, singing with luminous and rosy sound and fine-spun lyricism. And any coloratura soprano would covet Freni's ability to toss off Juliette's roulades and runs and trills in the lighthearted, show-stopping waltz that she sings in the masked ball scene that begins the work. Some impressive French artists take supporting roles and Alain Lombard elicits a transparent and stylish performance from the orchestra and chorus of the Paris Opera.

A fine alternative, on RCA, is a 1995 recording with Plácido

Domingo and Ruth Ann Swenson in the title roles. Domingo's performance may come as a surprise. At the time he had long been immersed in his weighty Wagner roles, repertory that drew upon the dark colorings and natural heft of his voice. But he ably adapts his husky sound to the lyrical necessities of Roméo. Swenson can rightly be faulted for her often slurry diction. And some may find her portrayal lacking in profile and interpretively cautious, though to me she captures Juliette's girlish petulance. Still, for sheer beauty of tone, beautiful placement of the voice, exquisite phrasing, and effortless agility, Swenson is hard to top. The robust baritone Kurt Ollmann makes a hotheaded Mercutio. The rich-toned mezzo-soprano Susan Graham steals her few scenes as the page boy Stéphano. Leonard Slatkin conducts the Munich Radio Orchestra in a surely paced account of the score and must be given credit for inspiring such good work from his leading singers. This is the one Gounod opera that lives up to his early reputation.

EMI Classics (two CDs) 5 65290 2
Alain Lombard (conductor), Orchestra Chorus of the National Theatre of the Paris Opera; Corelli, Freni, Gui, Lublin

RCA Victor Red Seal (two CDs) 09026-68440-2
Leonard Slatkin (conductor), Chorus of the Bavarian Radio and the Munich Radio Orchestra; Domingo, Swenson, Graham, Ollmann

28. GEORGE FRIDERIC HANDEL

(1685–1759)

Giulio Cesare in Egitto (Julius Caesar in Egypt)

Nicola Francesco Haym, librettist, based on work by Giacomo Francesco Bussoni

First performance: London, King's Theatre, February 20, 1724

Though George Frideric Handel showed exceptional musical talent from an early age, his father, a barber-surgeon in the service of the Duke of Saxe-Weissenfels in Halle, Germany, tried to prevent him from studying music. Law was the profession Handel's father had picked for him. But when Handel was nine, the duke heard George furtively playing the chapel's organ and, mightily impressed, persuaded the boy's father to let him receive solid musical training.

Details of Handel's early life are rather sketchy, but it's generally conceded that a childhood trip to Berlin to hear opera incited a passion for the theater in the aspiring composer. In his early adulthood Handel started learning the craft from the inside. In 1703, at eighteen, he won employment as a second violinist and continuo harpsichord player in the orchestra of the opera house at Hamburg. There he became an upstart apprentice to the company director, Reinhart Kaiser. Two years later he wrote his first opera, *Almira,* for that theater. By 1707 Handel was off to Italy to absorb firsthand the styles and idioms of Italian opera. Eventually, he wound up in London, where Italian opera had been introduced in 1705. Handel stoked the growing curiosity among Londoners for Italian opera and wrote the first Italian work specifically intended for London audiences, *Rinaldo,* produced at the King's Theatre in 1711.

Looking back with today's perspective, the idea of a German composer writing Italian operas for English-speaking audiences may seem curious. But Londoners took to this exotic and vocally astounding theatrical genre, and Handel was as gifted an impresario as he was a composer. His reign as London's dominant provider of Italian operas lasted over thirty years, even surviving a passing challenge by a rival company, the Opera of the Nobility, founded by a band of aristocrats, headed by Frederick, Prince of Wales, no less, who thought the presumptuous German had gotten too independent and successful. Their move just galvanized Handel's supporters.

As an opera composer Handel adhered closely to the standard practices of Italian opera, though he allowed German and even French influences into his works and adapted the genre to his own ends. Still, as was the Italian way, solo singing came first. Handel went searching through Italy to find Italian prima donnas to bring to London, where many won ardent followings, like Francesca Cuzzoni, who created the role of Cleopatra. But the singers who ruled the day and most astounded audiences were the castratos. And the premiere production of *Giulio Cesare* had three, including the superstar Senesino in the title role. Typically, only at the end of each act did the solo singers group together for an ensemble or chorus.

On the surface, the opera would seem to have been bound by the conventions of the time. Dialogue was delivered and the plot was advanced through continuo-accompanied recitative; the characters voiced their thoughts and emotions in numbered "da capo" arias: a three-part form in which a declaratory A section was followed by a contrasting and typically slower and more reflective B section, which led to a recapitulation of the A section, this time with additional and usually fancier ornamentation of the singer's choice. The formal elements of Handel's operas were becoming obsolete even during his lifetime. This surely accounts for the virtual disappearance of his works in the later nineteenth and early twentieth centuries. Handel's operas were assumed to be archaic and dramatically absurd.

But it's wrongheaded and unfair to view a Handel opera as a series of arias connected by recitative. What set these works apart was the stunning ingenuity, endless variety, and sheer beauty of Handel's music, and the trenchant effectiveness of his recitatives. If the plots sometimes seem knocked together, Handel was an insightful dramatist whose music tapped into the psychological states of human behavior.

The revival of interest in Handel operas started in the 1950s and became a genuine phenomenon in the 1980s with the burgeoning of the period instrument music movement, thanks to conductors, singers, and stage directors who recognized the powerful dramatic impact of Handel's music. Consider, for example, *Giulio Cesare in Egitto*, which was introduced at the King's Theatre in 1724.

The libretto is based on Caesar's visit to Egypt in 48–47 B.C. Though most of the characters are historical, most of the plot is fiction. Handel seized on the story as a chance to explore the interaction of two timeless human fascinations: sex and politics. When the opera begins Egypt is ruled jointly by Cleopatra and her younger brother, Ptolemy. Caesar has come to Egypt with his forces in pursuit of his archrival, the Roman general Pompey, whom he has defeated in battle. Caesar is hailed by the Egyptians as he enters the country. Pompey's wife, Cornelia, and her son, Sextus, plead for reconciliation and Caesar is asked to make peace. But just then the Egyptian general Achilles arrives bearing a gift he thinks will please the Roman emperor: the head of Pompey. Caesar is aghast.

Pompey's killing was ordered by Ptolemy, something Cleopatra has just learned when we meet her in scene 2. She resolves to seduce Caesar in an attempt to become sole ruler of Egypt. In a chillingly brilliant and coolly determined aria, she disparages her younger brother as an amateur who squanders his time and authority in pointless sexual conquests. She knows how to use sex to gain power.

But in act 2 Cleopatra's plan is complicated by her vulnerability to Caesar. Disguised as Lydia, a wronged noble lady, but arrayed in finery and sitting on the throne of Virtue, Cleopatra sings one of Handel's most lushly seductive arias, "V'adoro, pupille." She finds herself truly falling for the dashing Roman emperor, who is portrayed in this opera as a man in his twenties, though in fact he was fifty-four when he encountered Cleopatra. She is not accustomed to being rattled by romantic feelings. When later, against Cleopatra's wishes, Caesar charges off to face the conspirators who are plotting his downfall, she sings the grief-filled aria, "Se pietà," in which her poignant pleas to heaven to assuage her torment are mingled with sighing countermelodies in the violins.

The plot keeps taking sudden and improbable twists. Cleopatra and Ptolemy raise armies against each other. Ptolemy's is defeated;

Cleopatra is sentenced to death. But Caesar vanquishes the Egyptian forces and in a grand final scene appears hand in hand with the triumphant Cleopatra, though the fleet horn fanfares and almost enforced hardiness of the final chorus seem Handel's way of introducing some doubt about the rightness of the outcome.

Structurally the opera is marred in the final half of its third act by a succession of awkwardly inserted arias for secondary characters. But the circumstances of the premiere demanded that the celebrated artists singing these roles each have a moment to shine. Also, as the scholar Anthony Hicks has pointed out, there are too many suicide attempts and assaults on Cornelia's virtue for one evening at the opera. But the astounding richness of the arias provides a satisfying trade-off for the dramatic stiffness.

There have been several important recordings of this work. The best overall performance is the most recent and hence most easily available: an Archiv release from Deutsche Grammophon with Marc Minkowski conducting Les Musiciens du Louvre, a remarkable period instrument ensemble based in Paris. This live performance, recorded at the Vienna Konzerthaus in 2002, offers a cast of impressive singers (practically a feast of mezzo-sopranos) who understand both the musical style and the dramatic impact of this great work. The mezzo-soprano Marijana Mijanović brings dusky, rich colorings, intelligence, and temperament to the title role. Magdalena Kožená, a rising Czech mezzo-soprano, gives a dynamic and vocally alluring performance as Cleopatra. The great mezzo-soprano Anne Sofie von Otter makes an impassioned Sextus (Sesto), and yet another exceptional mezzo-soprano, Charlotte Hellekant, is a noble and affecting Cornelia. The dynamic countertenor Bejun Mehta excels as the scheming Ptolemy (Tolomeo). From this fine cast and orchestra Minkowski draws a lucid-textured, tellingly paced, and continually involving performance.

Archiv Produktion, from Deutsche Grammophon (three CDs) B0000314-0
Marc Minkowski (conductor), Les Musiciens du Louvre; Mijanović, Kožená, von Otter, Hellekant, Mehta

29. GEORGE FRIDERIC HANDEL

(1685–1759)

Orlando

Anonymous libretto adapted from Carlo Sigismondo Capece's *L'Orlando* (1711), after Ludovico Ariosto's *Orlando furioso*

First performance: London, King's Theatre, January 27, 1733

A breakthrough in the revival of the Handel operas was a 1982 production of *Orlando* at the American Repertory Theatre in Cambridge directed by the brash, brilliant, and sacred-cow-skewering Peter Sellars, then just twenty-four. Working dynamically with the sensitive conductor Craig Smith and an exemplary cast, Sellars and his production team showed that contemporary imagery, when imaginatively conceived, far from sinking a Handel opera in gimmickry, can make today's audiences connect viscerally with the dilemmas, passions, anguish, and ironies of Handel's characters.

Orlando is a stunning masterwork, for me George Frideric Handel's most psychologically resonant opera. The title character is drawn from Ariosto's epic poem *Orlando furioso*. In the opera, Orlando, the renowned knight and crusading hero of Christendom, has grown weary of seeking glory through combat, so he turns his attention to love. But the magician Zoroaster, an invented character not found in the Ariosto poem, determined to prod Orlando back on the path of valor, leads him to an enchanted forest where romantic entanglements and jealousies drive him mad. As in Ariosto, Orlando suffers from unrequited love for Angelica, the queen of Cathay, who has spurned numerous adoring royal suitors and fallen hard for Medoro, an African prince. Lending another layer of complexity to the story, the opera introduces the character of Dorinda, a shepherdess in helpless love with Medoro, who deserted her upon encountering the regal and dazzling Angelica.

In the libretto the opening scene is set in the country against the backdrop of a mountain on top of which stands Atlas holding up the heavens on his shoulders. In the foreground stands Zoroaster, leaning on a stone and contemplating the movements of the stars.

The synopsis of the Sellars production began: "The scene opens at Mission Control, Kennedy Space Center, Cape Canaveral. Zoroaster—scientist, magician, and Project Supervisor—is studying distant galaxies of the solar system."

In his orange astronaut's suit, the American Repertory Theatre Orlando (the role was double-cast with the countertenor Jeffrey Gall and the baritone Sanford Sylvan alternating performances) cut an endearingly romantic and dashing figure. Image after image in the production took you to the core of this work. Instead of our meeting Dorinda in a pastoral dale, this Dorinda appeared in a clearing in the Everglades as she emerged from a parked camper in cutoff jeans and a bright blouse. Angelica was not some bejeweled and begowned aristocrat but a handsome heiress in smart riding clothes. And when the libretto calls for a large fountain to rise magically from the earth to shield Medoro from the crazed and jealous Orlando, in the Sellars production a real drinking fountain spouting water rose up from the stage floor—an image that paid charming homage to the popular effects produced by the baroque stage machinery of Handel's day.

This landmark production would not have been so powerful had the musical performance not been so vibrant. Virtually every note and every repeat in the score was honored. And though the fine cast sang in the original Italian, they seemed confident that the stage pictures and costumes were conveying to the audience what was really going on and who the characters really were.

Though Handel mostly adhered to the formal dictates of baroque opera, this work abounds in unconventional forms. There are just a handful of typical da capo arias. And Orlando's mad scene, which should fill you with pity and terror, is as experimental a stretch of music as Handel ever wrote.

Of course, you will not have the Peter Sellars production to guide you when listening to *Orlando* at home. But a 1996 recording of the work with William Christie conducting the estimable Les Arts Florissants will create stage pictures galore in your imagination. Christie is widely regarded as a leading figure in the early music movement. But it's not his understanding of baroque performance practices that makes his work here so gripping. It's that he finds ways to inspire, prod, drive, and, at times (from all reports), intimidate his singers and musicians into playing with full-bodied passion and dramatic fervor.

The title role is sung by Patricia Bardon, a rich-toned mezzo-soprano in an impetuous and poignant performance. The soprano Rosemary Joshua as Angelica, the contralto Hilary Summers as Medoro, the soprano Rosa Mannion as Dorinda, and the hale and hardy bass Harry van der Kamp as Zoroaster all give nuanced and involving performances.

In 1982 traditionalists who may have been hoping that scholars and smart critics would slam the Sellars *Orlando* instead learned that respected opera historian Edward Dent, a pioneer at the start of the Handel revival in the 1950s, had been a consultant to the production. And Andrew Porter, then the widely read critic of *The New Yorker,* wrote that the performance "discovers all Handel's richness, variety, wit, humanity and genius."*

The opera ends with absolute psychological rightness. Zoroaster, who has allowed Orlando to go mad, cures him, but not without issuing a cautionary message. All our thoughts, he explains, travel through impenetrable darkness guided by blind love. Only the illumination of reason can deliver us from the abyss.

Erato (three CDs) 0630-14636-2
William Christie (conductor), Les Arts Florissants; Bardon, Joshua, Summers, Mannion, Van der Kamp

*February 22, 1982.

30. GEORGE FRIDERIC HANDEL

(1685–1759)

Alcina

Anonymous libretto after cantos VI and VII of Ariosto's *Orlando furioso*

First performance: London, Covent Garden Theatre, April 16, 1735

Many of George Frideric Handel's operas have elements of allegorical fantasy, but the best of these, indeed one of the finest Handel operas, is *Alcina*. Handel wrote it for the newly built theater at Covent Garden, which opened in 1732. (The current Royal Opera House, which opened in 1858, is the third to occupy that site.) *Alcina* abounds with dance sequences and choruses that reveal the influence of French opera. Still, the work is essentially an Italian opera seria with a glorious score and a playful and resonant story open to multiple interpretations.

Alcina, a beautiful sorceress, lures heroes to the enchanted island where she reigns. Inevitably she grows bored with her captives and turns them into rocks, streams, wild beasts, and trees. Her latest conquest is Ruggiero, a handsome knight. Mesmerized by Alcina, Ruggiero completely forgets about his virtuous fiancée, Bradamante, who arrives at the island searching for him and disguised as her brother, a warrior. Supported by Melisso, her trusted friend and governor, Bradamante is determined to wrest her beloved Ruggiero back to reality.

Other characters add romantic intrigue to the story. There's Morgana, Alcina's obliging sister, who becomes immediately enthralled with the warrior whom Bradamante pretends to be (called Ricciardo); and Oronte, Alcina's general, who adores Morgana and seethes with jealousy over her interest in "Ricciardo"; then there is the young boy Oberto, who has come to the isle to find his father, whom he believes to be one of Alcina's victims.

Though the roundelay of sexual attractions becomes absurdly complex, Handel's intent is to explore the absurdities of such attractions. If our romantic choices are so prone to confusion and whim, the opera suggests, then succumbing to someone else's vanquishing allure becomes the easier choice. The heroes are meant to be seen not entirely as victims but as complicitous in Alcina's ploys.

The opera invites an imaginative production. A striking 2003 staging at the New York City Opera, directed by Francesca Zambello, depicted the transformed heroes as a roster of male dancers costumed (by Martin Pakledinaz) as trees. With spindly branches growing from their fingers and wearing shaggy earthen pants, these bare-headed and bare-chested tree-men looked achingly vulnerable as the sorceress's captives.

But *Alcina* also invites imaginative singing. And a live 1999 recording of a performance at the Palais Garnier (an Opéra National de Paris production) is as splendid as you could hope for. The performance brought together the conductor William Christie and his esteemed early music ensemble Les Arts Florissants with some leading opera singers who are in no sense early music specialists. The soprano Renée Fleming sings Alcina with sumptuous sound, agile technique, and exquisite taste. A highlight is her meltingly poignant account of the somber aria "Ombre pallide" in act 2. The mezzo-soprano Susan Graham makes a fiery and rich-toned Ruggiero and is especially impressive in the Neapolitan-style showpiece aria, "Sta nell'Ircana," in which her bravura vocal flourishes are fortified by ringing high horns in the orchestra. As Morgana the coloratura soprano Natalie Dessay gives a radiant and wonderfully spontaneous performance, deftly executing the vocal gymnastics of the role. The contralto Kathleen Kuhlmann as Bradamante and the bass Laurent Naouri as Melisso are also excellent.

A palpable sense of collaboration comes through here. Christie brings his expertise and feeling for the baroque opera idiom; Fleming and her starry colleagues lend operatic glamour; and everybody sounds energized by working with and learning from one another.

Erato (three CDs) 8573-80233-2
William Christie (conductor), Les Arts Florissants; Fleming, Graham, Dessay, Kuhlmann, Robinson, Naouri, Lascarro

31. PAUL HINDEMITH (1895–1963)

Mathis der Maler

Paul Hindemith, librettist

First performance: Zurich, Stadttheater, May 28, 1938

It's hard to imagine that *Mathis der Maler*, a humane and distinguished opera about the sixteenth-century German painter Matthias Grünewald, was the work of a composer who as a brash youth fifteen years earlier wrote a salacious, one-act expressionistic shocker called *Mörder, Hoffnung der Frauen* (*Murder, Hope of Women*). The composer Paul Hindemith fully wanted his early opera to shake up audiences. Set in antiquity, it depicts a violent erotic encounter as observed by dual trios of warriors and female servants. He must have been satisfied that so many people at the work's 1919 Stuttgart premiere were duly distressed.

Hindemith had started his career as a diligent violist in the orchestra of the Frankfurt Opera. By his twenties he was a superbly skilled musician and composer. Instilling professional expertise in young musicians would become the focus of his later years as a college professor, especially at Yale University.

But as a young man reacting against the post-Wagnerian romanticism that many German composers would not shake off, Hindemith saw the theater as a way to take on the establishment. Of course, he didn't count on Adolf Hitler turning up at a 1929 performance of his iconoclastic comic opera *Neues vom Tage,* where the future Führer was scandalized to see a soprano taking a bath onstage.

By the time Hitler came to power in 1933, Hindemith had turned his back on his rebellious early stage works and dedicated himself to fostering understanding between contemporary composers and audiences. But the Nazis remembered his past, branding him a musical Bolshevist and impeding his performances. This experience, in part, led Hindemith to explore the plight of the artist in times of political upheaval, the subject matter of *Mathis der Maler,* his masterpiece, composed over two years (1933–1935).

Set in Mainz at the time of the Peasants' War in 1525, with a libretto by Hindemith loosely based on the life of Grünewald, the opera questions whether art can be meaningful when it cannot help those who suffer from want and injustice. In the first of seven tableaus, Mathis admits to Schwalb, the passionate and rash leader of the peasants, that a picture can hardly convert anyone to a cause. "Why should you worry about the arts?" Mathis asks. The arts "live close to God and obey their own laws."

As the streets fill with violence and the Catholic hierarchy orders a pile of Lutheran books to be burned in a bonfire near the marketplace, Mathis realizes that he can no longer isolate himself. He becomes an ally of the peasant revolt. But as the hostilities continue, Mathis is dismayed to see that with each fleeting victory the peasants become the oppressors and violate every principle they supposedly had been fighting for.

Hindemith wanted his opera to be elegant and powerful but musically comprehensible to audiences. So the contrapuntal writing is less dense than in other works of that period and the harmonic language is essentially tonal, texturally transparent, and easy on the ears. Hindemith also incorporates hymns and songs in his score, and even in moments of arching lyricism the vocal lines tend to follow the contours and rhythms of conversational German.

Yet just below its radiant and wistful harmonic surface the music teems with intricacies. And though much of the score is given over to subdued exchanges of dialogue and ruminative soliloquies, there are gripping dramatic episodes, like the frenzied book burning scene and the harrowing orchestral music that depicts Mathis's vision of the temptation of Saint Anthony, a scene that the real-life Grünewald painted on the Isenheim altar.

Actually, the music for "The Temptation of Saint Anthony" was written before the opera was composed, as the third movement of Hindemith's *Mathis der Maler* Symphony. The composer worked out his ideas for the opera in this score, which became his greatest and best-known concert piece. Its first movement, "Angelic Concert," with its calmly industrious counterpoint and angelic celestial chorales, became the orchestral prelude to the opera. No overture in any opera touches me more. The second movement, "Entombment," halting, harmonically pungent, and unbearably sorrowful music, was used in the opera to accompany the funeral for Regina, the peasant leader Schwalb's modest, decent, and brave daughter.

The only important and top-notch recording of *Mathis der Maler* offers Rafael Kubelik conducting the Bavarian Radio Orchestra and Chorus. After a long period when this 1977 recording was unavailable, EMI Classics brought it out again. So you should be able to find it. Dietrich Fischer-Dieskau brings his elegant baritone voice, keen intelligence, and affecting dignity to his portrayal of Mathis. The husky-voiced tenor James King is a volatile and self-questioning Cardinal Albrecht. Urszula Koszut gives a beautifully vulnerable performance as Regina. Kubelik conducts the score with palpable devotion and a sure sense of its dramatic structure.

The first performance took place in Zurich in 1938. The Nazis prevented its production in Germany until 1946, after the war.

EMI Classics (three CDs) 5 55237 2

Rafael Kubelik (conductor), Bavarian Radio Chorus and Orchestra; Fischer-Dieskau, King, Koszut, Wagemann

32. LEOŠ JANÁČEK (1854–1928)

Jenůfa

Leoš Janáček, librettist, after a play by Gabriela Preissová

First performance: Brno, National Theatre, January 21, 1904

The Moravian composer Leoš Janáček was a late bloomer. Though his slow start inhibited his development in opera, paradoxically it allowed him time to reexamine the existing genre and devise fresh approaches that made him one of the truly original opera composers of the early twentieth century.

The son and grandson of Czech schoolmasters who taught music,

Janáček had a small-town upbringing. Fortunately for the history of opera, his house grew so crowded that the boy was sent off at eleven to the city of Brno to be a chorister at a monastery, where he received a solid musical education. There he heard opera, though not often, since he was always scraping for money, but enough to nurture his ambitions to compose for the stage.

After organ studies in Prague and conservatory training in Leipzig and Vienna, Janáček followed the family business and became the director of the Brno Organ School. He was fifty before *Jenůfa,* his third opera but a breakthrough work, was produced in Brno. Slowly the reputation of *Jenůfa* spread and interest in Janáček's operas grew. In 1924, twenty years after its premiere, *Jenůfa* received influential productions at the Vienna State Opera and the Metropolitan Opera. Janáček had achieved international renown. Four years later he died.

Based on his instrumental and orchestral works, Janáček appears to be a skilled, accessible, and colorful Czech nationalist composer, not unlike many others of his time. But Janáček's operas are far more daring and contemporary, and with good reason.

In writing operas, the characters and story lines provoked Janáček to loosen the tonal moorings of his harmonic language and spike his music with wayward modal excursions and jolts of dissonance. Also, while many eastern European opera composers evoked the atmosphere and folk music of Moravian village life, Janáček, given his childhood and sympathies, did so with striking authenticity. Most of all, though, Janáček was fascinated to the point of obsession with the flow and contour of the Czech language. He used to go around with a notepad jotting down the pitches and rhythms of conversations he overheard. In his operas, he eschewed tunefulness in order to write what he called his "speech-melody." Consequently, when a character breaks into a truly lyrical moment and a long melodic line sounds from the orchestra, the effect is doubly poignant. Finally, Janáček's operas are daringly through-composed works with highly charged exchanges of dialogue and frequent soliloquies. The inexorable narrative pacing almost never stops to make room for a set-piece aria or ensemble.

After enduring tense working relationships with the librettists for his first two operas, Janáček decided to write his own libretto for

Jenůfa. He would be the sole or co-librettist for all but one of his eight other operas. It's not coincidental, I think, that my three favorite Janáček operas are all adaptations of existing plays. The composer found it more effective to write music for existing plays with proven dramatic impact.

Jenůfa, adapted from a play by Gabriela Preissová, is a story of a winsome young woman in a remote rural village of Moravian Slovakia in the late nineteenth century who is nearly crushed by the oppressive, small-minded moralizing of her severe stepmother, who has raised her, and her judgmental neighbors. The stepmother is called the Kostelnicka (or sacristan) because she tends the town's chapel and enforces its ethical codes. When the opera begins, a soft repeated note on the xylophone evokes the relentless spinning of the town's mill wheel, and that mill is a focal point of the story. Steva, a dashing young man and the town's resident rake, has inherited the mill from his dead parents, making him a local big shot. Working for him there, in a subservient role, is Steva's burly half brother, Laca, who seethes with resentments and shares Steva's interest in the lovely Jenůfa. But the young woman is smitten with Steva. By the end of act 1, twisted with jealousy over Jenůfa's rebuffs, in a fit of impotent and hideous anger, Laca slashes her cheek with a knife, scarring her permanently. Let's see how Steva will like that rosy cheek now, Laca screams.

Act 2 is dominated by the Kostelnicka. Five months have passed and Jenůfa, who has been kept hidden at home, has just given birth to Steva's son. As a girl the Kostelnicka had married a drunken blowhard, now dead, and she is determined to prevent her stepdaughter from making the same pathetic mistake. Moreover, as the town's self-appointed upholder of righteousness, she cannot abide the shame of the illegitimate birth that has taken place under her roof. By the end of the act, exasperated by her repeated arguments with the shaken but stubborn Jenůfa, the Kostelnicka goes off with the baby and, we later learn, drowns him in a river. This may be the most demented of mad scenes in all of opera. The Kostelnicka is a challenging and irresistible role for a powerful dramatic soprano.

In act 3, some workmen have found the frozen corpse of a baby, and in a chilling moment the Kostelnicka confesses what she has done. As the Kostelnicka is led off to stand trial, Jenůfa comes to understand what drove her stepmother to this abominable act and forgives her. Ultimately, the opera is a story of redemption, for by the final scene the shattered Jenůfa and the guilt-ridden Laca take refuge in their unromantic yet calming mutual regard.

The conductor Sir Charles Mackerras, an important champion of the Janáček operas, especially in England, found a compelling ally in the Swedish soprano Elisabeth Söderström, who brought a rich voice, expressive nuance, and stylistic sensitivity to her portrayals of Janáček's tormented heroines. Together, starting in the mid-1970s, they began recording the major Janáček operas. So despite some competition from recordings with mostly Czech casts, the classic 1982 Mackerras version with Söderström as Jenůfa remains the best overall choice. The molten Czech mezzo-soprano Eva Randová makes a mesmerizing Kostelnicka. The husky-voiced Polish tenor Weislaw Ochman is a volatile Laca, and the Slovak tenor Peter Dvorsky lends Steva an appropriately dashing and slick touch. Lucia Popp, the exquisite Hungarian soprano, is wonderful in the smaller role of Karolka. And Mackerras inspires undulant, intense, and vividly colored playing from the glorious Vienna Philharmonic.

Decca (two CDs) 414 483-2

Sir Charles Mackerras (conductor), Vienna Philharmonic Orchestra; Söderström, Randová, Ochman, Dvorsky, Popp

33. LEOŠ JANÁČEK (1854–1928)

Kát'a Kabanová

Leoš Janáček, librettist, after a play by Alexander Nikolayevich Ostrovsky

First performance: Brno, National Theatre, November 23, 1921

In 1881 Leoš Janáček, then twenty-seven, married Zdenka Schulzova, his piano pupil, who was not quite sixteen. They settled later that year in Brno, where Janáček became the director of the local organ school. From the start their marriage was unhappy.

Janáček was a nationalistic Czech from a family of music teachers with little means; Zdenka was the daughter of a convention-bound middle-class German family. Having children further strained their relationship and brought tragedy into their lives. Their firstborn, Olga, grew into a combative young woman who died at twenty. Their second child, a boy, lived only two years, dying of meningitis.

Though Janáček undermined his marriage through involvements with other women, the relationship that truly excited him does not appear to have been romantic. Late in life, in 1917, Janáček met Kamila Stösslova and her husband, David Stössel, an antiques dealer. Kamila was twenty-six, Janáček was sixty-two, and he adored her. Their intense friendship is documented in over seven hundred letters from the composer to Kamila. (Only a handful of her replies survive.) In 1921 Janáček wrote to Kamila that when he met her during the war for the first time, he saw how a woman could truly love her husband. As such he was inspired to write *Kát'a Kabanová*, the first opera of his important late period. The opera presents a poignantly sympathetic, though ultimately tragic, portrait of a lovely young married woman who commits adultery.

The opening of *Kát'a Kabanová* is a masterstroke of concise and effective scene setting and character depiction. The story takes place in the town of Kalinov on the banks of the Volga in the 1860s. The orchestral introduction sets the scene in music of transfixing ambiguity. A resonant sustained chord in the lower strings swells and evolves into a wistful melody punctuated by a softly insistent motif in the timpani. As the music grows more agitated it seems to evoke the constant flowing of the river, the cyclical patterns of life, and the forces of fate at play in the story.

A sprightly theme, like some modal Moravian folk song, breaks out and the first scene begins, set in a park near the Volga, where Kudrjáš, a young chemist and engineer, invites Glasa, a servant in the nearby Kabanov house, to admire the afternoon sunlight flickering on the river. Soon, the merchant Dikoj, Kudrjáš's employer, approaches with his nephew, Boris, who is enduring yet another rebuke from his blustery uncle over his supposed laziness. And in a few conversational exchanges the dynamics of the entire story are laid out.

Boris puts up with his bossy uncle's abuse, he explains, because the inheritance his parents left to him and his sister is under his control. But Boris's days have been enlivened, at last, by his love for a married woman, he confides to Kudrjáš. It's Kát'a, the winsome young wife of Tichon, the weak-willed son of Kabanicha, a stern, judgmental, and possessive mother, and the widow of a rich merchant.

The conversational exchanges occur over a restless and harmonically charged orchestral backdrop that conveys the emotional subtext of the gossip and chitchat. But when Kát'a enters the music turns luminous and tender, as if Janáček is sanctifying Kát'a (the stand-in for Kamila?) and building up sympathy for this beleaguered young wife before the full story of her confining married life is revealed. The shift in mood signaled by her entrance music has been compared by the Janáček scholar John Tyrrell, among other critics, to Puccini's sublime entrance music for Butterfly, surely a model.

Kát'a can do no right as a wife in the eyes of her mother-in-law. Kabanicha reproaches her for showing too much affection for Tichon in public, but also for not putting on a properly sorrowful public face when her husband is sent away on business. That Kát'a and Boris, who have oppressed home lives in common, give in to their longings is inevitable.

But Kát'a, unable to bear her guilt, confesses her sin, provoking the stinging condemnation of Kabanicha. Having failed at marital constancy, the only thing expected of her, Kát'a, anguished and disoriented, drowns herself in the river. Finally Tichon stands up to his mother, accusing her of driving Kát'a to suicide. But Kabanicha's only response is to make a public show of thanking the townspeople for their expressions of solicitude. As the music crests with grating orchestral chords, an offstage chorus sings a wordless and mystical benediction on the good-hearted Kát'a.

In 1951, Charles Mackerras, then just twenty-six, conducted *Kát'a Kabanová* in what was the first performance of a Janáček opera in Britain. In 1976 he and the soprano Elisabeth Söderström recorded the work, the first of what became an essential series of Janáček opera albums. That recording, with the Vienna Philharmonic, is the one to have. Though Söderström sounds vocally too mature for the Kát'a role, she brings throbbing intensity, rich colorings, and vulnerability to her portrayal. The impassioned mezzosoprano Nadezda Kniplová gives a volatile and vocally earthy performance as Kabanicha.

Mackerras recorded the opera again in 1997 with the distinguished Czech soprano Gabriela Beňačková in the title role, a mostly Czech cast, and the Czech Philharmonic Orchestra. Beňačková sounds past her prime; and for me there is too much wobbly intensity in the mezzo-soprano Eva Randová's Kabanicha. Still, this rhapsodic and idiomatic performance of an opera just shy of canonical status is a worthy alternative to Mackerras's 1976 recording.

Decca (two CDs) 421 852-2
Sir Charles Mackerras (conductor), Vienna Philharmonic; Söderström, Kniplová, Dvorsky, Krejcik

Supraphon (two CDs) SU 3291-2 632
Sir Charles Mackerras (conductor), Chorus of the Prague National Theatre, Czech Philharmonic Orchestra; Beňačková, Randová, Straka, Kopp

34. LEOŠ JANÁČEK (1854–1928)

Věc Makropulos (The Makropulos Case)

Leoš Janáček, librettist, after a play by Karel Čapek

First performance: Brno, National Theatre, December 18, 1926

The Makropulos Case, though Leoš Janáček's penultimate opera, was the last he lived to see in production. It is arguably his most musically sophisticated work, and clearly asks the most of the orchestra. Despite the convoluted twists of the story, adapted from a play by Karel Čapek, a black comic thriller that Janáček saw in Prague in 1922, the opera is ingeniously structured. But to succeed on stage and entice audiences, *The Makropulos Case* requires a cast of singers with considerable acting skills and presence. With the right leading soprano the opera can be riveting. I will never forget hearing Anja Silja's transfixing portrayal in a gripping production from the Glyndebourne Festival in England presented at the Brooklyn Academy of Music in 2001.

The backdrop to this darkly metaphorical story, set in Prague in 1922, is *Gregor v. Prus,* a lawsuit that has dragged on in the courts for nearly one hundred years—a Byzantine dispute over the estate of Baron Josef Prus, who died in 1827. Emilia Marty, an acclaimed opera soprano of the day, has taken an interest in the case, and seems curiously familiar with the long-gone parties to it. As we eventually discover, Marty knew them all personally. She was born Elina Makropulos in Crete in 1585, making her 337 years old. Elina's father, court physician to the Holy Roman Emperor Rudolf II, gave her an experimental life potion when she was sixteen. Clinging to mortality, if only from habit, Elina has invented and retired numerous identities over the centuries. The time has come for her to take the potion again, but the document with her father's formula is entangled among the papers of *Gregor v. Prus.*

The multiple strands of the case, like the strands of the plot, can be hard to unravel. At times the first act seems a thicket of legalistic explanations from quarreling lawyers. Of course, Janáček intended the audience to find the jargon confounding. The case is a metaphor for the pointless paperwork and ephemeral attachments that accrue to every human life. What Marty comes to realize is that without those attachments longevity is meaningless.

Though Janáček's highly chromatic harmonic language is boldly inventive, the real modernism of the score comes from the daring independence Janáček created between the vocal lines, predominantly delivered in quasi-recitative, and the teeming, restless, unhinged orchestral music. Bringing coherence and clarity to this frenetic score is a challenge. Sir Charles Mackerras, the renowned Janáček interpreter, does this and more in his compelling 1978 Decca recording with the Vienna Philharmonic, a performance that fully captures the music's rhapsodic sweep and restrained intensity. Mackerras's long-time collaborator, Elisabeth Söderström, had a career milestone in her portrayal of Marty, a woman who must hold fascination for every person she encounters. Söderström's radiant and emotionally coy singing makes her Marty at once charismatic and exasperating. The supporting cast, which includes many Czech singers, is also excellent, especially the tenor Peter Dvorsky as Albert Gregor, a party to the case who is still consumed by it.

A Supraphon recording made in 1965–1966 in the Czech Republic, though not as sonically satisfying, offers an idiomatic account of the opera with an impressive cast of Czech and Eastern European singers. The soprano Libuse Prylova, if not as vocally glamorous as Söderström, gives a volatile and intriguing portrayal of Marty. The Prague National Orchestra brings passion and stylistic authority to its performance under Bohumil Gregor. And given Janáček's near obsession with conveying the rhythms and contours of the Czech language in his vocal lines, it's a pleasure to hear the text sung so crisply by native speakers.

Decca (two CDs) 430 372-2
Sir Charles Mackerras (conductor), Vienna State Opera Chorus and the Vienna Philharmonic; Söderström, Dvorsky, Krejcik, Czakova

Supraphon (two CDs) 10 8351-2 612
Bohumil Gregor (conductor), Prague National Chorus and Orchestra; Prylova, Zidek, Vonasek

35. GYÖRGY LIGETI (b. 1923)

Le Grand Macabre

Michael Meschke and György Ligeti, librettists, after a play by Michel de Ghelderode

First performance: Stockholm, Royal Opera, April 12, 1978

The Hungarian composer György Ligeti, a colossus among twentieth-century composers, received his training at the Budapest Academy

Composer György Ligeti

within the culturally restricted confines of a Soviet-bloc country. So his early music, beholden to Bartók, reveals a lack of acquaintance with the radical currents of contemporary music at the time.

Paradoxically, his isolation may have benefited him. When Ligeti left Hungary in 1956 to immerse himself in the music and culture of Western Europe, he combined a voracious curiosity about innovation with a healthy skepticism about dogma, especially the dogma of the hardcore twelve-tone serialists who claimed the intellectual high ground. Instead, trusting in his acute ear for harmony and sonority and illimitable imagination, Ligeti drew from all camps, experimented with atmospheric effects (the musical equivalent of sound collages) and repetitive rhythmic structures, and was not afraid to introduce clear tonal harmonies and fetching melodies into otherwise pungently atonal works.

Everything came together in his audacious two-act opera, *Le Grand Macabre,* an apocalyptic romp with a libretto by Ligeti and

Michael Meschke (adapted from a play by Michel de Ghelderode), which had its premiere in 1978 at the Royal Opera in Stockholm. The story is set, to quote the composer, in "the rundown but nevertheless carefree and thriving principality of Brueghelland in an 'anytime' century." The place appears to be a land of peasants, creatures, monsters, and grotesqueries right out of a Brueghel canvas.

When the opera opens in an abandoned graveyard we meet Piet the Pot, a kind of "realistic Sancho Panza," as Ligeti puts it, who is a professional wine taster and consequently always tipsy. His nemesis is Nekrotzar, the "Great Macabre" of the title, who arises from an opening grave, a "sinister, shady, demagogic figure, humorless, pretentious, and with an unshakeable sense of mission," in Ligeti's words. That mission is to announce to the citizenry that he is Death incarnate and has come to destroy the world that very night.

A delicately beautiful couple, Amanda (a soprano) and Amando (a mezzo-soprano), turn up at the graveside looking for a quiet place to make love. Meanwhile, Astradamors, the court astrologer, who works in a cluttered place that seems to be a combination of observatory, laboratory, and kitchen, is enduring a combative relationship with the bullying Mescalina, the mistress of the house, who whips Astradamors, pricks him with a spit, and dangles a horrid spider over his mouth. When Nekrotzar appears Mescalina is intrigued by his allure of power and sexual promise. But Nekrotzar bites her in the neck like a vampire and she falls lifeless to the floor, which delights Astradamors.

The land is ruled by the ineffectual, infantile, and gluttonous Prince Go-Go, who is manipulated by two oppositional advisers, the White and Black Ministers. But after bizarre twists, when the end of the world arrives with a cannon blast in the orchestra, it is Nekrotzar who falls to the ground. Has Death died?

It's unclear. In the epilogue everyone reappears in bafflement. Has the world ended? Have they died and been resurrected, only to return to the same routine of drink, excess, dissension, and lovemaking? Was Nekrotzar a powerless phantom?

Listeners timid about contemporary music might be put off at first by the grating harmony, raspy vocal style, and sheer modernistic bedlam that pervade Ligeti's music. But open yourself to the work and you'll discover an arresting score with awesome energy, constant invention, and breathtaking musical effects. The tone of the opera is clear from the short overture, scored for twelve motor horns. But after the comic impact of the honking horns registers, you are transfixed by the intricacy of the musical interplay.

Piet the Pot appears in the opening scene singing a fractured version of a "Dies irae" theme against the bleating convolutions of the orchestra. Yet in the midst of the frenzy Ligeti will change the mood in an instant, as in the love duet for Amando and Amanda, with its wistful, intertwining vocal lines and hauntingly ethereal orchestral backdrop. In the final scene, the principals utter the opera's quizzical moral: "Fear not to die, good people all! No one knows when his hour will fall. And when it comes, then let it be. . . . Farewell, till then, live merrily!"

The music is structured as an elaborate passacaglia (a variation form built on a repeated ground bass line). The elusive harmony and every-which-way counterpoint combined with the formal structure vividly convey the ambiguous tone that Ligeti intends.

In the original production a great deal of the text was spoken. But experience with subsequent productions led Ligeti to feel that the spoken dialogue was ineffective. He revised the score and set more of the text to music. The White and Black Ministers, originally spoken roles, became singing roles. Ligeti has suggested that the libretto, originally written in German but performed in Swedish at the premiere, be translated into the most appropriate language for the purposes of the production. Dramatic comprehension was more important to him than matching his music to the contours of the text.

The existing recording of Ligeti's 1997 version of the work (his last, he has said) was taken from a live performance in Paris in 1998, a coproduction by the Théâtre de Châtelet and the Salzburg Festival, performed in English translation. Esa-Pekka Salonen conducts the Philharmonia Orchestra and the London Sinfonietta Voices. His palpable excitement over the opera comes through in every incisive and colorful moment of this dynamic performance. The cast is excellent, with the resonant bass-baritone Willard White as a menacing Nekrotzar, the agile countertenor Derek Lee Ragin as a whiny Prince

Go-Go, and the tenor Graham Clark as a slurpy-tongued Piet the Pot. The soprano Laura Claycomb and the mezzo-soprano Charlotte Hellekant as the lovers Amanda and Amando bring a welcome touch of longing to this hell-bent and exhilarating opera.

Sony Classical (two CDs) S2K 62312

Esa-Pekka Salonen (conductor), London Sinfonietta Voices, Philharmonia Orchestra; Claycomb, Hellekant, Ragin, White, Clark, van Nes, Olsen

36. JULES MASSENET (1842–1912)
Werther

Edouard Blau, Paul Milliet, and Georges Hartmann, librettists, after Goethe

First performance: Vienna, Hofoper, February 16, 1892

The operas of Jules Massenet were once hugely popular and influential. Even so, in his day Massenet weathered a fair share of critical jibes. The composer Vincent d'Indy complained of the "discrete and pseudo-religious eroticism" in the works. Some French critics, affronted by the curious mixture of Wagnerian sweep and French refinement, dubbed Massenet "Mademoiselle Wagner." Still, most of his operas claimed the stage and had strong adherents, among them Puccini. Recently, *Thaïs, Hérodiade,* and *Manon* have found a formidable champion in the exquisite soprano Renée Fleming.

Still, like many opera buffs I find Massenet's operas by and large musically thin and dramatically cloying. The lyricism that pervades the scores can seem trite and tiresome. Works like *Hérodiade* flow by with a pervasively sweet and charming musical surface despite the intensity of the scenes depicted. I'm not as down on the scores as some critics, like my *Times* colleague Bernard Holland who in a memorable phrase in a review of *Thaïs* described Massenet as more a paver than an excavator: "His smooth, intermittently lovely, often bland musical line smoothes over human anguish into bump-free blacktop."* Still, I could essentially do without these operas.

With one exception: *Werther*. This is Massenet's most musically distinguished and psychologically insightful work. Based on the Goethe play, *Werther* tells the story of an aimless young courtier in late-eighteenth-century Germany, a dabbler in poetry intoxicated with his own perceptions of life, who is seeking refuge in the country from sapping emotional entanglements and the loss of a loved one. Werther falls instantly and helplessly in love with the good-hearted Charlotte, the lovely oldest daughter and surrogate mother to the children of the widowed Bailiff (the manager of the royal estate at Wetzlar). That Charlotte promised her dying mother to marry the eligible businessman Albert just makes her more appealing to Werther: she is the idealized, unattainable woman. And this time Massenet's involving score palpably brings to life Goethe's feckless, self-absorbed, and passionately tragic hero. Here Massenet allows the surface beauties of the music to be disturbed by bouts of anguished intensity.

But only if you have the right tenor in the leading role. You can't miss with the classic EMI recording from 1969 with Nicolai Gedda as Werther on the company's Great Recordings of the Century series. Gedda doesn't quite have the vocal heft for the role's heated outbursts, but he gives a beautifully shaded, supply phrased, and excitingly spontaneous performance. The soprano Victoria de los Angeles sometimes ventured into mezzo-soprano repertory, and this Charlotte was one such time—a disarmingly melancholic, vocally honey-toned, and lyrically sensitive portrayal. The conductor Georges Prêtre's affection for the opera comes through palpably in this ardent and distinguished performance, with the Orchestre de Paris. The soprano Mady Mesplé as Sophie and the baritone Roger Soyer as Albert are other crucial members of this stylistically informed cast.

For a more recent version with up-to-date engineering try the 1999 account, also on EMI, starring Roberto Alagna and Angela Gheorghiu. EMI touted opera's "love couple" too much for their own good, but this recording finds them at their respective bests.

New York Times, December 17, 2002.

Alagna brings vocal charisma and elegant diction to Werther, and Gheorghiu sings Charlotte with dusky vocal colorings and psychological insight. Thomas Hampson makes a vocally robust and sadly flummoxed Albert. Antonio Pappano elicits responsive playing from the great London Symphony Orchestra.

Puccini lovers should note the sequence of subdued, richly chromatic, descending orchestral chords that occur right after the initial outburst in the prelude to act 1. A suspiciously similar chord sequence found its way into *Tosca*—the music associated with Angelotti. Puccini was no fool.

EMI Classics (two CDs) 5 62630
Georges Prêtre (conductor), Orchestre de Paris; Gedda, de los Angeles, Mesplé, Soyer

EMI Classics (two CDs) 5 56820 2
Antonio Pappano (conductor), London Symphony Orchestra; Alagna, Gheorghiu, Hampson, Petibon

37. OLIVIER MESSIAEN (1908–1992)

Saint François d'Assise

Olivier Messiaen, librettist

First performance: Paris, Opéra, November 28, 1983

Olivier Messiaen's only opera, *Saint François d'Assise,* is the wondrous, exuberant, and uncompromising work of a seminal twentieth-century composer and profound Catholic mystic. It is also almost impossibly daunting to produce. The score, lasting nearly four hours, calls for an orchestra of some 120 players, including ten percussionists (five alone are needed for mallet instruments, like the xylophone and marimba), three performers on the ondes martenot (the electronic instrument that creates eerie sci-fi sounds), and a chorus of one hundred. This intensely complex work seems even longer than it is because Messiaen consciously disregarded the conventions of musical drama and instead strove to create a heightened form of opera that transcends time. It's not surprising that since its 1983 premiere in Paris it has seen scant productions and was first produced in the United States only in 2002 by, appropriate to its subject, the San Francisco Opera.

Yet there are so few works that dare to be extreme, and this is one. In *Saint François* you have a towering genius of a composer enthralled with a vision that will not be contained. At every moment you can almost hear Messiaen saying, "I don't care what an opera is supposed to be, I'm writing the work of my soul and my inspiration."

Rather than telling a biographical story of the thirteenth-century saint, the opera, with a libretto by Messiaen, depicts Francis's inner spiritual journey. We see him discussing the nature of perfect joy with his brethren in Christ, isolating himself in a prayer cell, and forcing himself to confront human suffering by kissing an embittered leper. He engages in a dream encounter with an inquisitive angel, and delivers a sermon to the birds, losing ties to earthly space and time. We witness Francis praying to be wounded with the stigmata of Christ to overcome his feelings of unworthiness, until in the work's conclusion he is ushered by the angel to his death and granted his longed-for state of perfect joy.

Musically there is nothing like this work in all of opera. The text is set with slow-moving, gently lyrical vocal lines, often unaccompanied, as if every syllable is meant to be pondered. But the score is jolted repeatedly by jumpy, rhythmic percussion volleys—glorious clanking outbursts, like some heady mix of Balinese gamelan music and cutting-edge contemporary orchestra fare. Yet, the score shifts constantly between this hard-driving music and the almost timeless "music of the invisible," as Messiaen called it, characterized by lush, luminous, otherworldly, and strangely beguiling waves of pungent harmony. For Messiaen the realm of the spiritual is an astounding and disorienting place.

Only musicians and singers of formidable skill who are as inspired by this opera as its composer was in writing it can grapple with its challenges. The conductor Kent Nagano presided over such a performance at the Salzburg Festival in 1998, and Deutsche Grammophon was there to record it live for a landmark release.

Messiaen was a mentor to Nagano, who conducts the score with palpable devotion. But Nagano brings the sensibilities of a California baby boomer to bear as well, which comes through in the incisive articulation of the rhythms and his willingness to let the music swing without any loss of reverence. He draws dynamic and rich-textured playing from the Halle Orchestra and full-bodied, ecstatic singing from the Arnold Schoenberg Choir. And the cast is magnificent. The bass-baritone José van Dam's performance in the title role may be the high point of this essential artist's career. The soprano Dawn Upshaw brings heavenly radiance to the role of the Angel. The tenor Chris Merritt gives an anguished and potent performance as the Leper, who first lashes out and then unburdens himself to Francis. Messiaen was quite dubious about the viability of opera in the twentieth century. Paradoxically he may have written one of that century's greatest operatic works.

Deutsche Grammophon (four CDs) 445 176-2
Kent Nagano (conductor), Halle Orchestra, Arnold Schoenberg Choir; van Dam, Upshaw, Merritt

38. CLAUDIO MONTEVERDI (1567–1643)

Orfeo

Alessandro Striggio, librettist, after a play by Ottavio Rinuccini

First performance: Mantua, Ducal Palace, February, 24, 1607

Opera as we know it was more or less invented in the late 1590s in Italy, in Florence especially, by composers, poets, and academicians who, inspired by their studies of ancient Greek tragedy, met together and sought to create a modern-day Italian form of continuous musical drama. There had been musical dramas before this, of course, entertainments and pastorals and liturgical plays and such. But this new band of neoclassical Florentine creators wanted to develop an integrated and heightened genre of musical drama.

The breakthrough work in this effort came in 1600 with Jacopo Peri's *Euridice,* with a libretto by Ottavio Rinuccini. Peri's "dramma per musica," as it was called, employed a new style of setting text, "stile rappresentativo," characterized by declamatory vocal lines that followed the contours and rhythms of human speech sung over a slow-moving harmonic accompaniment. With this innovation recitative was born.

If Peri's *Euridice* was the first real opera, Claudio Monteverdi's *Orfeo,* composed in 1607, was the first great one, the first work of genius. At the time Monteverdi, who had already earned a reputation as a daring composer of madrigals for voices and instrumental ensembles, was employed at the court of the prosperous Duke of Mantua, and *Orfeo* was composed for a performance during the carnival season at the Mantuan court. So Monteverdi had considerable resources at his disposal, including a large instrumental force, dancers, and choristers.

Monteverdi was indebted to Peri and the other early operatic creators. But with the savvy intuition of a natural theater man he understood that the new recitative style, while an effective technique for setting dialogue, advancing the story, and giving voice to ruminations of the characters, could get pretty dull if stretches of it went on too long. Dramatic pacing and musical variety were essential, he believed. From his experience in madrigals he had learned how to reflect the imagery of words in vivid music. He drew from this knowledge, along with his knowledge of song and dance and his feeling for instrumental colorings. The resulting work is at once a courtly entertainment and a profoundly felt and deftly paced musical drama.

Of course, there were protocols to be followed for this commissioned work. So it begins with a rousing orchestral toccata, played three times, then segues into a harmonically rich and haunting prologue, structured as a set of variations over a repeated bass pattern, in which "La Musica," the spirit of music, pays compliments to the audience, especially the benevolent duke and his family, and introduces herself as a power that can soothe troubled hearts or arouse passions from the coolest of men. The Orpheus and Euridice myth, a fable about the power of Orpheus's poetry and music to charm all listeners, was an aptly metaphoric story with which to inaugurate a new musical art form.

The first act and half of the second are essentially a pastoral drama. The newlyweds Orfeo and Euridice celebrate their love amid nymphs and shepherds. Then, however, comes word from Silvia, a messenger, of Euridice's tragic fate, and here Monteverdi's dramatic genius and psychological insight come through powerfully. The messenger tries to give the news, but at the mention of Euridice's name, Orfeo breaks into agitated recitative outbursts in which the underlying harmony becomes unhinged. Trying to calm Orfeo, the messenger brings the music back to the central key and admits the worst: Euridice is dead. In a masterstroke of understatement, Orfeo sings just a two-note sigh, "Oime" ("Alas"). Then the messenger slowly tells the horrid story: Euridice was bitten by a poisonous snake. Stunned and halting, Orfeo reacts, building slowly into a tempest of anger in which he swears to travel to the underworld itself and win Euridice back from Pluto. Later, in act 4, the scene in which he has his chance to charm Pluto, Orfeo sings an aria that in each verse becomes increasingly elaborate, beguiling, and enriched with wondrous instrumental effects.

Though there are extensive documents of the first presentations of Orfeo, performers of this opera today must engage in a fair amount of guesswork as to what the style of singing and instrumental playing was actually like. Performances on early instruments are much preferable. But I prefer accounts that also treat Orfeo as a compelling dramatic work for singers and audiences today. To this end the 1985 Archiv recording conducted by John Eliot Gardiner is just about ideal. Gardiner brings his scholarly insights as a leading figure in the early music movement to bear, but elicits wonderfully fresh, buoyant, and responsive playing from the English Baroque Soloists and robust singing from the Monteverdi Choir. The cast boasts an elegant and impassioned Orfeo in the tenor Anthony Rolfe-Johnson, and a vulnerable and sweet-toned Euridice in the soprano Julianne Baird.

The mellow mezzo-soprano Anne Sofie von Otter is riveting as the anguished messenger bearing the tragic news. And the bass-baritone Willard White makes a chilling Pluto in the scene in Hades.

Archiv Produktion (two CDs) 419 250-2
John Eliot Gardiner (conductor), The Monteverdi Choir, The English Baroque Soloists; Rolfe Johnson, Baird, von Otter, Tomlinson, White

39. CLAUDIO MONTEVERDI (1567–1643)

L'Incoronazione di Poppea
(The Coronation of Poppea)

Gian Francesco Busenello, librettist

First performance: Venice, Teatro S.S. Giovanni e Paolo, 1643

Between Claudio Monteverdi's first opera, *Orfeo,* from 1607, and his last, *L'Incoronazione di Poppea,* produced in 1643, almost every-thing about his life, his career, and the overall state of opera in Italy changed. Opera was born as a plaything of princes. *Orfeo* probably had no more than three presentations, each at the ducal palace in Mantua. But in the 1630s the public's curiosity about opera could no longer be stemmed. The first public opera house in Italy, to which anyone with the money could buy admission, opened in 1637 in Venice. Since 1613 Monteverdi had been employed in Venice as director of music at the Basilica of Saint Mark's, the most prestigious musical post in Italy. He also took holy orders in 1632, probably as a means to ensure his financial well-being as he approached old age.

The demands of a paying public forced changes in the opera genre. Subject matter, whether historical, mythological, or fictitious, had to be accessible, even sensational. Producers, now worried about turn-ing a profit, compelled creators to keep the demands for instruments, choristers, and dancers to a minimum, though a high premium was placed on virtuoso singers. And it was essential that the music of an opera be appealing to general audiences.

On all these counts *L'Incoronazione di Poppea* provided an ideal subject. Gian Francesco Busenello's involving libretto, with its sure-handed evocation of vernacular conversation, focused on the historical emperor Nero's love affair with Poppea, the wife of the noble Roman lord Otho, here called Ottone. Nero's tutor, Seneca, tries to convince the emperor to return to his wife, Ottavia. But the voluptuous and manipulative Poppea is determined to become the new empress. As the opera opens, Ottone, whom Nero had conveniently stationed in Lithuania, has returned to Rome, desperate with grief and madness over the inconstancy of his wife. He is persuaded by the highborn Ottavia, Nero's wife, to kill Poppea. But Ottone lacks the guts to act decisively. Disguised as a lady of the court, he attempts to stab Poppea but is stopped by Cupid, who protects her. Seneca takes his own life; Ottavia is banished. Poppea is crowned amid the celebrations of the populace, and the opera ends with Poppea and Nero singing the most blissfully beautiful love duet imaginable.

Is the message of the opera that love, even ruthlessly immoral love, conquers all? On one level *Poppea* is a bleakly satirical look at the Roman court that contemporary Venetians would have found riveting. Moreover, Monteverdi's audience would have known the full story, namely, that Nero eventually murdered Poppea. So this love tale would have been taken in context, much the way audiences today can enjoy John Adams's *Nixon in China* knowing how the Nixon presidency ended.

Monteverdi was nearly seventy-five when he composed this work, which pulses with the inspiration only a master composer and dramatist could command. The score is rich with arias, ensembles, and dialogue that vividly flesh out the characters from all stations. In the second scene, for example, as the sun rises, we meet sleep-deprived soldiers who have spent yet another night standing guard outside Poppea's palace as Nero shares her bed inside. What can they do? one soldier tells his partner. After all, Cupid blesses this union, to which the other replies: "Curses on Cupid, as well as Poppea, Nero, Rome, and the whole stinking army. I never get a chance to relax for even a single hour."

The minor characters are all memorable, like Valletto and Damigella, the page and lady-in-waiting to the empress, who are young and in love and adorable. They prefigure countless operatic couples to come, like Mozart's Masetto and Zerlina in *Don Giovanni*. Monteverdi gives the spurned Ottavia music of poignant elegance and high nobility. But the slightly old-fashioned cast to her music invites the audience to find her aggrieved outpourings somewhat tiresome.

The scores to most of Monteverdi's operas are lost and there are lapses in the manuscripts for this one as well. Only scant instrumental parts exist. Clearly Monteverdi inserted instrumental interludes into a production as needed, some composed by him, some by others. Certain ritornellos (orchestral refrains) from *Poppea* exist only in the form of figured bass lines. It's possible that even the beguiling final duet, "Pur ti miro," was not originally composed by Monteverdi.

As with *Orfeo,* I prefer performances of *Poppea* that are historically informed yet bring out the opera's contemporary resonances. For this reason I again recommend the conductor John Eliot Gardiner, whose Archiv release, from a live 1993 performance in London, is superb. Gardiner makes judicious choices of instrumental interludes, some of which were composed for this recording by Peter Holman using Monteverdi's original bass lines. Though he keeps the instrumental forces modest, Gardiner employs a richly diverse and continually varying roster of continuo instruments to accompany the recitative, including lutes, guitars, virginals, organs, and harps. The English Baroque Soloists give a lithe, urgent, and engrossing performance and the cast is consistently excellent, with the soprano Sylvia McNair as an alluring Poppea, the soprano Dana Hanchard as an impetuous Nero (a role originally written for a male castrato), the mezzo-soprano Anne Sofie von Otter as an achingly indignant Ottavia, and the countertenor Michael Chance as an anguished and pliable Ottone. That opera in Italy developed from the early Florentine efforts to Monteverdi's *Poppea* in just over forty years represents a dynamic growth spurt that would not be equaled until the early decades of jazz.

Archiv (three CDs) 447 088-2
Sir John Eliot Gardiner (conductor), The English Baroque Soloists; McNair, Hanchard, von Otter, Chance

Mozart Operas: An Introduction

The preliminary sketches that survive from the Mozart operas make clear what extraordinary compositional facility he brought to the job. In writing an aria, all Mozart needed to jot down was the vocal setting of the text and a rudimentary bass line, with here and there a rhythmic motif or a chord or two. No doubt, he had already formulated everything else in his mind: inner harmonies, orchestration—all the musical intricacies.

Actually, Mozart's facility was hard-won. He was arguably the best trained opera composer ever. One reason that his father, Leopold, left home in Salzburg for tours with the family throughout Austria and Europe was to show off the wunderkind boy as a prodigy pianist and instrumental composer in hopes of securing a royal patron. But the other goal was to expose young Wolfgang to the various styles of French, German, and especially Italian opera, then the dominant style even in Germany and England. In England Mozart worked with Johann Christian Bach, the youngest son of Johann Sebastian, who, in the curious cultural ways of the day, had turned himself, a German, into an expert provider of proper Italian opera for the London public.

By the age of nine Wolfgang could improvise recitatives and arias in the Italian manner and evoke the called-for emotional state. In late 1772, the sixteen-year-old Mozart, on an extended visit to Milan, had a triumph when his *Lucia Silla* was performed at the Regio Ducal. It's interesting to think how his life might have turned out had Mozart been able to secure a post and stay there. Maybe he would have lived to sixty and composed another dozen Italian operas. But the archbishop in Salzburg, who employed Leopold and considered the gifted young Wolfgang part of the deal, called him back home.

Mozart's extensive training may explain his skill and expertise. But nothing explains his instinctive feeling for the theater. He was so obsessed with music it's hard to imagine that he had room within himself for anything else. Mozart was uncurious about history and unabashedly apolitical. Though he lived through the French

Revolution you search his letters in vain for anything other than the most oblique references to this continental cataclysm. He had no feeling for nature and no interest in the visual arts. In his letters home during his wide-ranging travels he describes everything he heard and nothing he saw.

Reports suggest he was self-absorbed and rather uncouth. Yet his operas betray an uncanny insight into the human condition. Respectful of tradition, he didn't set out to revolutionize the genre. Yet, as he explored the various comic and dramatic operatic styles, his determination to humanize the characters had the same result. If *Idomeneo* was Mozart's first genuine masterpiece in the opera seria tradition, a work beholden to the French lyric tragedies of Gluck, he found his own ingenious approach, creating a work of gravity and elegance with an inexorable dramatic sweep, and composing poignant arias in which virtuosic display for its own sake is dispensed with. In his breakthrough work *Le Nozze di Figaro,* he demonstrated that opera buffa, a low-brow genre, could be intense, expansive, and musically sophisticated. Through his opera buffas Mozart explored class conflicts, societal mores, and the battle between the sexes. And, though *Die Zauberflöte* retains the essential character of the German singspiel, complete with spoken dialogue, Mozart turns this whimsical fairy tale into a profound morality play that still abounds with comic zaniness.

Like many people drawn to the theater, Mozart loved the collaborative process. He preferred to wait until an opera he was working on was cast so that he could compose arias with particular singers in mind, or, as his father put it, so he could "fit the costume to its figure," an approach old Leopold thought imprudent. Mozart would have a lot to talk about with Stephen Sondheim, who likes to work the same way. Rather than chafe when challenged by singers, Mozart was quick to accommodate their needs. When *Don Giovanni* was presented in Vienna in 1788, the year after its Prague premiere, the tenor singing Don Ottavio complained that the florid aria "Il mio tesoro" was too difficult. No problem. Mozart obligingly replaced it with the tenderly lyrical "Dalla sua pace." Today, it's standard practice for tenors to sing both, which necessitates awkwardly inserting the latter into a place in the plot where it doesn't quite fit. But who cares when you get to hear such astounding music?

Mozart was rare among opera composers of his day in that he undertook projects for which he had no commission. In the mid-1780s, desperate for a suitable subject, he read and rejected dozens of librettos, then started cajoling the sought-after Lorenzo da Ponte into working on something with him. Da Ponte, who had studied for the priesthood in Italy but was expelled for committing adultery, moved to Vienna in 1783 and won an appointment as poet to the Imperial Theater. Though he worked with every important composer in the city, he might be forgotten had he not collaborated with Mozart on *Le Nozze di Figaro, Don Giovanni,* and *Così fan tutte,* works that brought opera buffa to its glory. Piled-up debts forced da Ponte to flee to the United States in 1805, where he eventually wound up teaching Italian literature at Columbia University and writing a risqué autobiography fashioning himself a latter-day Casanova.

The da Ponte librettos inspired Mozart to reinvent the operatic ensemble. Previously, in most comic operas, the plot was advanced and information imparted during the recitatives. Arias and ensembles were for summing up feelings. But in Mozart's ensembles characters intrude upon one another, often in disguise, climb in and out of closets and windows, get into scrapes, uncover secrets, concoct revenges—all while the music keeps ambling along, with trios segueing seamlessly into quartets, quintets, and sextets, typically culminating in an up-tempo, everyone-onstage finale.

The melodic and harmonic ingenuity of Mozart's operas has been frequently commented upon. Less attention has been given to his inventive use of rhythm and dance elements, which is why I find *Rhythmic Gesture in Mozart,* a 1983 book by Wye Jamison Allanbrook, so important. An insightful music historian, Allanbrook analyzes *Le Nozze di Figaro* and *Don Giovanni* to demonstrate how virtually every aria and ensemble in those operas evokes a commonplace dance meter that would have resonated with Mozart's audiences. The composer chose the rhythmic character of a particular aria, Allanbrook suggests, even before he settled on its melody and key. In effect he had a vocabulary of rhythmic gestures and dance meters that produced specific associations with his listeners, just as a film-score composer today might evoke swing music, or blues, or a fox-trot, or a rock riff to tell audiences something about the nature of a character or the dramatic situation.

Allanbrook begins her discussion with an example from the act 2 finale of *Figaro*. The Countess, Figaro, and Susanna, having just barely managed to outwit the latest machination of the Count, turn to him and, for a fleeting moment, seriously ask him to give up already, to stop trying to sabotage the marriage of Susanna, whom he lusts for, to Figaro, his valet. Their subtly intense plea takes the form of a poignant musette-gavotte, a dance form associated with the pastoral play and with pastoral virtues of natural order, bucolic peace, and true love. Obviously, most operagoers today would not pick up that association. Even so, there is something haunting about this passage. It always got to me. After I read Allanbrook's study I had more insight into why.

Moreover, we know that Mozart was quite a nimble dancer himself and churned out dozens of dances for chamber ensemble and for orchestra. True, he also made some quick money with these pieces. But he did it out of love for the dance. So Allanbrook's analysis seems completely convincing.

Mozart is the only composer in history who reached the summit of greatness in both instrumental music and opera. But many of his instrumental works, notably the piano concertos, can be heard as de facto mini-operas, with their dramatically shifting scenes, face-offs between soloist and orchestra, ruminative soliloquies for individual instruments, and stretches of wordless recitative. Mozart was also the first opera composer to create a body of work that entered the repertory shortly after his death and remains at its core today.

40. WOLFGANG AMADEUS MOZART

(1756–1791)

Idomeneo

Giovanni Battista Varesco, librettist

First performance: Munich, Residenztheater, January 29, 1781

For a young man who never doubted his own brilliance, Mozart was actually humbled when he received a commission in 1780 from the Bavarian court at Munich to write a major work, an opera seria, for performance during the carnival season early the following year. He had already composed ten works for the stage, but nothing of the scope and seriousness required for this commission. Mozart's ambition kicked right in, though. He set about to produce an opera that would dazzle audiences and perhaps win him a permanent post in Munich so that he could finally escape his hometown, Salzburg, where he held the lowly appointment of court organist for the overbearing prince archbishop.

But first he had to do something about the libretto assigned to him: *Idomeneo,* an adaptation by Giovanni Battista Varesco, a wordy and conventional Italian poet, of an existing seventy-year-old French lyric tragedy. Mozart saw immense possibilities in the story of the noble Idomeneo, King of Crete, who nearly dies in a horrific storm while sailing home from the Trojan War. As his ship is destroyed, the king makes a last-ditch plea to Neptune: if the god will save him Idomeneo will sacrifice the first living creature he encounters onshore. When the storm calms and the king lands the first person he sees is Idamante, his son.

Taking matters in hand, Mozart, after arriving in Munich, demanded an extensive reworking of the libretto. Since Varesco was living in Salzburg, Mozart conveyed his needs through letters to his father, who served as go-between. In these letters the twenty-four-year-old composer is revealed to be already a savvy theatrical professional

Composer Wolfgang Amadeus Mozart

with a sure grasp of drama and pacing. The text was pruned and reshaped to Mozart's specifications.

Mozart's music similarly demonstrates a thorough knowledge of what was best in the serious opera traditions of Italy and France and a high regard for the reforms of Gluck, who cleared away some of the musical excess of serious eighteenth-century opera and introduced a beautifully austere classicism that in context sounded radical.

But Mozart broke new ground in *Idomeneo*. The score is wondrous for its harmonic daring, especially in stretches of dramatic recitative, its inventive use of the orchestra, and its innovative dramatic structure in which crucial arias and ensembles are folded into continuously flowing music. The score achieves great dignity and refinement.

Though revived regularly, *Idomeneo* remains Mozart's most overlooked mature opera. Fortunately there are several fine recordings.

As of this writing, the most satisfying overall is unavailable: the conductor Colin Davis's first recording from the early 1970s on Philips with the BBC Symphony Orchestra and Chorus. This magisterial performance offers an excellent cast headed by the American tenor George Shirley, who could be variable but is impressive here, singing with verve and style and deftly dispatching the fleet passagework in the bravura act 2 aria, "Fuor del Mar," when the disconsolate king says that the torrents of the seas are nothing compared to the rages of his heart.

You can't go wrong, though, with the 2001 recording on EMI Classics with Sir Charles Mackerras conducting the Scottish Chamber Orchestra and a superb cast, a fleet, bracing, and lucid performance informed by Mackerras's extensive work in the early music movement. The crucial role of Idamante, written for a castrato (and performed on the Davis recording by the tenor Ryland Davies), is here sung by the radiant mezzo-soprano Lorraine Hunt Lieberson, a consummate artist. The rich-voiced soprano Barbara Frittoli makes a fiery Elettra. And, in a daring bit of casting, Idomeneo is the British tenor Ian Bostridge, who brings dulcet lyricism, keen intelligence, and urgency to his portrayal, though ideally you want a voice with more heroic heft for "Fuor del Mar."

Heroic heft is what you get from Plácido Domingo on a fascinating 1994 Deutsche Grammophon recording with James Levine conducting the orchestra and chorus of the Metropolitan Opera. Levine's work is typically crisp, nuanced, expansive where called for, and stylistically insightful. The stellar cast includes Cecilia Bartoli as Idamante, Heidi Grant Murphy as a plangent Ilia, Carol Vaness, a soprano prone to stridency who here sings handsomely, as the volatile Elettra, and the baritone Thomas Hampson doing ably in the tenor role of Arbace, the king's confidant. And just for fun, the recording offers the bass-baritone Bryn Terfel in a bit part: a godly voice from afar. Domingo brings a resplendent sound tinged with sadness and a quality of tragic grandeur to his work.

Alas, because he cannot technically execute the florid runs of "Fuor del Mar," he sings a simplified substitute version of the aria that Mozart wrote for an amateur production in Vienna that he financed in hopes of jump-starting his stalled operatic career. The alternate version is an acceptable compromise in the opera house when you are in Domingo's presence. But it's a disappointment on a recording.

EMI Classics (three CDs) 5 57260 2
Sir Charles Mackerras (conductor), The Scottish Chamber Orchestra; Bostridge, Hunt Lieberson, Frittoli, Rolfe Johnson.

Deutsche Grammophon (three CDs) 447 737-2
James Levine (conductor), Metropolitan Opera Orchestra and Chorus; Domingo, Bartoli, Vaness, Grant Murphy, Hampson, Terfel

41. WOLFGANG AMADEUS MOZART

(1756–1791)

Die Entführung aus dem Serail (The Abduction from the Seraglio)

Gottlieb Stephanie the Younger, librettist, freely adapted from a libretto by Christoph Friedrich Bretzner

First performance: Vienna, Burgtheater, July 16, 1782

In early 1781 the vainglorious prince archbishop of Salzburg, accompanied by a typically large entourage of retainers, traveled to Vienna to tend to his ailing father. Traveling separately from far-off Augsburg was Mozart, who held the constricting post of court organist to the archbishop. Mozart found Vienna "magnificent," as he wrote to his father, and "for my Metier the best place in the world." The twenty-five-year-old Mozart convinced himself that in Vienna he would find fresh opportunities to give concerts, win commissions, make some real money, and establish an independent career. By midsummer his rebelliousness provoked a bitter break with the archbishop. To the utter dismay of his father, Mozart decided to remain in Vienna on his own.

He must have felt that the heavens supported his boldness, for no sooner had he cut himself free than a commission fell into his lap to write a three-act singspiel for the Burgtheater based on a libretto by Christoph Friedrich Bretzner titled *Belmont und Constanze*. The work was to be performed in conjunction with the visit to Vienna of the Russian grand duke.

Mozart was excited at the prospect of writing a comic opera with spoken dialogue in his native tongue for a popular theater. Though generally pleased with the libretto, as usual he wanted changes and improvements. Gottlieb Stephanie the Younger, who ran the theater and had secured Mozart the commission, worked with him to shape up the text.

Though the visit of the grand duke was postponed, the sections of the opera that had already been composed were so popular with Stephanie and the singers that a production was scheduled for the next year. The premiere performances of *Die Entführung aus dem Serail* (*The Abduction from the Seraglio*), as the opera was finally titled, were triumphant and its fame quickly spread outside of Austria. Within three years there were productions in Warsaw, Bonn, Frankfurt, Leipzig, and elsewhere.

One lingering criticism of the opera is that Mozart lavishes too much musical richness on this slender comedy, a tale of an ardent young Spanish nobleman, Belmonte, who travels to an exotic pasha's palace in Turkey to rescue his fiancée, Konstanze, who is being held captive by the smitten pasha along with her perky English maid, Blonde. There is, for example, Konstanze's act 2 aria, "Martern aller Arten," in which the threatened young woman defiantly declares that she would welcome pain or any kind of torture rather than betray her Belmonte and succumb to the pasha's advances. This nine-minute aria with its long orchestral introduction and obbligato parts for solo flute, oboe, violin, and cello, and its vocal gymnastics replete with extravagant coloratura runs and roulades, sounds like some hybrid of a tour de force showpiece and a concerto grosso. Yet while poking fun at Konstanze's ostentatious virtue Mozart gives the soprano such stunningly difficult music to sing that the aria is at once hilarious and riveting.

I think Mozart knew just what he was up to in this work. He instinctively understood that for comedy to be effective it must be played straight, the characters must take themselves seriously, and Mozart's music allows them to do so. The poignant ambiguity in the score starts with the overture, which opens with an effervescent Allegro section evocative of Turkish martial music complete with cymbals and drums. But all of sudden this Allegro in C major gives way to a slow middle section in C minor, a pensive melody in a halting triple meter. The bright Allegro returns to conclude the overture. When the curtain goes up and we see Belmonte, just arrived outside the pasha's palace and bent on rescuing his Konstanze, he sings a gentle major-mode version of that pensive slow music from the orchestra. It's a marvelous touch. Though he sounds confident, there is an echo of doubt in his music.

I prefer performances of this opera that, instead of milking it for easy laughs, respect the richness of the music and the depth of the characterizations. Karl Böhm's 1974 recording with the Staatskapelle Dresden Orchestra finds just the right balance between frothiness and complexity, between vitality and introspection, and his superb cast is right with him: Arleen Auger as Konstanze, Reri Grist as Blonde, Peter Schreier as Belmonte, and, most of all, the booming German bass Kurt Moll as an endearingly befuddled Osmin, the overseer of the pasha's country house, who is searching in vain for love. One curiosity is that the spoken dialogue is performed by actors who double for the singers. But quite of bit of dialogue is cut, which makes sense on a recording.

Another excellent choice, available on Deutsche Grammophon's Originals series, is the landmark recording from 1954 with the Hungarian conductor Ferenc Fricsay leading the Berlin RIAS Symphony Orchestra. By using reduced orchestra forces and favoring fleet tempos and transparent textures, Fricsay anticipated the period instrument movement. The performance features a cast steeped in the Germanic tradition: Maria Stader as Konstanze, Rita Streich as Blonde, Josef Greindl as Osmin, and, most fascinating of all, the great Swiss tenor Ernst Haefliger as an exceptionally elegant Belmonte.

Deutsche Grammophon (two CDs) 429 868-2
Karl Böhm (conductor), Staatskapelle Dresden Orchestra; Auger, Grist, Schreier, Moll

Deutsche Grammophon (two CDs) 289 457 730-2

Ferenc Fricsay (conductor), Berlin RIAS Symphony Orchestra; Stader, Streich, Haefliger, Greindl

42. WOLFGANG AMADEUS MOZART

(1756–1791)

Le Nozze di Figaro (The Marriage of Figaro)

Lorenzo da Ponte, librettist, after a comedy by Pierre-Augustin Caron de Beaumarchais

First performance: Vienna, Burgtheater, May 1, 1786

Perhaps the most helpful thing to know in approaching *Le Nozze di Figaro* is that it's, in effect, a sequel, an operatic treatment of the second in a trilogy of plays by the French ancien régime writer Pierre-Augustin Beaumarchais written over a period of twenty years. The composer Giovanni Paisiello had scored a triumph in Vienna in 1783 with his operatic version of the first play, *Le Barbier de Séville (The Barber of Seville)*. In it, Figaro, the title character, who is not just a barber but a professional go-between and provider of services, chances upon the dashing young Count Almaviva, for whom he had briefly worked as a servant. His former master is pretending to be a poor student and serenading a pretty girl named Rosina, the ward of the stodgy old Dr. Bartolo, who intends to marry her. Figaro helps the count outwit Bartolo and win Rosina's love.

In the second play, some years have gone by and the count has grown bored in his marriage to Rosina, now the Countess Almaviva. Figaro, ensconced as the count's valet, is betrothed to perky Susanna, the countess's maid. But the inconstant count has his own designs on Susanna. Meanwhile, Dr. Bartolo, still smarting over having been duped, would love to exact some revenge.

It was Mozart's idea to capitalize on Paisiello's success and turn the second play, introduced in Paris in 1784, into an opera. But the seething grievances among the working classes that would culminate in the French Revolution caused the ruling aristocracy to fear a play in which quick-witted servants bamboozle a corrupt royal. Consequently, performances were banned in Vienna; da Ponte and Mozart had to soften the insurrectionist edges of the play to win permission to adapt it.

No problem, for through his music Mozart staged his own sly insurrection. For example, in the play when Figaro learns that the count is still trying to force Susanna to yield to him before her marriage, the valet denounces the inherited fortune and rank that endow the count with such power. "What have you done to gain so many advantages?" he says in a bitter soliloquy; "You took the trouble to be born, and nothing else."

In the equivalent moment in the opera, Figaro sings his act 1 aria "Se vuol ballare," in which he says, to paraphrase: "OK, Mr. Count. You want to dance? Fine. But you will dance to my tune." Mozart might have had Figaro explode with avenging anger. Instead this aria is a cool, courtly, but muscular minuet. Pizzicato violins suggest the plucked strings of Figaro's guitar, but insistent horn calls give an ironic nudge to his challenge. The musical subtext is rich: Figaro turns the aristocratic minuet into a vehicle for a servant's defiance.

Mozart was not much bothered by having to soft-pedal the play's politics. What drew him to the story were its romantic relationships. During all the imbroglio of act 1, as we see the menacing Count looking foolish, conniving to get Susanna into bed, we only hear about his wife. In an affecting dramatic stroke, act 2 begins with an intimate scene in which we finally meet the Countess, alone in her room, pining for the husband who has tired of her, sentiments she expresses in the poignant aria "Porgi amor." The Countess must turn to her maid, Susanna, as a sisterly confidante—hardly the aristocratic life she had imagined. In truth, Susanna is the type of woman that the younger Rosina would have related to immediately. Yet in act 3, as the two women concoct a plot to disguise themselves as each other and expose both the Count's unfaithfulness and Figaro's unfounded doubts about Susanna, the Countess, in the sublime aria "Dove sono," expresses bewildered sadness that she has been reduced to such demeaning extremes in an attempt to salvage her marriage.

In act 4, just before the entrapment scheme begins, the just-married but still virginal Susanna sings "Deh vieni, non tardar," a deceptively simple recitative and aria of stunning psychological complexity. Susanna knows that Figaro is secretly watching her; she also knows that he thinks, wrongly, that she, on her wedding night, is awaiting an assignation with the Count. Miffed, hurt, yet still in love with her thickheaded husband, she sings a purposefully ambiguous serenade, saying, in essence, "Enough already; stop all your plotting and just come to me, my love, I'm ready." She is at once teaching Figaro a lesson and inviting him to their first night of bliss.

The Beaumarchais play was considered not only politically dangerous but morally scandalous. So Mozart and da Ponte were forced to eliminate some of the sexual innuendo between the Countess and the young page, Cherubino, a pants role for a mezzo-soprano. Beaumarchais's Countess is hardly an innocent, for in the third play of the trilogy we discover that she has had a child by the young page. Mozart's Cherubino is safer, a typically hormonal adolescent with a crush on an older woman.

Still, it's important for any performance of *Figaro* to tap the dangerous currents of sexual desire and class resentment that lurk below the music's lithe surface. Though there are many fine recordings of this opera, two, both with the Vienna Philharmonic, achieve this multilayered richness extraordinarily. The conductor Erich Kleiber's 1955 account is available on Decca's Legendary Performances series, and it is indeed a legend. Kleiber was a renowned Mozart conductor and the orchestra playing breathes and flows with elegance and sparkle. The cast is exemplary, with the clear-toned lyric soprano Hilde Gueden as Susanna, the hearty and insightful bass Cesare Siepi as Figaro, the luminous soprano Lisa della Casa as the Countess, the robust bass-baritone Alfred Poell as the Count, and the bright-voiced Suzanne Danco as Cherubino.

For a more recent recording, try the conductor Claudio Abbado's 1994 account on Deutsche Grammophon, a superb achievement. Taking fleet tempos for the most part, Abbado elicits incisive, articulate, and supple playing from the Vienna Philharmonic. Yet the music making is wonderfully relaxed and natural. The cast has a dynamic Figaro and sweet Susanna in Lucio Gallo and Sylvia McNair. Bo Skovhus makes a virile Count and Cheryl Studer a regal yet sympathetic Countess. Cecilia Bartoli brings her tasteful musicianship, vibrant sound, and high spirits to the role of Cherubino.

Decca (three CDs) 289 466 369-2

Erich Kleiber (conductor), Vienna Philharmonic; Gueden, Siepi, Poell, della Casa, Danco

Deutsche Grammophon (three CDs) 445 903-2

Claudio Abbado (conductor), Vienna Philharmonic; Skovhus, Studer, McNair, Gallo, Bartoli

43. WOLFGANG AMADEUS MOZART

(1756–1791)

Don Giovanni

Lorenzo da Ponte, librettist, after an opera by Giovanni Bertati

First performance: Prague, National Theater, October 29, 1787

It's become fashionable in productions of *Don Giovanni* these days for stage directors to emphasize the story's bleakness and the title character's depravity. After all, the opera begins with a brutal attempted rape followed in short order by the cavalier homicide of the intended victim's aging father. Not content to portray Giovanni as a dashing nobleman turned lecherous Don Juan, directors routinely fill their productions with heavy-handed indicators of his evilness. A director of a Salzburg Festival production in 2002 peopled the stage almost continually with a silent chorus of bedraggled, vacant-eyed women in torn and bloodied garments who hover in the background, the ghostly victims of Don Giovanni's abuse and lust. In such productions the lighter elements of the opera are treated like the darkest of black comedy. If you laugh you are supposed to feel guilty about it.

Directors who approach *Don Giovanni* this way patronize the opera, called a "dramma giocoso," or jocular drama, on its title page. The prevailing attitude behind these unutterably grim stagings would seem to be: Mozart and his librettist, Lorenzo da Ponte, did not fully grasp the dangerous underside of their own opera, so let me help them out.

Actually, I think Mozart and da Ponte knew exactly what they were doing, which was something daringly ambiguous. The Don is a monster, but he's a charming monster. That he is also rich, threatening, and willfully amoral is part of his appeal. He ruthlessly attempts to seduce the stately Donna Anna, who is contentedly engaged to the young nobleman Don Ottavio. Yet at the same time we are invited to find Donna Anna laughably high-minded and Don Ottavio rather silly with his stiff rectitude. Donna Elvira, who, we find out, has had an affair with Giovanni and seems to think of herself as his spouse, spends most of the opera abjectly pursuing him, panting with desire, fulminating over his betrayal, and seemingly deranged, qualities powerfully captured in the fitful coloratura passagework running through her arias. Yet at the same time she is meant to be a pathetically risible figure. And if you really pay attention to the "Catalog Aria," in which the Don's beleaguered servant Leporello runs through the list of his master's conquests, you learn some truly gruesome information, for example, that the Don sometimes seduces older women just for the kick of adding them to his list. Still, if you are not cracking up during the "Catalog Aria" then the production has failed.

Virgil Thomson encapsulated the astounding ambiguity of the opera in a 1940 article for the *New York Herald Tribune*: "Don Giovanni is one of the funniest shows in the world and one of the most terrifying. It's all about love, and it kids love to a fare-ye-well. It's the world's greatest opera and the world's greatest parody of opera. It is a moral entertainment so movingly human that the morality gets lost before the play is scarcely started."

For these reasons I prefer performances of *Don Giovanni* that embrace its humor along with its grimness and keep the pacing lithe.

Of the many fine recordings, I keep going back to the first one I owned: the 1955 account with Josef Krips, a vibrant Mozartean, conducting the Vienna Philharmonic and a stellar cast headed by the incomparable bass Cesare Siepi in the title role and the exquisite Lisa della Casa as Donna Anna. The underrated Belgian soprano Suzanne Danco sings Donna Elvira impressively, Hilde Gueden is the dreamiest Zerlina imaginable, Anton Dermota the most elegant Ottavio, and the basso buffo Fernando Corena a truly comic and endearingly befuddled Leporello. Decca has reissued the recording on its Legends series. But if you have trouble finding it, look for the 1998 Deutsche Grammophon version with Claudio Abbado conducting the Chamber Orchestra of Europe. Abbado's performance combines old-school insight with an up-to-date sensibility informed by the early music movement. The playing of the orchestra is supple and lucid. The baritone Simon Keenlyside as Giovanni and the bass-baritone Bryn Terfel as Leporello are the standouts in the young cast, though Soile Isokoski as Elvira, Carmela Remigio as Anna, and the rest are strong. But Abbado's work is the special attraction.

Decca (three CDs) 466389; Legends series
Josef Krips (conductor), Vienna Philharmonic; Siepi, della Casa, Danco, Gueden, Dermota, Corena

Deutsche Grammophon (three CDs) 457 601-2
Claudio Abbado (conductor), The Chamber Orchestra of Europe; Keenlyside, Terfel, Isokoski, Remigio, Heilmann

44. WOLFGANG AMADEUS MOZART

(1756–1791)

Così fan tutte (roughly translated as All Women Do the Same)

Lorenzo da Ponte, librettist

First performance: Vienna, Burgtheater, January 26, 1790

If, as I suggested in the previous entry, *Don Giovanni* is often taken too seriously, *Così fan tutte* is not taken seriously enough. The plot, it's true, can be seen as heartless and silly. Alfonso, a cynical older bachelor in eighteenth-century Naples, is wryly amused to hear his young officer friends Guglielmo and Ferrando always bragging about the unassailable faithfulness of their girlfriends. Asserting that all women are fickle-hearted, Alfonso challenges the guys to a wager. They are instructed to announce that they have been called into battle, then to reappear in disguise and attempt to seduce each other's fiancées. The young men accept the bet. And the women succumb within the space of a day.

In its time *Così* was considered lesser Mozart at best and immoral at worst. But the opera's frothy surface cannot mask its eerie ambiguity and troubling undercurrents. That the women give in so readily to the strangers is presented as utterly risible, especially since Guglielmo and Ferrando are usually disguised as exotic Albanians or some such. That the guys are guilty of manipulative betrayal is apparently irrelevant.

Yet, as the evening progresses, the two determined men, despite themselves, get increasingly caught up in the demeaning game. The clear implication is that they actually have sexual relations with each other's girlfriends, though it all happens offstage. In comparison, Don Giovanni, despite repeated attempts, has not one successful seduction during the long day Mozart's opera recounts.

As presented, Fiordiligi and Dorabella, who are sisters, are widely thought to be a humorous homage to the Weber sisters, Aloysia and Constanze. When Mozart first met them in Mannheim it was the sixteen-year-old Aloysia who made his heart go pitter-pat. But by the time the Weber family and Mozart found themselves in Vienna in 1781, Aloysia was married. He switched his affections to Constanze, whom he soon married under pressure from Frau Weber and over the stern objections of his father.

To me, though, something deeper is at work in the opera's evocation of the Weber sisters. Could Mozart be suggesting that choosing a spouse is a more arbitrary endeavor than we might like to admit? Mozart lived every day of his curtailed life with his head full of music. Aloysia. Constanze. On some level what was the difference? This is just one troubling truth that *Così* explores.

Mozart's score is a triumph of ambiguity. Take the quintet in act 1 when Ferrando and Guglielmo arrive at the home of the sisters filled with anguish because they have been called up into action. As the orchestra begins an innocuous oom-pah-pah-pah pattern the two men, feigning upset, sing in halting, broken phrases, while the two women, truly crushed, yet perhaps laying it on a little thick, sing in achingly beautiful, long-spun lines. Meanwhile in the background Alfonso chortles to himself that if this absurd scene goes on another moment he is going to lose it. At first you laugh. But as the music turns more poignant and intense, you don't know what to feel. It's hilarious; it's horrible.

The sublime and deservedly famous trio that the sisters and Alfonso sing when the young men sail off, "Soave sia il vento" ("May the wind be gentle"), is music I'd like performed at my funeral. Even the moments of musical parody, like Fiordiligi's aria "Come scoglio," in which she asserts to the entreating Albanians that her fidelity is as firm as a rock against the seas, seem uncomfortably ambiguous. With the dramatic vocal leaps from low to high register and excessively florid runs, it could be a mockery of a grandly noble opera seria aria. Yet there truly is grandeur in this stirring music. At the same time it seems the music of a woman on the edge of a breakdown.

Both the psychological resonance and breezy comedy of *Così* come through best when the cast and conductor play it straight. I grew up with the classic recording conducted by Karl Böhm featuring Elisabeth Schwarzkopf, Christa Ludwig, Alfredo Kraus, and Giuseppe Taddei, a performance I still revere. But I recommend the 1994 account with Sir Georg Solti conducting the Chamber Orchestra of Europe. The cast is excellent: the soprano Renée Fleming is a radiant Fiordiligi, and the mezzo-soprano Anne Sofie von Otter a tenderly human Dorabella. The lyric tenor Frank Lopardo is at his best as Ferrando and the robust baritone Olaf Bär is a volatile Guglielmo. Solti is the draw here, though. He had a special affinity for *Così*. But in this live recording from Royal Festival Hall in London, made when Solti was eighty-one, he shows himself as having paid close attention to the early music movement. Working with this crack chamber orchestra, he conducts a lithe yet lyrically fine-spun performance.

I also treasure—and this may seem a curious choice—the historic 1952 recording of a landmark Metropolitan Opera production, performed in English translation, with Richard Tucker (Ferrando), Frank Guarrera (Guglielmo), Roberta Peters (Despina), Blanche Thebom (Dorabella), and, best of all, the great Mozartean soprano Eleanor Steber (Fiordiligi). Fritz Stiedry conducts a buoyant performance. Sadly, the opera is cut a bit. But it's terrific to hear the work performed with such crisp English diction. In 1952 *Così fan tutte* was a rarity. This recording captures the quality of excited discovery that permeated this important Met production.

Decca (three CDs) 444 174-2
Sir Georg Solti (conductor), The Chamber Orchestra of Europe; Fleming, von Otter, Lopardo, Bär, Scarabelli, Pertusi

Sony Classical Masterworks Heritage Opera series (two CDs) MH2K 60652
Fritz Stiedry (conductor), The Metropolitan Opera Orchestra and Choir; Steber, Thebom, Peters, Tucker, Guarrera, Alvary

45. WOLFGANG AMADEUS MOZART

(1756–1791)

Die Zauberflöte (The Magic Flute)

Emanuel Schikaneder, librettist

First performance: Vienna, Theater auf der Wieden, September 30, 1791

If I could zap myself back in time and attend the first performance of any opera in the repertory, I would choose the September 30, 1791, opening night of *Die Zauberflöte* (*The Magic Flute*) in Vienna. Sure, I would love to have been at the 1887 premiere of Verdi's *Otello* in Milan, or the 1865 premiere of Wagner's *Tristan und Isolde* in Munich, or any number of other openings. But I can imagine what those evenings must have been like. For all I've read about the premiere of *The Magic Flute,* I still don't have a clear idea of what kind of place the Theater auf der Wieden on the outskirts of Vienna was back then, or what kind of audience its productions attracted.

Though court composers and high-born music lovers routinely showed up at this theater, it was essentially a house for the common folk that offered lots of low-brow comedies that relied on stage machinery and all manner of contraptions for special effects. *The Magic Flute,* a singspiel with spoken dialogue, was tailor-made for the place. How could it not be? The librettist was the actor and singer Emanuel Schikaneder, who ran the theater and wrote the comic role of Papageno for himself to play. This fairy tale story with its vaguely Egyptian trappings, set in no specific locale or period, offers opportunities galore for spectacle. A monstrous serpent must be slain by three lady attendants to the mysterious Queen of the Night, who descends from on high. The hero is young Prince Tamino who agrees to search for the queen's abducted daughter, Pamina, guided by three wise boys and a magic flute that tames wild beasts. Creative stagecraft is required to depict the fearsome trials by fire and water that

Tamino and Pamina must endure. And Papageno, the rustic bird catcher who works for the queen and who is typically portrayed as rather birdlike himself, is an unabashedly hammy and crowd-pleasing character.

Yet, Mozart and Schikaneder, both practicing Freemasons, also made *The Magic Flute* an allegory about the quasi-religious rituals of this secret, liberal-minded brotherhood. For all its slapstick humor, the opera is deeply spiritual and musically sophisticated. The score abounds with catchy tunes and comic ensembles, like the quintet in which the Three Ladies punish Papageno for lying by sealing his lips with a padlock so all he can sing are muffled, but exactly pitched, grunts of "hmm, hmm, hmm, hmm." Mozart also ingeniously evokes older styles of music to make resonant dramatic points, as when the Two Armored Men who guard the gates to the hall of trials warn Tamino of its dangers in a grimly minor-mode melody accompanied by contrapuntal inner voices and a walking bass line in the orchestra, like some stern aria from a baroque oratorio.

More than in almost any other score, Mozart achieves his oft-articulated goal of writing music that provides surface delights to all but also subtleties only connoisseurs will appreciate. For example, the little song that Papageno sings to introduce himself, "Der Vogel-fänger bin ich ja," seems at first just a simple folk tune with a repetitive rhythmic pattern that swings along in a jaunty 2/4 meter. Yet, notewise, the tune is a string of two-measure units, each one different from the rest; there are no repetitions until the end of each verse. This crafty subtlety suggests to listeners, at least subliminally, that Papageno is a creature of spontaneity, that he lives for the moment and makes it up as he goes along.

Though charming and fanciful, the opera's spiritual dimension is what lingers with me. So I prefer performances that tap into that dimension and convey the magisterial qualities of the score. No performance has done so better than Otto Klemperer's astonishing 1964 recording for EMI Classics. With a cast that includes the hardy bass-baritone Walter Berry as Papageno, Klemperer certainly captures the earthy humor of the work. But overall, he takes spacious tempos, elicits radiant playing from the Philharmonia Orchestra, and makes the score sound as spiritually elevated as Mozart's Requiem.

As the Three Ladies, who almost always sing in ensemble, this recording recruited three illustrious artists, Elisabeth Schwarzkopf, Christa Ludwig, and Marga Höffgen, who sound like they are having great fun. The superb tenor Nicolai Gedda brings his sweet voice, lyrical ardor, and refined musicianship to the role of Tamino. The soprano Gundula Janowitz is in exquisite voice as Pamina. The resounding bass Gottlob Frick is an imposing Sarastro, the leader of the temple. And you will never hear a better Queen of the Night than the young Lucia Popp, who sails through the hazardous coloratura flights, complete with pinpoint high F's, singing always with luscious tone and perfect breath control. So many coloraturas sound strident and harsh in this role. Popp's way of conveying the queen's diabolical power is to sing this inhumanly difficult music with uncanny effortlessness and clarion beauty.

EMI Classics (two CDs) 5 55173 2

Otto Klemperer (conductor), Philharmonia Orchestra; Janowitz, Gedda, Popp, Berry, Frick

46. MODEST MUSSORGSKY (1839–1881)

Boris Godunov

Modest Mussorgsky, librettist, adapted from the historical tragedy by Alexander Pushkin

First performance: St. Petersburg, Mariinsky Theatre, January 27, 1874 (revised version)

In 1858, Modest Mussorgsky, then nineteen, resigned his commission with the Cadet School of Guards, a step that proved disastrous for the livelihood of his family but fortuitous for the history of opera. Born to privilege, he was afire with musical ambitions from an early age. But his family intended him for a career in the military. By 1857, determined to become a composer, especially in opera, he began studying with Mily Balakirev, a leader in the Russian Nationalist movement in music. But two years after giving up his commission the serfs were emancipated and his family ruined. For the rest of his life Mussorgsky had to hold down intermittent civil service jobs to support his career in music.

It's difficult to discuss *Boris Godunov,* Mussorgsky's most important work, because the opera exists in multiple versions, especially if you include various revisions and reorchestrations by several subsequent composers, notably Rimsky-Korsakov. In his authoritative entry on *Boris Godunov* in the *New Grove Dictionary of Opera,* the scholar Richard Taruskin points out that historical drama was the dominant theatrical genre in mid-nineteenth-century Russia, reflecting a widespread conviction that art had a "civic obligation," an "attitude that tends to flourish in states where open discussion of public policy is not permitted." Mussorgsky was hooked by the idea of an opera about the ruthless and tormented czar, who ascended the throne in 1598 after ordering the murder of the rightful heir, a young boy, Prince Dimitri. With his keen dramatic sense and psychological insight, Mussorgsky thought Boris could be an arresting operatic character, a flawed and self-defeating tragic hero.

At that time most Russian composers were trying to hone a distinctively Russian style of opera. Its hallmark was the naturalistic setting of words to music. But Mussorgsky took this principle in a radical direction, composing music that meticulously captured the flow, rhythm, accents, and contours of conversational Russian. Whole stretches of *Boris Godunov* have a quality of elegiac and lyrically charged recitative, though as the characters converse the orchestra often provides commentary through hymnal harmonies, plaintive melodies, and quotes of recurring themes and motifs.

Mussorgsky wrote his own libretto adapted from a historical tragedy by Pushkin. The first version of the opera, completed late in 1869, was a compact work in seven scenes grouped into four acts, called parts. Mussorgsky whittled down Pushkin's sprawling tale by boldly eliminating almost every scene in which Boris does not appear. Still, the opera was rejected when Mussorgsky submitted it to the selection committee for the Imperial Theatre. The reason given was the lack of a substantial female role. Eventually Mussorgsky returned to the score, made changes, and added the so-called Polish act (the third of four). Set first in a boudoir and then by a grand fountain at the Sandomierz Castle in Poland, the act centers on Grigory, formerly a novice from a Moscow monastery, who, outraged at Boris's abuse of power and criminality, has disguised himself as the Czarevich Dimitri and is trying to incite the enmity of the Polish people toward Russia. He is also seeking the hand of Marina, a Polish princess who has been scheming with the Jesuit priest Rangoni in order to marry Grigory, called the Pretender, and claim the Russian throne.

This second *Boris Godunov,* completed in 1872, premiered at the Mariinsky Theatre in St. Petersburg in 1874. Despite the enrichments of this version, Mussorgsky's orchestrations and other aspects of the score were deemed inadequate. After Mussorgsky's death at forty-two in 1881, in a well-meaning effort to bring a work he admired into the canon, Rimsky-Korsakov edited and reorchestrated the score. For decades afterward Rimsky-Korsakov's version was the standard. In 1940 Shostakovich orchestrated the score, and after the 1960s his version frequently turned up at the Mariinsky Theatre. Since the 1970s, though, it has been increasingly common to perform the work with Mussorgsky's orchestration. The original instrumental sonorities, though curiously spare and often unconventional, are strangely alluring and, to me, more appropriate to the naturalistic quality of the vocal writing.

Though the 1872 version of *Boris Godunov* is more conventional in structure and less radical in its naturalistic setting of text, many critics agree with Taruskin's assessment that it is superior to the first version, seldom performed today. In 1998 Philips released a special five-disc set of both versions, with the conductor Valery Gergiev and the forces of the Mariinsky Theatre (the Kirov Opera). The performance of the fascinating earlier version stars the great Russian bass Nikolai Putilin, who makes a chilling Boris. The 1872 version offers the powerful bass Vladimir Vaneev as a Boris palpably at war with himself, the heroic tenor Vladimir Galuzin as Grigory, and the lustrous mezzo-soprano Olga Borodina as Marina. Gergiev captures the restless sweep and psychological ambiguity of the 1872 *Boris,* with its world-weary choruses of oppressed Russian peasants and its scenes of coerced public rejoicing as Boris ascends the throne—thanks to the maneuvering of the cunning Boyars. Gergiev draws dusky and resonant tone from the strings, mournfully reedy colors from the winds, and steely flourishes from the brass.

Another recording to consider was released in 1977 by EMI Classics. Jerzy Semkow conducts the Polish Radio National Orchestra in a grimly beautiful and stirring performance. The elegant tenor Nicolai Gedda brings such vocal charisma to the role of Grigory that you can't help feeling sympathy for this manipulative character. With his gravelly bass voice Martti Talvela makes a poignantly volatile Boris. The czar's death scene is one of the most inspired episodes in all of opera. In a delirium of anguish and remorse Boris bequeaths his throne to his sweet young son, a mere child. Pressing his hands to his head, Boris feels like the pealing church bells are pounding within his brain.

And in an inspired touch, the revised version of the opera ends with a character called the Simpleton, the Fool. A crowd of insurgent peasants who have gathered in a forest hear that Boris has died and the pretender, Dimitri, has taken the throne. Rejoicing, they march off toward the city. The Fool knows better. In a few eerie phrases he sings softly that tears will flow and Russia's misfortunes continue.

Philips (five CDs) 462 230-2
Valery Gergiev (conductor), Chorus and Orchestra of the Kirov Opera of the Mariinsky Theatre; Putilin, Lutsuk (1869 version); Vaneev, Galuzin, Borodina (1872 version)

EMI Classics (three CDs) 7 54377 2
Jerzy Semkow (conductor), Polish Radio Chorus of Krakow and the Polish Radio National Orchestra; Talvela, Gedda, Kinasz, Haugland

47. MODEST MUSSORGSKY (1839–1881)

Khovanshchina

Modest Mussorgsky, librettist

First performance: Professional premiere of the work with Rimsky-Korsakov's orchestration—St. Petersburg, Mariinsky Theatre, November 7 (20), 1911

If you find yourself baffled by the story of Modest Mussorgsky's folk-music drama *Khovanshchina*, you will hardly be alone. The cluttered plot reflects the convulsive times the opera depicts.

Set in and near Moscow roughly around 1690, the opera is based on historical events conflated for narrative purposes. It concerns the struggle for dominance between the young Peter the Great and his half sister, Sophia.

Peter does not appear in the opera because censorship rules in Russia at the time forbade the depiction of czars onstage. Paradoxically, this restriction proved dramatically rich for it forced Mussorgsky to focus on the tragic factional strife among the Russian people as Peter came to power. A wave of revolts has broken out against the young czar, feared as an advocate for religious reform and Westernization. The uprising is spearheaded by the warlord Prince Ivan Khovansky and his son Andrei, allied with the Old Believers, a rigidly traditional religious sect. The opera's title translates as *The Khovansky Affair*.

The confusion in the opera was compounded by its genesis. Mussorgsky, who wrote his own libretto based on various historical sources, began composing the work in 1872 and was still at it when he died of complications from alcoholism in 1881, at forty-two. He completed a piano-vocal score, but was able to orchestrate only two short scenes, and the endings of two acts were left incomplete. Rimsky-Korsakov finished and orchestrated the score.

Folk-music drama and epic historical opera do not combine easily.

Yet, somehow Mussorgsky pulls it off. The endless variety of Mussorgsky's vocal writing, which faithfully captures the sputtered cadences and grainy colorings of the Russian language, is a hallmark of the music. Mussorgsky's melodic writing is steeped in the melancholic idiom of Russian folk idioms. But all the vocal lines—from the chantlike ruminations of the chorus to the sturdy exhortations of the royals to the wistfully fetching tunes of the commoners—are enshrined with poignant and churchly harmonies.

Because of this Mussorgsky tends to avoid counterpoint. You would think he was as fearful of Western influence as were the Old Believers. The closest you get to real independent part-writing is when some anthemlike melody in the chorus or woodwinds is accompanied by a walking bass line.

Khovanshchina can seem like the most ennobled (some would say overly ennobled) folk opera ever written. For all its wistful beauty, the subdued tone of the music can get tedious. You leap to attention during the fleeting moments of fast, highly charged music, as when Prince Ivan appears in regal garb atop a white horse as choral throngs sing somewhat forced anthems of praise.

No conductor balances a respect for the contemplative beauty of the score with a willingness to pump up its infrequent outbursts better than Valery Gergiev. His live 1991 recording with the forces of the Kirov Opera of the Mariinsky Theatre is the one to have. Gergiev, who finds the Rimsky-Korsakov orchestration overly lush, conducts an orchestration by Dmitri Shostakovich, which he prefers for its sparer textures. The impressive cast is headed by the stentorian bass Bulat Minjelkiev as Ivan, the powerhouse tenor Vladimir Galuzin as Ivan's calculating son Andrei, and the aptly nasal-toned tenor Alexei Steblianko as the paranoid Prince Vasily Golitsyn, a statesman loyal to Sophia.

Best of all is the great mezzo-soprano Olga Borodina in her youthful glory as Marfa, Andrei's former fiancée, who has become a devout follower of the Old Believers. With Marfa and Andrei, Mussorgsky introduced an invented story of thwarted love into this sweeping historical pageant. Yet Mussorgsky knew what he was doing. Marfa becomes a humane guidepost through the relentless political machinations. In the end, as Peter mobilizes a crackdown on

Conductor Valery Gergiev

dissent, Marfa joins the Old Believers in a mass suicide as they set fire to their own church. This folk opera literally ends in a blaze of tragedy.

Philips (three CDs) 432 147-2
Valery Gergiev (conductor), Chorus and Orchestra of the Kirov Opera of the Mariinsky Theatre, St. Petersburg; Borodina, Minjelkiev, Galusin, Steblianko

48. JACQUES OFFENBACH (1819–1880)

Les Contes d'Hoffmann (The Tales of Hoffmann)

Jules Barbier, librettist, after a play by Barbier and Michel Carré

First performance: Paris, Opéra-Comique, February 10, 1881

As a composer of lighter operatic fare, Jacques Offenbach, a German Jew turned Parisian Catholic, enjoyed unrivaled success in the middle decades of the nineteenth century. His specialty was the opéra bouffe, a tuneful concoction that typically took a satirical look at serious plays or myths, like Offenbach's *Orpheus in the Underworld,* a wickedly clever retelling of the woeful legend of Orpheus and Eurydice.

But in his mid-fifties, worried that his dozens of light operas were thought delightful but ephemeral, Offenbach seized on a subject that would allow him finally to demonstrate his depths as a composer: *Les Contes d'Hoffmann,* a play by Jules Barbier and Michel Carré, based on the fictional writings and real-life romantic exploits of E. T. A. Hoffmann—painter, author, composer, and lawyer, born in 1776, a court bureaucrat by day, an inebriated artist by night. Offenbach was occupied with this work, a musically rich and psychologically resonant *opéra fantastique,* from 1877 until his death at sixty-one three years later.

The haunting and complex prologue takes place in Luther's tavern in Nuremberg, right near the opera house where Hoffmann's current amour, Stella, is making her debut as Donna Anna in Mozart's *Don Giovanni.* An invisible chorus, the spirits of wine and beer, sets the supernatural tone of the work. Hoffmann's Muse, a mezzo-soprano who takes the form of Nicklausse, Hoffmann's sidekick and confidant, bemoans that the poet neglects his art for a dissolute life of drink and lovemaking. A group of boisterous students bursts in, followed by Hoffmann, and they demand that, as usual, he entertain them with one of his tales. Hoffmann obliges with a bitingly irreverent story about a dwarf named Kleinzack.

But as he relates the tale (a fetching and brilliant tenor aria), Hoffmann keeps lapsing into incoherent recollections of his dream of a sensuous woman. The students try to laugh but are too freaked out. Has Hoffmann finally lost it? Settling down, they urge Hoffmann to speak of his love life. This sets up the next three acts of the opera, each a reenactment of a tragic infatuation.

First we meet Olympia, a mechanical singing doll, the invention of Spalanzani, an eccentric physician. Wearing magic spectacles that Spalanzani lends him, Hoffmann sees Olympia as enchantingly alive and falls for her, only to have his ecstasy shattered when the villainous Coppelius, smarting over not having been paid for making the doll's eyes, smashes her to pieces.

If Olympia was the object of superficial infatuation, Antonia, the daughter of a violin maker, Crespel, is a symbol of achingly real but unattainable love. The beautiful young woman suffers from the fatal chest ailment that claimed her mother, and Crespel orders her to refrain from singing, Antonia's only pleasure, lest the effort and intensity worsen her condition. Hoffmann adores her. But Dr. Miracle, a nefarious quack who treated Antonia's mother, entices her into song, provoking Antonia's death and consigning Hoffmann to despair.

The tale of Giulietta, the Venetian courtesan, is a morality tale of idealized love. Tempted by the sinister magician Dapertutto, Giulietta lures Hoffmann into a state of possessive passion, then goads him into a duel with her current lover, Schlemil. Hoffmann kills his rival, only to find Giulietta in the embrace of a strapping servant.

In the epilogue back at the tavern, we finally encounter the mysterious and gifted Stella, in whom Hoffmann recognizes different aspects of his other loves. But Stella arrives on the arm of Counsellor Lindorf, Hoffmann's rival, and the poet collapses in a drunken stupor as Nicklausse urges him to channel his emotions into art.

To make manifest that the four loves are facets of an ideal woman, Offenbach thought the roles should be sung by a single soprano. Similarly, the villains who confront Hoffmann in each story—Lindorf, Coppelius, Dr. Miracle, and Dapertutto—were meant to be sung by a single bass.

Still, it's hard to say anything for certain about Offenbach's intentions because he left the score in a shambles at his death. The 1881 premiere of the opera, which had been completed by the composer Ernest Guiraud, was by all reports a travesty. The opera was performed in mishmash editions for decades until serious scholarly endeavors, especially during the 1980s, altered general perceptions of the work. The scholar Michael Kaye has compellingly extolled the value of some source materials and manuscripts that have turned up since. But, as the Offenbach scholar Andrew Lamb has suggested, it's impossible to know what final form the opera would have taken because Offenbach was a theatrical pragmatist ready to alter his works to accommodate the circumstances of a particular production.

Kaye's edition is the basis for a remarkable 1996 Erato recording drawn from a production at the National Opera of Lyon, conducted by Kent Nagano, with the tenor Roberto Alagna as Hoffmann. Though a grainy quality sometimes mars his voice, Alagna sings with informed French style and plenty of vocal flair. Portraying the four villains, the bass-baritone José van Dam is all the more menacing for the disarming elegance of his singing. In this performance Hoffmann's adored ones are sung by different sopranos, a practice that, however common, some scholars think a violation to the opera's essence. Still, the performances are splendid, with Leontina Vaduva as a poignant Antonia, Sumi Jo as a bright-toned Giulietta, and the stunningly brilliant coloratura soprano Natalie Dessay as Olympia. Among the cast are some distinguished French veterans, including the ageless tenor Michel Sénéchal as Spalanzani and the great baritone Gabriel Bacquier as Crespel.

The other choice, a 1972 Decca release, offers Joan Sutherland in resplendent voice as all four of Hoffmann's loves, a much younger Bacquier as the villains, and the conductor Richard Bonynge, who elicits a stylish and supple though low-keyed performance from the Orchestre de la Suisse Romande. The recording, made prior to the breakthrough scholarship of the 1980s, offers a cut version of the opera. Still, the reason to own it is Plácido Domingo's Hoffmann. What he lacks in idiomatic French style he makes up for with his impassioned and risk-taking singing. For Domingo, clearly, Hoffmann is a heroic tenor role and Domingo inhabits it. His singing is at once thrilling and unsettling, exactly the ambiguous reaction Offenbach surely wanted.

Erato (three CDs) 0630-14330-2

Kent Nagano (conductor), Chorus and Orchestra of L'Opéra National de Lyon; Alagna, van Dam, Vaduva, Jo, Dessay, Sénéchal, Bacquier

Decca (two CDs) 417363-2

Richard Bonynge (conductor), L'Orchestre de la Suisse Romande; Domingo, Sutherland, Bacquier

49. FRANCIS POULENC (1899–1963)

Dialogues des Carmélites
(Dialogues of the Carmelites)

Francis Poulenc, librettist, after a play by Georges Bernanos

First performance: Milan, Teatro alla Scala, January 26, 1957

Born in Paris in 1899, Francis Poulenc had a privileged and carefree childhood. His father was a prosperous manufacturer of pharmaceuticals, his mother an accomplished pianist. While mostly self-taught, Poulenc developed solid compositional skills. Still, early on he joined a band of composers dubbed Les Six, champions of inconsequence who led a backlash to the somber, post-Wagnerian French music of the day. Poulenc's works were insouciant, charming, and lucidly clear. Unapologetically gay and a charmer with a wicked wit, Poulenc was dubbed by a friend "half monk, half guttersnipe."

In the 1920s, though, he had a crisis of confidence about his music and undertook lessons with the composer Charles Koechlin to develop his technical know-how so he could create works of more seriousness. Inspired by the neoclassical music of Stravinsky, Poulenc began to experiment with elements of atonality. His musical crisis was followed by a spiritual crisis in 1936 when a close friend died in a car crash. After a pilgrimage to Notre-Dame de Rocamadour, he reembraced Catholicism and composed a beautifully subdued sacred work, *Litanies à la Vierge Noire*.

So when the Ricordi publishing house offered him a commission to write an opera for La Scala in Milan, Poulenc immediately chose as a subject a spiritually inspiring play he had seen in the early 1950s, the vestige of a failed screenplay based on the true story of a group of Carmelite nuns in Compiègne who defied the antireligious decrees of the French Revolution and were sent to the guillotine in 1794. Poulenc, typically a speedy and prolific composer, worked on *Dialogues des Carmélites* for three years, from 1953 to 1956.

Fashioning his own libretto, he devised an economical and urgent narrative focusing on Blanche, the daughter of the Marquis de la Force, a fearful young woman crippled with anxiety during the terrors of the revolution. It's 1789 and Blanche yearns to enter the order of Carmélites as a way to shield herself from the daily tyranny in Paris. At the convent in Compiègne she finds relief within this community of strong-willed women.

After Blanche's arrival the convent is badly shaken by the death of its ailing prioress, Madame de Croissy. Rather than offering the nuns under her charge an example of acceptance in the face of mortality, the prioress dies in a delirium of bitter anger and abject fear. Mostly the nuns avoid speaking at all of their leader's near-blasphemous death. Only the endearing Sister Constance, a chatterbox novice who just can't help it "if serving the Lord amuses me," as she says, tries to account for the prioress's anguish. Perhaps we do not die for ourselves alone, Constance tells Blanche; perhaps we die for one another, or even die one another's deaths. That must be it, Constance says. Perhaps the Lord gave the prioress "the wrong death, as a cloakroom attendant might give you the wrong coat." Maybe someone else will have a surprisingly easy time of dying.

Her deceptively simple words turn out to be prophetic. At the end of the opera, after the nuns have been arrested and condemned (all except Blanche, who had managed to escape), Constance is seized with fear when her turn comes for the guillotine. At that moment Blanche, hidden among the crowd of onlookers, emerges and joins her Carmelite sister on the path to martyrdom. They walk arm in arm, full of spiritual elation.

Poulenc, who acknowledged his debt to Mussorgsky, Monteverdi, Verdi, and Debussy in the dedication of this opera, used to apologize about the work's conservative harmonic language. "It seems my

Carmélites can only sing tonal music," he wrote; "you must forgive them."

There is little to forgive. Here Poulenc's subtle and intricate tonal language is by turns hymnal and haunting. Though scored for a large orchestra, the instruments are often used in smaller groups selected for particular effects and colorings. The most distinctive element of the score, though, is its wonderfully natural vocal writing, which captures the rhythms and lyrical flow of the libretto in eloquent music that hardly calls attention to itself yet lingers with you.

In a lesser composer's hands the final scene of execution might have been a mawkish disaster. In Poulenc's powerful depiction, the nuns sing a serenely wistful "Salve Regina" as one by one they march to the guillotine. With each offstage death the falling blade is evoked with a gnashing orchestra chord that slices through the music, momentarily interrupting the singing of the nuns, who then resume the "Salve Regina" with one less voice until finally just Constance and Blanche are left to sing together.

A few months after the Milan premiere of the opera, performed in Italian translation, *Dialogues des Carmélites* was given in Paris with a cast selected and coached by the composer. That cast recorded the work in 1958 under Pierre Dervaux, the principal conductor of the Paris Opera, and it remains the definitive account, available as part of the EMI Classics Great Recordings of the Century series. The old prioress is sung by the veteran contralto Denise Scharley, who reaches fits of despair in her disturbing enactment of the death scene. Mother Marie, the unflappable assistant to the prioress, and Madame Lidoine, the new prioress, are sung respectively by the earthy-voiced mezzo-soprano Rita Gorr and the radiant soprano Régine Crespin. The sweet lyric soprano Liliane Berton sings Constance. The emotional center of the performance is surely the Blanche of the soprano Denise Duval, who affectingly shows the character's growth from a tremulous young woman to an unquestioning martyr. Duval's purity of line and warm resonance ennoble her Blanche, one of the most memorable characters in twentieth-century opera.

EMI Classics (two CDs) 5 62768 2
Pierre Dervaux (conductor), Chorus and Orchestra of the Théâtre de l'Opéra de Paris; Duval, Crespin, Scharley, Gorr, Berton

50. SERGEY PROKOFIEV (1891–1953)

The Gambler

Sergey Prokofiev, librettist, after the novella by Fyodor Dostoyevsky

First performance: Brussels, Théâtre de la Monnaie, April 29, 1929

Only in recent years has *The Gambler,* Prokofiev's audacious second opera, based on the 1866 novella by Dostoyevsky, started gaining the attention it deserves in the West. When the Metropolitan Opera presented its premiere production of *The Gambler* in the spring of 2001 conducted by Valery Gergiev, audiences overall were stunned. How could such a riveting work not have made it to New York long ago? Yet this was the first Prokofiev opera ever performed by the Met.

Dostoyevsky's fascinating story centers on the snobbish and cunning denizens of a German spa in the imaginary city of Roulettenberg where casino gambling is the main attraction. Dostoyevsky understood the gambling addiction firsthand. Still, Prokofiev's music conveys the utter compulsion of this condition as viscerally as Dostoyevsky's prose.

Aleksey, the title character, is a young man with a university education who has lost his social standing through gambling debts and now tutors the children of a disdainful retired general. Aleksey is entranced by the general's stepdaughter, Paulina, who shares his gambling obsession but, as a dependent and eligible young woman, must be discreet about it. The general himself is deeply in debt to an obsequious French marquis, a loan shark who preys on vulnerable guests at the spa.

In the novella Dostoyevsky supplies long ruminations about the gambling mentality. Aleksey sees two classes of gamblers: the "gentlemanly sort" and the "plebian, mercenary sort," though he especially detests all the "fat and prosperous moralists" who gamble small sums thinking it less covetous.

These observations are missing from the opera, with a libretto by the composer. Instead Prokofiev relies on his brash and expressionist music to tap the story's psychological undercurrents. *The Gambler* is a brilliant yet youthful score, completed in 1917 before Prokofiev turned twenty-six, though he revised the opera for its eventual 1929 premiere.

The music abounds in gnashing dissonance and modernist strokes. Still, its true radicalism comes from Prokofiev's attempts to thwart all the conventions of opera. There are scant passages of soaring melody, no arias, and few times when two or more of the thirty-one characters sing at once. Instead, Prokofiev sets the wordy text to his own brand of lyrically enhanced dramatic recitative, which sits—sometimes uneasily—atop his teeming orchestral music: a pulsating and relentless succession of compact thematic episodes, sudden outbursts, buzzing rhythmic riffs, aborted melodic flights, and occasionally a reflective passage that cuts off just when you are settling into it.

Which recording to get? Without doubt the 1996 Philips recording with Gergiev conducting the forces of the Kirov Opera, from the Mariinsky Theatre in St. Petersburg. Gergiev has been waging virtually a one-man campaign to make Russian operas like *The Gambler* a repertory staple at the Kirov, as familiar to Westerners as the operas of Puccini. He considers Prokofiev as major a figure in twentieth-century opera as Britten, and he may be right.

The distinctively throaty colors and sounds of the Russian language are embedded in Prokofiev's vocal lines. For that reason Russian casts bring a special authority to the opera and Gergiev's on this recording is consistently impressive. The title role is taken by the powerhouse tenor Vladimir Galuzin, who brings ringing tone and fervor to his singing and wallows in the character's shameless obsession. Also fine is the soprano Ljubov Kazarnovskaya as Paulina, who sings with lustrous sound and volatility. Gergiev conducts a surging and rhapsodic account of the score, and milks every patch of lyricism for all its worth. But you have to listen carefully or those fleeting melodic snatches flit by before you know it. The Kirov Orchestra, with its dusky string tone, reedy woodwinds, and mellow brass, plays the music with an authority that says, "Move over, everyone else, this music is ours."

Philips (two CDs) 289 454 559-2
Valery Gergiev (conductor), Kirov Opera Chorus and Orchestra, Mariinsky Theatre, St. Petersburg; Galuzin, Kazarnovskaya, Alexashkin, Gassiev

51. SERGEY PROKOFIEV (1891–1953)

Semyon Kotko

Sergey Prokofiev and Valentin Katayev, librettists

First performance: Moscow, Stanislavsky Theatre, June 23, 1940

By including Prokofiev's *Semyon Kotko* on my list of essential operas I'm not suggesting that this little-known work is more important to the repertory than some operatic staples like Gounod's *Faust* that did not make the cut for this guide. But Prokofiev's strangely gripping opera is essential to those who want to understand how opera, like other art forms, has been used as a vehicle for political propaganda by composers intent on reaching success whatever it took.

In 1933, after spending fifteen restless years in the West, Prokofiev returned to Russia, frustrated and as intensely ambitious as ever. His timing was terrible, for Stalin had propounded the artistic doctrine of socialist realism. So Prokofiev tried to get with the program. One result was *Semyon Kotko,* his fifth opera, based on an obsequiously Stalinist novella by Valentin Katayev.

The story centers on a demobilized Russian soldier who returns to his isolated Ukrainian peasant village just after World War I and is politically enlightened by the Bolsheviks, who defend the common folk against brutal German occupiers and corrupt counterrevolutionaries.

With *Semyon Kotko,* written in five acts, Prokofiev hoped to win both popular acclaim and Soviet approval while maintaining artistic integrity. Perhaps there was too much integrity in his score and insufficient propaganda, because the opera failed dismally at its 1940 Moscow premiere.

Yet it is a riveting work. Prokofiev, who wrote the libretto with Katayev, had to contend with strictures imposed by Soviet censors who insisted that the novella's revolutionary themes be treated with heroic grandeur. So he tried to compose in a less veiled, more popular vein. His earlier operas, like *The Gambler,* were astringent scores of onrushing dramatic and musical continuity. *Semyon Kotko* is the opposite, an episodic opera of purposefully contrasting scenes calculated for clear dramatic effects. Still, the music proves that a skillful composer can be at once accessible and ingenious.

Wistfully lyrical outpourings for the peasant characters, some fashioned from Ukrainian folk music, are accompanied by lush orchestral writing of melting harmonic sonorities and striking instrumental effects that ennoble the characters. There are also stock comic bits, like the scene for busybody female villagers who ogle Semyon, a real curiosity when he returns from the battlefield.

A major plot line concerns the plight of the mismatched lovers Semyon and Sofia, the daughter of a rich peasant, Tkachenko, who plots against the Bolsheviks and hopes to marry his daughter to the heir of a prosperous landowner. Yet for the requisite love duet Prokofiev came up with something hauntingly original: the smitten Semyon sings soaring avowals while the fretful Sofia chatters in nervous patterns of steady eighth notes, both cushioned by radiant, swaying orchestral harmonies.

To make the propaganda explicit Prokofiev provides gnawing, dissonant, and angular music for the invading German officers. The extended final scene of act 3, one of the most arresting episodes in all of opera, is essentially a mad scene for Lyubka, the spirited fiancée of Tsaryov, a husky sailor and a loyal Bolshevik who is executed by the invaders. As the crazed woman sings in anguish, the orchestra churns on and on in weighty, ominously repeated drones amid the wails of the chorus.

Though *Semyon Kotko* has long been tainted by its subject matter, the conductor Valery Gergiev utterly believes in the work. His landmark recording with the Kirov Opera of the Mariinsky Theatre in St. Petersburg was recorded live in 1999 at the Grosser Saal concert hall in Vienna. Gergiev's cast, headed by the powerful tenor Viktor Lutsiuk in the title role, vividly conveys the rough-hewn, guttural colors and beauties of the Russian language, which Prokofiev sets with naturalistic immediacy. Tatiana Pavlovskaya brings her cool, gleaming voice to the role of Sofia, sounding here like a Russian Karita Mattila. As Lyubka, Ekaterina Solovieva sings that amazing act 3 finale with a dusky timbre and pitiable anguish. Viktor Chernomortsev's brawny voice is just right for Tsaryov, Lyubka's hapless fiancée. The incisive, insistent performance, by turns ravishing and harrowing, that Gergiev draws from his company testifies to his conviction in this compromised yet fascinating work.

Philips (two CDs) 289 464 605-2
Valery Gergiev (conductor), Kirov Opera Chorus and Orchestra, Mariinsky Theatre, St. Petersburg; Lutsiuk, Pavlovskaya, Chernomortsev, Solovieva

52. SERGEY PROKOFIEV (1891–1953)
Betrothal in a Monastery

Mira Alexandrovna Mendelson and Sergey Prokofiev, librettists, after a comic opera libretto by Richard Brinsley Sheridan

First performance: Prague, Narodni Divadlo Theatre, November 3, 1946

Betrothal in a Monastery, an ebullient, inventive, and humane comedy, could be called Prokofiev's *Falstaff.* Following the dismal reception of *Semyon Kotko* in 1940, a propagandistic work with which Prokofiev tried but failed to curry favor among Soviet authorities, he wanted to write something entertaining and safe. At the time his common-law wife, Mira Alexandrovna Mendelson, was collaborating with a friend on a translation of the British playwright Richard Sheridan's 1775 comic opera libretto *The Duenna,* and Prokofiev became intrigued with that work. He ended up writing his own libretto, working closely with Mendelson.

As Richard Taruskin points out in his entry on this work for the *New Grove Dictionary of Opera,* Sheridan's *The Duenna* is an outlandish parody of the typical, tried-and-true eighteenth-century comic opera genre in which "a ward or daughter outsmarts her parent or guardian to marry the suitor of her choice." In the opera, set in eighteenth-century Seville, Don Jerome, a Spanish grandee, intends to marry his daughter, Louisa, to Isaac Mendoza, a wealthy Portuguese Jew. By the end of the opera, after disguises, ploys, and mistaken identities galore, three—count 'em, three!—confused couples wind up properly matched in socially appropriate and romantically acceptable unions: Mendoza with Louisa's chaperone, the Duenna of the title; Ferdinand, Don Jerome's son, with Louisa's friend Donna Clara, whose father had intended her for life in a convent; and Louisa with the impoverished and strapping Don Antonio. Sheridan's text includes lyrics for some twenty set-piece songs. So music was part of the mix from its first conception.

Naturally, much of the dialogue is set to lithe and snappy vocal lines. Yet in every place where a phrase in the text or a turn in the story allows it, Prokofiev writes music of disarming lyricism. These moments, though fleeting, lend the score a warmth and resonance without inhibiting the opera's comic pacing. And the orchestra abounds in harmonic intricacies, rhythmic displacements, and brassy bouts of sarcasm. Yet the complexities are there for your delectation only if you care to pay attention. What Prokofiev achieves reminds me of Mozart's comments about three piano concertos he composed in 1782–1783. "There are passages here and there from which connoisseurs alone can derive satisfaction," he wrote; "but these passages are written in such a way that the less learned cannot fail to be pleased, though without knowing why."

Betrothal in a Monastery may represent a retrenchment for Prokofiev. Still, it's a completely delightful and musically brilliant opera that would be performed in the West as often as *Falstaff* if more non-Russian singers were comfortable with the Russian language. Performing opera in translation is an honorable practice, but perhaps not in this case. Much of the spark, humor, and inventiveness of the score comes from the pungent way Prokofiev sets his native tongue.

Therefore, the recording to have (once again in this repertory) is Valery Gergiev's live 1997 performance with the Kirov Opera at the Mariinsky Theatre in St. Petersburg, the company that gave the opera its 1946 Russian premiere. You may quibble with the vocal qualities of this or that singer. But overall from start to finish the cast—headed by the bright tenor Nikolai Gassiev as Don Jerome, the dusky contralto Larissa Diadkova as The Duenna, the robust tenor Evgeny Akimov as Don Antonio, and the shimmering soprano Anna Netrebko as Louisa—performs the work with a stylistic authority and palpable pleasure that will draw you right in. Gergiev conducts a buoyant and vibrant performance, though he is not afraid to make the most of every raucous interruption, startling harmonic shift, and dangerous dissonance.

Philips (three CDs) 289 462 107-2

Valery Gergiev (conductor), Kirov Opera Chorus and Orchestra, Mariinsky Theatre, St. Petersburg; Gassiev, Gergalov, Netrebko, Diadkova, Akimov

53. SERGEY PROKOFIEV (1891–1953)

War and Peace

Sergey Prokofiev and Mira Alexandrovna Mendelson, after Leo Tolstoy's novel

First performance of the full-evening version with thirteen scenes: Moscow, Bolshoi Theater, December 15, 1959 (though this production made cuts in the score)

As befits the epic Tolstoy novel that is its source, Prokofiev's *War and Peace* is a sprawling opera, nearly four hours of music with thirteen scenes that move from mansions and ballrooms in Moscow and St. Petersburg to battlefields during Napoleon's failed Russian campaign in 1812. The opera, which Prokofiev composed in the early 1940s and revised several times before his death, calls for a large chorus (one hundred or more is typical), a sizeable orchestra, and enough singers to cover sixty-eight roles (some doublings are possible).

The idea of creating an opera from Tolstoy's monumental novel, with its hundreds of characters, complex subplots, frequent sermonizing, and historical tracts, might have seemed foolhardy. But Prokofiev, who wrote the libretto with Mira Alexandrovna Mendelson (at the time his common-law wife), assumed that his audience knew the novel intimately. In a way, he conceived of his opera as a series of musical dramatizations of key scenes and characters.

The pacing is at times intentionally deliberate. Prokofiev tries to emulate the rambling conversations that are the essence of the novel's aristocratic scenes by giving his characters time to gossip, exchange confidences, and voice asides. The ingenious qualities of the music come through in the subtle details. The orchestra enshrouds the vocal lines with harmonically pungent commentary. The score abounds in elusive tunes like the insinuating waltz that Natasha and Prince Andrei first dance to, tunes that you can't quite get out of your head but can't quite get straight in your memory.

Tolstoy's philosophical ruminations are replaced by stirring patriotic choruses for the defiant Russian people. While composing the opera, Prokofiev came under pressure from Stalin's All-Union Committee on Arts Affairs to turn it into a propaganda vehicle for the Soviet war effort. If those brassy choruses are somewhat bombastic, there is a subtext of foreboding in Prokofiev's clashing harmonies and asymmetrical phrases.

Though the opera of necessity does only a glancing job of telling Tolstoy's story, the essence of the novel comes through palpably. This is due, I think, to the slightly bitter, at times ironic tone of Prokofiev's music, which eerily captures the detached, wry, and ironic tone of Tolstoy's narrative voice. Both works present epic events with a sardonic attitude that paradoxically makes the human tragedies all the more poignant.

Among conductors on the scene today, Valery Gergiev owns this work, and his recording, taken from live performances in 1991 with the Kirov Opera at the Mariinsky Theatre in St. Petersburg, is the one to have. Though *War and Peace* abounds in stirring choral scenes and tumultuous battle reenactments, Gergiev never goes for superficial excitement. Instead he emphasizes the music's bittersweet elegance and harmonic richness, lending the opera an affecting gravity. He draws luminous yet incisive playing from the orchestra, and husky, robust singing from the chorus.

The excellent cast brings stylistic authority and arresting involvement to its work. There are consistently impressive performances from the baritone Alexander Gergalov as Prince Andrei, the soprano Yelena Prokina as Natasha, the mezzo-soprano Svetlana Volkova as Natasha's winsome cousin Sonya. The tenor Gegam Gregorian is Count Pierre, who is chuckled over in society for being chubby and decent but takes heroic action when his friends and country are endangered. Also fine are the tenor Yuri Marusin as the two-timing Prince Anatol Kuragin, and the mezzo-soprano Olga Borodina, an international star today, as Countess Bezukhova.

Another choice is the 1961 recording from the Bolshoi Theater in Moscow, conducted by Alexander Melik-Pashayev, the same company that presented the first relatively complete performance of the opera's thirteen-scene final version in 1959 six years after the composer's death. The radiant Natasha of the great soprano Galina Vishnevskaya is just one strong attraction of this recording, which also offers the virile baritone Yevgeny Kibkalo as Prince Andrei.

Philips (three CDs) 434 097-2
Valery Gergiev (conductor), Orchestra and Chorus of the Kirov Opera, Mariinsky Theatre, St. Petersburg; Gergalov, Prokina, Gregorian, Borodina, Marusin

Melodiya (three CDs) 74321 29350 2
Alexander Melik-Pashayev (conductor), Chorus and Orchestra of the Bolshoi Theater, Moscow; Kibkalo, Vishnevskaya, Petrov, Arkhipova

54. GIACOMO PUCCINI (1858–1924)

Manon Lescaut

Domenico Oliva and Luigi Illica, librettists, based on a novel by Abbé Prévost

First performance: Turin, Teatro Regio, February 1, 1893 (revised version, Milan, Teatro alla Scala, February 7, 1894)

As a young music student Puccini allied himself with a group of artists, authors, journalists, and composers who called themselves the Scapigliatura Milanese, which means the Disheveled Ones from Milan. The movement, which had sprung up in the 1860s and 1870s, aimed at modernizing Italian art, music, and theater. In the field of opera this meant debunking the grand old man of Italian opera, Verdi, and looking to Germany and France for new directions. Wagner provided a model of advanced harmonic thinking, continuous structure, and sophisticated use of melodic motifs (an Italian version of Wagner's leitmotif technique). Massenet's penchant for realism strongly influenced the "verismo" movement in Italian opera.

Puccini had earned a sufficiently strong response to his early operatic efforts, especially *Le Villi,* that he was taken into the Ricordi publishing house. By the time Puccini announced his intention to write *Manon Lescaut* he had distanced himself from the Scapigliati. Selecting *Manon Lescaut* was a brazen act, since Massenet's 1884 opera on the same subject, based on a novel by Prévost, had been a major success.

Ricordi tried to dissuade Puccini from the idea, but the composer, then in his early thirties, was doggedly intent. Still, as the scholar Julian Budden has written, *Manon Lescaut* had the most tormented genesis of any Puccini opera, which is saying something. In getting this work to the stage Puccini went through five librettists, who were so demoralized by the experience that none of them wanted his name on the title page of the original printed score. At the time Puccini was also embroiled in a domestic crisis. In 1884, just when *Le Villi* had brought him some renown, he became involved with a married woman, Elvira Gemignani, who had to flee her incensed husband when she became pregnant by Puccini (their son, Antonio, would be Puccini's only child). At the time of *Manon Lescaut* Puccini's life with Elvira was an ongoing scandal.

Yet, operatically, the pigheaded composer seems to have known what he was doing. No Puccini opera was more immediately acclaimed than *Manon Lescaut*. The work quickly assumed a place in the repertory. There are miscalculations in the opera, especially in comparison with the seamless professionalism of Massenet's version. But (forgive me, French opera devotees) I find Puccini's the more dramatically compelling and musically inspired work.

Early in the first act, amid a public square in Amiens teeming with soldiers and townsfolk, we meet the dashing Cavalier des Grieux, a poor student despite his title. Puccini shows his mastery at quickly establishing character through the beguiling tenor aria "Tra voi belle, brune o bionde," in which Des Grieux coyly searches among a crowd of students for a woman to love. Everything about Des Grieux's smooth-talking charm comes through in this jaunty aria. Manon, the lovely young sister of an overprotective yet unprincipled brother, Lescaut, a sergeant in the royal guard, is bound for a convent school. But she captivates Des Grieux, who is undone by her allure, as he makes clear in the rhapsodic and demanding aria "Donna non vidi mai." An ingenious love duet follows, which begins with clipped, halting, and conversational phrases that evolve into passionately lyrical outbursts.

Puccini never set a more cynical story. Geronte, a treasury official, has also been captivated by Manon and convinces Lescaut that he would like to elope with the young girl. But Manon impulsively runs off with Des Grieux. When Geronte discovers what has happened, Lescaut assures him that his sister is too fond of luxury to endure poverty with the young Des Grieux. A fair and often expressed criticism of the opera is that, unlike Massenet's *Manon*, Puccini's version omits a scene showing the lovers contending with deprivation in Paris, making Manon miserable. Instead Puccini's story skips to the elegant salon of Geronte, where, to satisfy her need for finery, Manon has become his mistress.

When Des Grieux appears and pleads with Manon to escape with him, she agrees but stops to gather up her jewelry. That hesitation gives Geronte time to arrive with guards and have her arrested for theft. Manon is exiled to Louisiana along with "the other prostitutes." But Des Grieux smuggles himself aboard her ship.

The final act takes place in a "vast desert near the outskirts of New Orleans." That there are no vast deserts in Louisiana is something Puccini and his collaborators apparently did not realize. They must have assumed the state was just like Texas. Still, Puccini's music and dramatic imagination carry the day. Manon sings "Sola, perduta, abbandonata," a scene and aria in which her abject humiliation and despair are searingly conveyed in Puccini's grimly subdued music. Des Grieux, who has been scouring the land for shelter, returns to find Manon dying.

The title role is a tour de force for a spinto soprano, that is, a voice capable of lyrical elegance and dramatic grit. But Des Grieux may be the killer role. I grew up wearing out the exciting 1954 recording with Licia Albanese and Jussi Björling. Albanese's voice was perhaps somewhat light for the role, but her affecting singing wins your heart. Björling's thrillingly sung Des Grieux has everything: insouciance, burnished power, impetuosity. The baritone Robert Merrill makes a vocally robust yet conniving Lescaut. Jonel Perlea conducts the Rome Opera Orchestra and Chorus in a supplely paced performance.

A more recent and very classy recording, though, is the 1992 Decca version starring Mirella Freni and Luciano Pavarotti. By this stage of Freni's career her voice had lost some of its rosy bloom. But the added weight, dusky colorings, and fearless intensity of her singing more than compensate. Pavarotti, in good voice, brings vocal charisma and stylistic insight to his impressive portrayal. The reason to get this recording, though, may be the conducting of James Levine, whose palpable respect for this score comes through consistently. With the Metropolitan Opera Orchestra and Chorus, he conducts an organic yet volatile performance and captures the symphonic sweep of Puccini's orchestral writing in this breakthrough Italian opera.

RCA Victor (two CDs) 60573-2-RG

Jonel Perlea (conductor), Rome Opera Orchestra and Chorus; Albanese, Björling, Merrill, Calabrese

Giacomo Puccini

Decca (two CDs) 440 200-2

James Levine (conductor), Metropolitan Opera Orchestra and Chorus; Freni, Pavarotti, Croft, Taddei

55. GIACOMO PUCCINI (1858–1924)
La Bohème

Giuseppe Giacosa and Luigi Illica, librettists, after Henry Murger

First performance: Turin, Teatro Regio, February 1, 1896

My live introduction to Puccini's *La Bohème* when I was a teenager could not have been more glorious. It took place in 1965 at the Metropolitan Opera—the *old* Met in its final season. I had a partial-view seat way up in the fourth ring close to the stage. The renowned Renata Tebaldi sang Mimi and the elegant and underappreciated Hungarian tenor Sandor Konya was Rodolfo. I remember everything about that enthralling performance, even the fact that, at least from my vantage point, Tebaldi appeared to be actually eating vanilla ice cream during the scene at the Café Momus.

I've attended remarkable performances of this beloved Puccini opera since. I've also endured more than my share of routine runthroughs. *La Bohème* remains too popular for its own good. But I was not prepared to be so deeply affected by a performance I reviewed for the *Boston Globe* in 1991 at the New England Conservatory performed in an English translation. As I watched the cute, earnest, and endearingly awkward student singers throw themselves into these iconic roles I was struck anew by the opera's powerful emotional insights. The lives of most music students—who must hold down jobs to support their studies, who live together, share expenses, catch meals where they can, and often look a little hungry—are much like the lives of Puccini's bohemians, characters based on real people. The source for the opera was Henry Murger, an impoverished writer in Paris who fashioned an account of life on the Left Bank among penniless artist friends into a series of stories published during the 1840s.

Puccini was drawn to the stories because they told his story, too. When he was a student at the conservatory in Milan, Puccini shared an attic flat with his younger brother and a poor cousin. They spent one another's money, ate one another's food, wore one another's clothes. It was a life of daily humiliation and chronic insecurity. Of course there were also good times and lots of kibitzing, something Puccini captures in the opera's garret scenes when the guys horse around and trade bad puns.

But Puccini, his brother, and his flat mate were pursuing professional training and had clear career goals. The bohemians of *La Bohème* are aimless, self-proclaimed artists who don't seem all that consecrated to their respective arts. The ambitious five-act drama Rodolfo is writing means very little to him, it would seem, since on a whim he sacrifices it to the iron stove in the garret for a few minutes of warmth on a wintry Christmas Eve. The male bohemians talk of lovemaking but shun attachments. Not once does anyone mention his family. They are charming guys, but also dropouts.

Romance gets introduced into the opera through its two female characters: Musetta, a vivacious and determined young woman keenly aware of her own allure, who has been having an on-again/off-again affair with Marcello, the painter; and, of course, Mimi, the frail and winsome seamstress who shows up with her spent candle at the garret door and—in every opera buff's favorite magical moment—captivates Rodolfo instantaneously.

Yet, Mimi introduces something else into this bohemian circle: illness. It's fine to be poor and carefree when you are young and healthy. But life-threatening illness is an adult problem demanding adult responsibility. The sensitivity shown by Puccini and his librettists, Giuseppe Giacosa and Luigi Illica, in presenting this element of the story makes *La Bohème* in the end such a timeless and unflinching tragedy.

Though Rodolfo adores Mimi, he can no longer ignore her worsening health. What can he possibly do for her? By act 3, when Marcello tries to pry from his pent-up friend the real reason for his latest breakup with Mimi, Rodolfo finally admits the truth: Mimi is ill, probably dying. What he tells Marcello, translated to the lingo of the '60s, is: "Mimi's real sick and I can't hack it, man."

These themes come through in the opera's well-crafted and impressively economical libretto. But it's Puccini's ingenious, impassioned, and lyrically soaring music that makes the opera so disarming and true. There is less of the lush orchestral richness that characterized *Manon Lescaut*. *La Bohème* is an ardent but lighter-textured score run through with recurring, subtly varied melodic motifs associated with characters, places, and events (Puccini's own version of Wagner's technique of leitmotifs). These motifs are deployed with a sophistication that gives the opera its emotionally powerful undertow. For example, in the final scene when the dying Mimi is brought back to the garret by Musetta, the other bohemians decide to give the guilt-ridden Rodolfo and the dozing Mimi some time alone. When they leave, Mimi tells Rodolfo in a forlornly beautiful melody accompanied by steady, quiet minor chords that she was only pretending to be asleep so everyone would leave for a moment. But when she finally dies and Rodolfo cries out her name in anguish, that same minor theme returns, now performed by vehement violins accompanied by steady chords of blasting brass. This time, the music tells us, Mimi is not pretending to be asleep.

Though it can be wonderful to experience *La Bohème* in an opera house performed by a young cast that look like Puccini's bohemians, the opera has provided defining roles to some of the great singers of the era. Perhaps my fondness for the 1959 recording featuring Renata Tebaldi as Mimi stems from my introduction to the opera at the Met. By any standard, though, this Decca recording with Tullio Serafin conducting the orchestra and chorus of the Academy of Saint Cecilia in Rome is among the best. Serafin, a masterly Puccini stylist, leads a richly nuanced account of the score with often spacious tempos that allow the singers to shape the phrase with arching lyricism. The sheer warmth and sublime beauty of Tebaldi's voice does not distract you from the tenderness and vulnerability of her singing. The great tenor Carlo Bergonzi, in vibrant voice, sings Rodolfo, the sweet-toned lyric soprano Gianna D'Angelo is a perky Musetta, and the other bohemians are veterans of Italian opera in impressive form: Ettore Bastianini as Marcello, Cesare Siepi as Colline, and Renato Cesari as Schaunard.

Tenor Carlo Bergonzi

Another cherished *La Bohème,* also from Decca, is the 1972 record-ing with Luciano Pavarotti, sounding splendidly youthful, as Rodolfo and Mirella Freni as a vocally exquisite Mimi. Though the conductor Herbert von Karajan and the players of the great Berlin Philharmonic may not seem a dream roster for this Italian opera chestnut, they give a supple, nuanced, and, in places, effectively restrained performance, and they sound like they absolutely adore the music.

Arturo Toscanini conducted the 1896 premiere of *La Bohème,* so his live 1946 recording with the NBC Symphony Orchestra, com-memorating the opera's fiftieth anniversary, is an important docu-ment. Though I grew up with it and admire the cast, especially Licia Albanese as Mimi, I have come to find Toscanini's tempos somewhat driven. I can't imagine Puccini allowed the pacing to be so breathless at the premiere. But it remains an essential recording in the discogra-phy of opera.

Sir Thomas Beecham also has a direct connection to the opera, since he consulted with Puccini in 1920 in London, raising numerous questions about confusing details in the published score. Beecham's 1956 recording, available on EMI's Great Recordings of the Century series, while spirited and lithe, is more leisurely and expansive than Toscanini's. And the cast is incomparable: the disarmingly lovely soprano Victoria de los Angeles as Mimi, the thrilling tenor Jussi Björling as Rodolfo, the agile soprano Lucine Amara as Musetta, the virile baritone Robert Merrill as Marcello, with John Reardon as Schaunard, and Giorgio Tozzi as Colline. If you could only have one *La Bohème* in your collection, this may be the best overall choice. But I can't imagine being without Karajan's account and, of course, my beloved Tebaldi's.

Decca (two CDs) 411 868-2
Tullio Serafin (conductor), Orchestra and Chorus of the Academy of Saint Cecilia, Rome; Tebaldi, Bergonzi, D'Angelo, Bastianini, Siepi, Cesari

Decca (two CDs) 421 049-2
Herbert von Karajan (conductor), Berlin Philharmonic, Chorus of the German Opera, Berlin; Freni, Pavarotti, Harwood, Panerai, Ghiaurov, Maffeo

EMI Classics (two CDs) 5 67753 2
Sir Thomas Beecham (conductor), RCA Victor Orchestra and Chorus; de los Angeles, Björling, Amara, Merrill, Reardon, Tozzi

NOTE: *As of this writing, the Toscanini recording of* La Bohème *is unavailable. But you can expect a re-issue to come out before long.*

56. GIACOMO PUCCINI (1858–1924)

Tosca

Giuseppe Giacosa and Luigi Illica, librettists, based on a play by Victorien Sardou

First performance: Rome, Teatro Costanzi, January 14, 1900

In 1895, Puccini saw a production in Florence of *La Tosca*, a French melodrama by the popular playwright Victorien Sardou written as a vehicle for Sarah Bernhardt. Actually, Puccini found Bernhardt's performance rather mechanical. But he seized on the play as an ideal source for an opera.

Compressing Sardou's wordy play (five acts, twenty-three characters) into a taut, three-act libretto drew the exacting composer into another drawn-out tussle with his beleaguered librettists, Giuseppe Giacosa and Luigi Illica. Detractors of the opera assert that its swift dramatic pacing comes at a price. Without the revealing details of the play, set in Rome in 1800 at the time of Napoleon's victory at the Battle of Marengo, the motivations of Puccini's characters are illogical, critics say, and the opera seems little more than a manipulative melodrama, with religious pageantry, sadism, torture, an attempted rape, a murder, an execution, and two suicides crammed into just over one hundred minutes of music.

Yet, Sardou's play disappeared long ago, while within a few years of its 1900 premiere, Puccini's *Tosca* was translated and performed in over twenty languages, including Norwegian, Croatian, and Hebrew. It seems destined to remain a repertory staple.

This is because Puccini's music can convey in an instant what Sardou's speechifying characters never make clear in a full evening. Yes, it's helpful to know, as we learn from the play, that Tosca, a celebrated, wealthy soprano, is at that time thrilling audiences at the Teatro Argentina in Rome. Still, that she is a diva is vividly clear from the entrance music Puccini provides. When Tosca comes to the Church of Sant'Andrea della Valle, where her lover Mario Cavaradossi is painting a mural, she is seized with jealousy when she finds the chapel door locked, for no good reason, and hears, she is sure, rustling clothes and whispered voices inside. She strides in, struggling to maintain her bearing and dignity as her eyes desperately search every alcove for evidence of some betrayal. Immediately, the orchestra begins the pliant, alluring love theme that Mario will soon sing so ardently, music that assures the audience immediately, and before long, Tosca, too, that she has no rival.

Only in the play do we learn of Floria Tosca's childhood as a wild, orphaned country girl, rescued and raised by an order of Benedictine nuns, bound for the veil until the beauty of her voice was recognized and the pope himself released her to a life in music. Yet Puccini tellingly conveys Tosca's fascinating attitude toward religion. In the first act, her music animates Tosca's sudden shifts from beatific moments of prayer to fleeting kisses with Mario, right in the presence of the Madonna's statue. Tosca is devout. Yet, she is carrying on an illicit affair, which is, of course, a sin. But she has an intensely personal relationship with the Madonna. They talk, in a sense, woman to woman. The Madonna will understand, Tosca is convinced, that as a theatrical professional her life simply cannot adhere to convention.

Again, in the play we learn much more about Mario's background and politics. He is a wealthy descendent of a patrician Roman family, who was brought up in Paris during the revolution and now sides with the anti-royalist republicans in Rome. By painting the mural in the chapel, he is trying to mislead the royalists about his true sympathies, so that he can better aid his allies in the underground.

The essence of his character comes through, and then some, in his first aria, "Recondita armonia." Standing back from his depiction of the Magdalena for a moment, he sacrilegiously compares the blond allure of the unknown woman who has been coming to the chapel in prayer, whom he has painted into the mural, with the dusky, dark-eyed southern charms of his passionate Tosca.

The villain of the opera, Scarpia, is the police chief in Rome. But, it must be remembered, he is a baron, a royalist, appointed to this post to quash by any means the rising rebellion. Puccini painstakingly conveys the gallant and patrician sides of Scarpia's character. When Tosca returns to the chapel to change the evening's plans she has made with Mario, Scarpia dips his hand in holy water so that Tosca may touch her fingers to his own and cross herself. For a few phrases, his music is soothing, stately, and deceptively gracious. But slowly the harmonies twist, the tension bursts forth, and Scarpia's sick lechery comes through: the more Tosca loathes and fears him, the more he desires her.

In this score Puccini again borrows Wagner's technique of using leitmotifs, that is, short themes and motifs associated with characters and incidents in the story. The most obvious is the three-chord blast that opens the opera, the motif of Scarpia, three unrelated harmonies that suggest the fitfulness of his nature and actions. But, in no other score does Puccini use this technique with more subtlety. Scarpia's unmistakable three-chord motif gets tucked discreetly into the most unlikely places, as in the opening of act 3, atop the Castel Sant'Angelo, when dawn rises, distant church bells ring, and the coming execution of Mario is momentarily forgotten. Just before a far-off shepherd boy begins to sing a song, you hear Scarpia's three chords in the orchestra, turned into an insistent, rhythmic stutter. It's as if the baron is saying: "You citizens of Rome may not yet know of my fate, but even from the grave I am going to defeat Mario and claim Tosca."

Few recordings of operas are deemed absolutely ideal, but among that select group is the 1953 *Tosca* with Maria Callas, Giuseppe di Stefano, and Tito Gobbi in the leading roles, and Victor de Sabata conducting the orchestra and chorus of La Scala. This is one of the great Callas portrayals, passionate, complex, volatile, and impressively sung. The character of Tosca, after all, is a Callas-like diva, which is why Mario affectionately calls her by her last name, "my Tosca." De Sabata was as renowned in mid-twentieth-century Italy as Toscanini, and his conducting is spellbinding. Di Stefano and Gobbi are in top form. EMI Classics wouldn't dare let this recording go out of print.

Among several other worthy accounts, I especially admire the 1973 RCA Red Seal recording with Leontyne Price's beautifully sung and deeply affecting Tosca, Plácido Domingo's youthful, virile Mario, and Sherrill Milnes's chilling Scarpia, with Zubin Mehta conducting the New Philharmonia Orchestra.

Soprano Maria Callas as Tosca

EMI Classics (two CDs) 5 56304 2

Victor de Sabata (conductor), The Orchestra and Chorus of La Scala, Milan; Callas, di Stefano, Gobbi

RCA Red Seal (two CDs) RCD2-0105

Zubin Mehta (conductor), New Philharmonia Orchestra; Domingo, Milnes, Price

57. GIACOMO PUCCINI (1858–1924)

Madama Butterfly

Giuseppe Giacosa and Luigi Illica, librettists, based on play by David Belasco

First performance: Milan, Teatro alla Scala, February 17, 1904 (revised version, Brescia, Teatro Grande, May 28, 1904)

Madama Butterfly was adapted from a potboiler of a play by David Belasco that Puccini saw in London in 1900. Though he understood scant English, Puccini was captivated by the story as a subject for an opera. In some ways he may have benefited by not really being able to follow the dialogue. Belasco's play was a superficial melodrama. But Puccini had an instinctive sympathy for the character of Butterfly and immediately sensed what a powerful work the opera could be.

Madama Butterfly invites kidding. The vocally demanding title role has attracted a long line of chunky prima donnas who look rather ridiculous portraying an adolescent geisha girl. But in the right performance the opera remains Puccini's most emotionally shattering work.

Given the era they lived in, Puccini and his librettists, Giuseppe Giacosa and Luigi Illica, had precocious insight into the issues of racism that Belasco bobbled in the play. All that saves the character of Lieutenant Pinkerton, a U.S. Navy officer stationed temporarily in Nagasaki, from being the biggest cad in all of opera is that he can be seen as a product of the early twentieth century. Pinkerton seems oblivious to the racism behind his cavalier courtship of young Cio-Cio San, whose friends call her Butterfly. And the revised version of *Madama Butterfly*, the most commonly performed, actually softened Pinkerton's callowness.

Consumed with desire for the smitten Butterfly, Pinkerton arranges a marriage ceremony and rents for a pittance a nuptial house with a 99-year lease. He takes neither commitment seriously. Sharpless, the American consul, tries to warn Pinkerton that Butterfly views her impending marriage with profound seriousness. But Pinkerton laughs at the idea that anyone could consider such a marriage legitimate. Someday, he sings to a melodic strain from the "Star-Spangled Banner" orchestrated with mock pomposity, he will take a real wife, an American wife.

Puccini also painfully conveys Butterfly's own internalized racism. To her Pinkerton is a wondrous man, a strapping and commanding figure in his white dress uniform. He is not at all like Japanese men. He laughs heartily, says what he thinks, and exudes willful energy. Butterfly feels deep pride that Pinkerton has chosen her.

Then comes act 2. Three years have passed with no word from Pinkerton. Sharpless and the marriage broker Goro explain to Butterfly that in Japanese law a husband's abandonment renders a marriage null and void. They try to persuade her to accept the marriage proposal of Prince Yamadori, the Japanese equivalent of a rich young Kennedy, as David Henry Hwang characterized him in his play *M. Butterfly*. Yet, Butterfly, though destitute, turns him down. She considers herself an American wife.

The ending of the opera suggests that Puccini and his librettists perceived that suicide is as much a lashing out as an act of despair. Pinkerton has finally returned, but with his real American wife, Kate. Though racked with guilt over what he now sees as his cruel treatment of Butterfly, he still intends to claim his young son and bring him to America.

Abjectly humiliated, Butterfly agrees to relinquish the boy, but only if Pinkerton comes for him in person. At the moment of her husband's arrival, Butterfly stabs herself. Pinkerton has driven her to this, and he will have to live from now on with the horrid image of her death imprinted in her memory.

Trying to invest his lushly chromatic harmonic language with a touch of Asian color, Puccini incorporated some half dozen Japanese folk melodies into the score. Still, the music abounds with Italianate lyrical outpourings. A soprano singing Butterfly must be demure on the surface but turbulent within. A tenor singing Pinkerton must make this self-indulgent character sympathetic. Puccini gives him the means to do so. For example, in the act 1 love duet—the longest, most elaborate, and most raptly beautiful in all of Puccini—Pinkerton can convey that his feelings for Butterfly are more than lust. At that moment he is truly enchanted by his trusting child bride.

As to recordings, a sure choice is the classic 1958 Decca account with Renata Tebaldi in the title role. Tebaldi prepared the role with a Japanese drama coach in an effort to move discreetly and look petite. Still, Tebaldi's Butterfly looked like a tall, striking, well-fed, and friendly Italian lady. But she sang the music incomparably. Reviewing her first Butterfly at the Metropolitan Opera in 1958, Jay Harrison of the *Herald Tribune* wrote that, despite all the cherry blossoms, *Madama Butterfly* is an "Italian product and that is the way Miss Tebaldi sang it . . . with the beauty and glory of the grand Italian style." True enough, but on this recording, Tebaldi does more, shaping gentle phrases with supple grace, tenderness, and touching restraint. The entire cast is top-notch, with the stylish tenor Carlo Bergonzi as Pinkerton, the distinguished mezzo-soprano Fiorenza Cossotto as Suzuki, and the sturdy baritone Enzo Sordello as Sharpless. Tullio Serafin draws a dynamic yet elegant performance from the orchestra and chorus of the Academy of Saint Cecilia.

A 1959 recording from EMI Classics offers the sweet-voiced and innocent Butterfly of Victoria de los Angeles and the charismatic Pinkerton of Jussi Björling, so vocally gleaming you don't care he's a louse. Gabriele Santini conducts the forces of the Rome Opera in this affecting recording.

But the other recording to consider—and some will find this a surprising choice—is the 1955 EMI account with Maria Callas as Cio-Cio San and Herbert von Karajan conducting the forces of La Scala. Callas performed the role onstage only three times (in Chicago the same year this recording was made). Perhaps she thought she was too intense a presence for this demure character. Still, her recorded portrayal is riveting. In a fascinating twist Nicolai Gedda, as Pinkerton, sings with honeyed sound and lyricism, while Callas's Butterfly is earthy and impetuous, which introduces an intriguing ambiguity into their relationship. At a crucial moment of the love duet Butterfly, ecstatic with joy, compares herself to the moon goddess. Singing in melting tones, Gedda's Pinkerton says, "You haven't told me you love me yet," then asks if the moon goddess knows the words that satisfy desire. She does, Butterfly answers, though perhaps she's unwilling to utter them "for fear of dying of it." Callas brings such tremulous intensity to this aching phrase you almost can't bear it. Can happiness like this ever be true? Butterfly is afraid to believe it. With good reason, it turns out.

Decca (two CDs) 425 531-2
Tullio Serafin (conductor), Orchestra and Chorus of the Academy of Saint Cecilia, Rome; Tebaldi, Bergonzi, Cossotto, Sordello

EMI Classics (two CDs) 7 63634 2
Gabriele Santini (conductor), Orchestra and Chorus of the Rome Opera; de los Angeles, Björling, Pirazzini, Sereni

EMI Classics (two CDs) 5 56298 2
Herbert von Karajan (conductor), Orchestra and Chorus of La Scala, Milan; Callas, Gedda, Danieli, Borriello

58. GIACOMO PUCCINI (1858–1924)

Turandot

Giuseppe Adami and Renato Simoni, librettists, based on a drama by Carlo Gozzi

First performance: Milan, Teatro alla Scala, April 25, 1926

Turandot is five-sixths of a masterpiece. Puccini died in 1924 at sixty-five before he completed the extensive final scene that begins roughly halfway through the third and last act. Even so, *Turandot* is Puccini's most adventurous and accomplished score.

Some opera historians have suggested that long before Puccini's death (from complications of surgical treatment for throat cancer) he was stumped by the ending of the opera and unsure of what to do about it. A notorious procrastinator who needed quantities of cigarettes and coffee and a jolt of panic to get himself into a composing state, Puccini had been working on *Turandot* in fits and starts since 1921. He was clearly not in creative decline, because up until the stopping point his music ventured into new realms of inspiration and harmonic daring. Still, something about the scene daunted him.

Puccini and his beleaguered librettists, Giuseppe Adami and Renato Simoni, compounded the difficulty by the way they modified the source for the opera, a dramatic fable by Carlo Gozzi. In ancient Peking the icy Princess Turandot nurses a hatred of all men. Suitors who seek her hand must answer three riddles that she poses or die. So far everyone attempting the challenge has failed. Then a mysterious stranger comes to town, Prince Calaf in disguise, the son of an exiled Tartar king. Calaf solves the riddles and demands his reward. But the horrified Turandot casts about frantically for an escape from her pledge.

Puccini and his librettists made Turandot's hatred of men even more grisly than in Gozzi. Consequently, in the final scene Calaf would have to melt Turandot's resistance solely through the power of his love, an unmotivated transformation that would need to be conveyed only through music.

Puccini excelled at projecting powerful emotions in conflict. He was not so good, though, at conveying ambiguity. For him feelings, however misguided, were strong things. He could compose a happy love scene with premonitions of tragedy, as in *La Bohème*. But Turandot's psychologically murky change of heart baffled him.

At his death he left thirteen pages of sketches, which take the final scene only to the crucial early moment when Calaf kisses the princess. The task of completing the score was entrusted by Puccini's publisher to the Neapolitan composer Franco Alfano, who composed the rest essentially from scratch based on Puccini's sketches and his own guesswork.

Alfano's ending (he actually composed two, the second and shorter one being the more commonly heard) represents solid professional work. But the music is uninspired, abounding in blatant and brassy orchestral proclamations representing Turandot's romantic breakthrough (breakdown?). Also, *Turandot* is Puccini's most harmonically experimental score. Alfano's more timid harmonic language takes the final scene back to the mainstream Italian verismo tradition.

Various composers have tried their hand at finishing the final scene. By far the boldest and most interesting completion was Luciano Berio's. Though a brainy modernist, Berio had a love of opera, a flair for drama, and a lyrical bent. In his completion he showed us where Puccini's harmonic explorations might have led him. And Berio ends the opera in a state of emotional uncertainty. Turandot's declaration of love is quizzical, as if to say, "What's happening to me?" The chorus of Peking citizens responds not with Alfano's hosannas but with guarded expressions of amazement. Berio's ending drew equal measures of cheers and jeers when I heard it at the Salzburg Festival in 2002. It's probably too radical a solution to catch on. Opera companies are likely to stick with Alfano's yeoman job, though I much prefer Berio's.

But inconclusiveness does not dim the greatness of Puccini's final work. Two classic recordings capture all the sweep, imagination, and exotic flavor of Puccini's impressive score.

In 1959 RCA recorded the opera with a dream cast. The title role was a Birgit Nilsson specialty and this recording captures her vocally dazzling portrayal. Nilsson's Wagnerian soprano voice lacked the subtlety and colorings that certain Italian roles in her repertory demanded. But her cool Nordic power, lean vibrato, and, in the last act, vulnerable warmth ideally suited the icy Peking princess who discovers love. The tenor Jussi Björling's lyrically impassioned Calaf, throbbing with vocal intensity, will flatten you, I promise. Even when Björling sings with burnished sound there is a melancholic cast to his voice, a quality that makes his Calaf a sympathetic figure even in his most defiant and obtuse moments.

Renata Tebaldi brings her honeyed voice and tremulous expressivity to the crucial role of Liù, the slave girl who loyally guides and protects her blind and dethroned master, Calaf's father King Timur. Liù has always loved Calaf from afar. Her death scene, in which her wistfully beautiful phrases are spun through with lingering traces of ethereal dissonance in the orchestra, gives a tantalizing hint of where Puccini might have headed as a composer. Giorgio Tozzi makes a no-nonsense and vocally dignified Timur. Though you may wish Erich Leinsdorf had brought a bit more pliancy and warmth to his conducting, he elicits a dynamic performance from the orchestra and chorus of the Rome Opera.

The other recording is Decca's 1972 account with Zubin Mehta conducting the London Philharmonic Orchestra, the John Alldis Choir, and a sterling cast. Throughout his career I have found Mehta's conducting frustratingly inconsistent. But here he delivers an arresting performance, vividly colored, beautifully subdued when called for, and full of giddy exuberance when the music turns sinister. Mehta and the Decca executives persuaded Joan Sutherland to sing Turandot, a role she never sang in the theater. The bel canto prima donna may have seemed a curious choice for Puccini's icy princess. It's not surprising that Sutherland has the requisite power and gleaming high notes. But Mehta draws feisty temperament, verbal clarity, and rhythmic incisiveness from Sutherland, qualities often missing in her bel canto roles. It makes you wonder what her career might have been had she worked more often with conductors who challenged her, rather than playing it safe with her husband, the conductor Richard Bonynge, who kept her comfortable.

Luciano Pavarotti gives a surprisingly impetuous and vocally radi-

Composer Giacomo Puccini

ant performance as Calaf. Newcomers to *Turandot* who only know the familiar tenor aria "Nessun dorma," Pavarotti's signature tune at the Three Tenors concerts, will be fascinated to hear him sing it in its proper dramatic context. Montserrat Caballé's Liù may lack a degree of emotional spontaneity, but she sings with disarmingly luminous sound and floating pianissimo high notes. Nicolai Ghiaurov brings his sturdy bass and sure dramatic instincts to the role of Timur. You even get the venerable British tenor Peter Pears in a cameo as Turandot's father, the aging Emperor Altoum.

At the 1926 premiere of *Turandot* in Milan, Arturo Toscanini, who was conducting, put down his baton at the place where Puccini's own score ended and announced that he would not continue. (At subsequent performances he conducted the Alfano ending.) That moment, as some historians have suggested, could be seen as the sadly inconclusive ending point to the thriving, hundred-year era of Italian opera.

RCA Victor (two CDs) 09026-62687-2
Erich Leinsdorf (conductor), Orchestra and Chorus of the Rome Opera; Nilsson, Björling, Tebaldi, Tozzi

Decca (two CDs) 414 274-2
Zubin Mehta (conductor), London Philharmonic Orchestra, John Alldis Choir; Sutherland, Pavarotti, Caballé, Ghiaurov

59. HENRY PURCELL (1659–1695)
Dido and Aeneas

Nahum Tate, librettist

First performance: According to the *New Grove Dictionary of Opera* and other sources, it was at a girls' boarding school at Chelsea before December 1689.

Henry Purcell wrote only one true opera, *Dido and Aeneas,* a fifty-minute miracle. It's hard to hear this extraordinary work without bemoaning what might have been, and how the course of opera in England, not to mention music history, might have changed.

In seventeenth-century England the public was largely indifferent toward opera. Among cultured circles the genre was scoffed at. England proudly, and rightly, one could argue, claimed the high ground in drama. But to most Brits, theater was theater and music was music. Mixing a few songs, dances, and choruses into a play was one thing. But sung-through opera was an absurdity. Some attempts to introduce Italian and French opera into England during the 1670s went nowhere. John Dryden, the poet laureate of the kingdom, famously declared that the English language and even the English temperament were incompatible with opera.

But Purcell was keyed up to change all this in the mid-1680s when he composed *Dido and Aeneas*. Born in London, he had been trained as a chorister in the Chapel Royal, won a position as composer to the king, and eventually became an organist at Westminster Abbey and the Chapel Royal. His posts required him to churn out countless odes, anthems, marches, and such for royal occasions. But theater music increasingly excited him.

The circumstances under which *Dido and Aeneas* was written remain obscure. In his lifetime there seems to have been only one performance, this at a boarding school for girls in Chelsea. Nothing came of this performance.

Dido and Aeneas is a high tragedy and a completely sung-through opera. Given the brevity of the work, which may have been imposed, Nahum Tate's libretto necessarily compresses the story of Aeneas's romantic sojourn in Carthage with the widowed Queen Dido. In many ways the opera is stylistically beholden to French and Italian approaches to dance music, arias, and ensembles. Purcell's great breakthrough came with his ingenious solution to the challenge of setting the English language to music. With its clipped rhythms, choppy flow, and hard consonants, English was thought resistant to musical setting, at least in the operatic style involving long stretches of sung dialogue. Purcell's recitative captured the asymmetrical flow and choppy contours of the English tongue. Even in moments of lyrical outpouring he managed to set words in a way that kept them clear. In a good performance, the words of *Dido and Aeneas*, lifted and energized by the music, should leap off the stage at you.

Actually, though Tate's text is poetic and elegant, the story as he tells it has huge narrative holes. We never learn why the Sorceress and her coven of witches despise Dido and plot her death. But the Sorceress is a beguiling character, who sings only in pungent recitative spiked with chortling "ho, ho, ho's" and accompanied by rich, four-part string harmonies.

There are good reasons why Dido's lament in act 3 is among the most famous arias in all of opera. The Sorceress has conjured a false image of Mercury to appear before Aeneas and instruct him to sail away. Being a compliant sort, Aeneas listens to the god. (If truth be told, this operatic Aeneas comes off as a wimp.) Purcell employs a standard descending ground bass pattern in this lament, a device right out of Venetian opera. Over the slowly treading repeated bass figure, the shattered Dido spins out lyrically poignant expressions of her grief and prepares to die, for death can be the only result when a love as strong as hers for Aeneas is thwarted.

In the aria, every time the harmony that fills in the textures between the melody and the bass line seems about to rest on a chord of resolution, the music takes another harmonic turn and leaps forward, creating a sense of cyclic, endless anguish and subdued agitation. And when the queen sings the high sustained cries of "Remember me," the ground bass and the soulful chords in the orchestra just grind on, as if there is nothing to be done. Not until Isolde's "Liebestod" from Wagner's *Tristan und Isolde* would another heartbroken operatic heroine express such a plaintive and powerful yearning for death.

There are some classic recordings of *Dido and Aeneas,* but the most recent release (as of this writing) is the one I'd recommend. A 2003 recording on the Veritas label offers the captivating American mezzo-soprano Susan Graham as Dido, the distinctive British tenor Ian Bostridge as Aeneas, and Emmanuelle Haïm conducting Le Concert d'Astrée, a period instrument ensemble that gives an articulate, undulant, sensitive, and tellingly detailed performance. Bostridge's light tenor voice lends a boyish vitality and welcome earnestness to Aeneas. Graham balances her full-bodied operatic fervor with a knowing sense of English baroque style. The soprano Camilla Tilling makes a lovely Belinda, Dido's confidante, and the contralto Felicity Palmer has a hoot of a time as the Sorceress. European Voices, an impressive choir, does affecting work.

I also love a 1959 recording that Benjamin Britten conducted with the English Opera Group Orchestra and the Purcell Singers. The fine cast is headed by Claire Watson as Dido and Peter Pears as Aeneas. Britten performs from his own edition for the score, and some scholars may quibble with his realization. What comes through for me is the palpable love of the great British opera composer of the twentieth century for the masterwork of a man who might have been the leading British opera composer of the early eighteenth century.

That Purcell really could have changed attitudes had he lived longer is suggested by the conversion he inspired in Dryden. A few years after his put-down of opera as unsuitable for the English, Dryden collaborated on two semioperas with Purcell, *King Arthur* and *The Indian Queen,* and became the composer's biggest booster.

Veritas (one CD) 72435 45605 2 1
Emmanuelle Haïm (harpsichord and musical direction), Le Concert d'Astrée and the European Voices; Graham, Bostridge, Tilling, Palmer

BBC Music (one CD) BBCB 8003-2
Benjamin Britten (conductor), English Opera Group Orchestra and the Purcell Singers; Watson, Pears, Sinclair, Mandikian

60. MAURICE RAVEL (1875–1937)
L'Enfant et les Sortilèges (The Child and the Spells)
Colette, librettist

First performance: Monte Carlo Opera, March 21, 1925

Maurice Ravel, a small and painfully shy man, was living a quite solitary existence when in the midst of World War I he was asked by the director of the Paris Opera to collaborate on a fantastical ballet with the author Colette. The subject of the work appealed to him immediately. A young boy, bored with his homework and grounded by his mama, smashes furniture, rips pages from a storybook, and torments his pets. But then, in his imagination, his victims—animals and objects alike—speak to the child, chastising his wickedness and pitying his isolation.

Ravel soon envisioned the work more as a short opera than a ballet and Colette agreed. She delivered the libretto to him in 1918. By this point in his career, though, Ravel was a terribly slow worker. He spent five years on the score, which turned into a one-act work of some sixty minutes. The premiere, with ballet sequences by the young Balanchine, wound up taking place in Monte Carlo.

The time Ravel lavished on the opera paid off: *L'Enfant et les Sortilèges* is among his most ingenious and enchanting works. While Ravel is always identified with the impressionist movement in French music, by nature he was a neoclassicist and at his best when he turned to older musical forms as models. This opera offered limitless possibilities to do so.

In a brief orchestral prelude, two oboes are heard playing a succession of seemingly aimless intervals (parallel fourths and fifths), music that eerily captures the state of mind of the restless child we soon meet, who cannot focus on his math homework.

His kindly mother encourages him to concentrate, but when this fails she instructs the boy to stay at his desk and get to work. Left alone, the child vents his indignation in a fit of destruction. As he torments his pet squirrel and tomcat, the orchestra squeals with gnashing bitonal chords reinforced by a piano. Now spent, the child heads to an armchair, which eerily moves away from him to some wonderfully galumphing music. The old armchair and a Louis XV couch then sing a delightfully stiff minuet.

The orchestral chaos builds as the furniture and other objects complain to the child about the abuses he has inflicted: he has kicked holes in the chairs, pulled the pendulum from the grandfather clock, ripped the wallpaper to shreds. In a poignant chorus that evokes Renaissance dance music, with its modal harmonies and lightly tapping drums, the tattered shepherds and shepherdesses sing a forlorn song from the wallpaper.

Finally the tormenters relent and the moon comes out, as the black tomcat and its white mate in the garden sing an endearingly whiny duet. In his perceptive entry on the work in the *New Grove Dictionary of Opera*, Roger Nichols points out that Ravel and Colette, both cat lovers, would never have demeaned the species by having them sing in human language. Instead Ravel devised a cat text of "miinhous" and "moâous" and such, "on the linguistic accuracy of which Ravel lavished the greatest care," Nichols writes.

During scene 2, in the garden outside, the child is accosted by some trees whose bark he has cut with a penknife, as well as the bat and the dragonfly, whose spouses he has blithely killed. The orchestra erupts in an earthy Frogs' Dance that effectively sets up the climactic episode. Sensing the child's vulnerability, the animals confront him. A brawl follows in which the squirrel, who has just sung melancholically of the years he lost locked up in the child's cage, is injured. In a breakthrough act of sympathy the child binds the squirrel's wounded paw with a ribbon. Wandering bitonal harmonies in the orchestra finally gain some grounding and the animals join in a contrapuntal anthem in praise of the child's newfound kindness.

Naturally, the opera invites imaginative stage direction and scenic designs. But magical effects of the aural kind abound in the 1965 recording by the conductor Lorin Maazel and the Orchestre National de la R.T.F. Those who read my reports in the *New York Times* on Maazel's tenure as music director of the New York Philharmonic will know that I have been less than happy with his work. But at his best Maazel is a powerful musician, and he's at his best in this incisive yet sensitive and brilliantly colored account of the opera. The slight coolness of his approach allows the menacing dimension of the score to come through, something often missing in performances that emphasize the music's dreaminess. The cast is excellent, especially the clear-toned soprano Françoise Ogéas as the child and the dusky-voiced mezzo-soprano Jeanine Collard as the mother, or "Maman," as the child calls her in the final moments of the opera when, forced to acknowledge his hateful behavior, he finally admits to his longing for his mother.

As an extra bonus the Maazel performance is available on a specially priced, two-disc set from Deutsche Grammophon's Originals series, coupled with Ravel's early opera *L'Heure Espagnole* and short works by Stravinsky and Rimsky-Korsakov.

Deutsche Grammophon (two CDs) 449 769-2
Lorin Maazel (conductor), Orchestre National de la R.T.F.; Ogéas, Collard, Berbié, Gilma, Herzog

61. NIKOLAY RIMSKY-KORSAKOV

(1844–1908)

The Legend of the Invisible City of Kitezh and the Maiden Fevroniya

Vladimir Nikolayevich Belsky, librettist

First performance: St. Petersburg, Mariinsky Theatre, February 20, 1907

Rimsky-Korsakov's penultimate opera, *The Legend of the Invisible City of Kitezh and the Maiden Fevroniya,* has been called the Russian *Parsifal,* and in its own soft-spoken way the work is just as raptly beautiful, deeply spiritual, and musically colossal as Wagner's final masterpiece. The story is fashioned from numerous Russian epics, legends, songs, and traditional tales, including "The Life of Peter, Prince of Murom, and His Wife Fevroniya," as set down in 1547, the year of their canonization.

In his illuminating essay on this work for *The New Grove Dictionary of Opera,* the musicologist Richard Taruskin writes that Belsky's libretto itself has become a document of Russian religious thinking. The opera combines Christian and pre-Christian Slavonic beliefs, melding history, folklore, and religious mystery. While God is clearly responsible for the miracle at the center of the opera, Taruskin points out, supernatural agents play a part as well and Fevroniya is portrayed as an apostle of pantheism who sees God present in all the world's creatures.

While the theological and historical resonances of the opera are fascinating to contemplate, and surely contribute to its hold on audiences, it's entirely possible to just sit back, bask in the spellbinding music, and get caught up in the fairy tale. The opera begins with an orchestral prelude titled "In Praise of the Wilderness," enchanting music in which wistful tunes thread through a quivering, hushed, harmonically restless orchestral backdrop. This is music every bit as ingenious and alluring as the "Forest Murmurs" scene of Wagner's *Siegfried,* to which it has often been compared. Then we meet Fevroniya, a young maiden forest-dweller who lives in harmony with the animals and has devised powerful herbal remedies for sicknesses and ills. A hunter who has lost his way chances upon the young woman and they fall instantly in love. He has never met such a calmly wise and wholesomely beautiful woman. She is overcome by his strapping handsomeness and heroic mien. He announces his intention to marry her, but hunting horns draw him away. Soon his men approach and Fevroniya learns that she is now betrothed to Prince Vsevolod, son of Prince Yuri of Kitezh.

Things look promising in act 2 when the young couple is celebrated by the citizens of Lesser Kitezh and the prince is hailed for taking a common-born bride, though the scheming town drunk Grishka and a group of rich citizens express snippy discontent with what they consider his rash and inappropriate choice.

Suddenly Lesser Kitezh is attacked by a band of Tatars. Fevroniya and Grishka are taken prisoner. The glorious city of Greater Kitezh, across the river, is the next target of the marauders. But a miracle occurs when Fevroniya prays that the great city be made invisible, a transformation accomplished in act 3 to mystical music of hazy textures, hymnal harmony, and pealing church bells. This being a legend, complications ensue. But in the final scene Vsevolod, who fought to the death in a battle with the Tatars rather than be taken captive, and Fevroniya are united in blissful happiness and eternal life in the invisible city of Kitezh.

Rimsky-Korsakov had conflicting impulses at work when he wrote this score. Like many non-German composers of the day, he was influenced by the arrogant Wagner but reluctant to admit it. Still, woven through the long, spacious expanses of post-Romantic Wagnerian-tinged harmony are folkloric tunes, exotic colors, and hymnal music that achieve a stately grace and give the score its Russian character. All these qualities clearly influenced the young Stravinsky, who began studying with Rimsky-Korsakov in 1903, the year the elder Russian started composing this opera. Whole swaths of Stravinsky's 1910 ballet score *The Firebird* are lifted, at least in spirit, from *Kitezh.*

When the Kirov Opera of the Mariinsky Theatre presented a

festival of Russian works at the Metropolitan Opera in 2003, a boldly imaginative production of *Kitezh* by Dmitri Cherniakov was the highlight. The staging was a playful but sensitive modern-dress conception that humanized the story: a prophet bird that briefly appears to guide Fevroniya to the invisible city was portrayed as a wizened Russian peasant woman lighting a cigarette and leaning out of a window, meant to be Fevroniya's portal to the heavens.

The opera received its 1907 premiere at the Mariinsky Theatre in St. Petersburg and the Mariinsky company's 1994 live recording is the one to have. The conductor Valery Gergiev adores this score and it comes through in his luminous, tellingly paced, and intricately textured performance. The soprano Galina Gorchakova as Fevroniya and the tenor Yuri Marusin as Prince Vsevolod head an impressive cast of singers who bring complete stylistic authority to their work. Every role is strongly sung, right down to minor ones, like Alkonost, a prophet bird, here the dusky-toned mezzo-soprano Larissa Diadkova.

Philips (three CDs) 462 225-2

Valery Gergiev (conductor), Chorus and Orchestra of the Kirov Opera, Mariinsky Theatre, St. Petersburg; Gorchakova, Marusin, Galuzin, Putilin, Ohotnikov

62. GIOACCHINO ROSSINI

Il Barbiere di Siviglia (The Barber of Seville)

Cesare Sterbini, librettist, after a play by Pierre-Augustin Caron de Beaumarchais

First performance: Rome, Teatro Argentina, February 20, 1816

Rossini's determination to write an opera based on Beaumarchais's play *Le Barbier de Séville,* the first in a trilogy of revolutionary French comedies, provoked a public outcry in Italy. The esteemed composer Giovanni Paisiello had already written a hugely popular operatic adaptation, *Il Barbiere di Siviglia,* introduced in 1782, two years before the premiere of Mozart's *Nozze di Figaro,* based on the second play in the trilogy. How dare Rossini, this upstart composer in his early twenties, write another?

But Rossini persisted and his *Barbiere* opened in Rome in 1816. The premiere was disrupted by a noisy contingent of Paisiello partisans. Still, Rossini's new approach to comedy and his brilliant score with its "abundance of genuine musical ideas," as Verdi would later comment, soon won out. Today Paisiello's charming little opera is a footnote and Rossini's *Barber of Seville* an enduring staple of the repertory.

From all reports, Rossini composed the opera in less than two weeks, though surely ideas must have been tossing around in his head for a long while. The overture, which today seems so brilliantly comic and appropriate, was actually recycled from an earlier work, a serious opera, *Aureliano in Palmira.* How is that possible?

I've long thought a key to Rossini's genius was his understanding that there is not that large a divide between the comic and the serious. Both in theater and in music, just a slightly different inflection, attitude, or pacing will turn a somber gesture into a silly one. You can understand how Rossini thought that this overture—for example, the grim minor-mode section when a nervous tune in the violins is accompanied by short, steady repeated chords in the orchestra—if conducted with the right nuance, would seem suspenseful in a comic way.

In this work Rossini created full-fleshed and complex characters. We identify with their foibles, plucky swagger, and exasperating dilemmas. The opera is rich with hilarious comic bits, though for a performance to work the singers must take themselves seriously.

In the first scene, for example, young Count Almaviva, who is disguised as a poor nobody, has hired a band of musicians to accompany him in a serenade beneath the balcony of a pretty girl he has seen from afar. After some hapless mess-ups as the musicians assemble and tune their instruments, Almaviva begins to sing his wistful and elegantly lyrical serenade. Suddenly the comedy seems tenderly real. Like innumerable young men before him, the love-struck count has been touched by a woman he doesn't even know, who turns out to be

Rosina, the young ward of the overprotective Dr. Bartolo, who intends to marry her. But there is an earnest intention behind the count's ploy: he wants to be loved for himself, not his position.

Figaro's famous "Largo al factotum" is funny, yes, because of its explosive energy and passages of Italian patter. But it's also an exuberant manifesto from a young man who loves his life. Figaro, formerly a servant to the count, is not just a barber. He's an arranger, a facilitator. You need a date, a spouse for your daughter, a message conveyed, a compromising situation untangled, an entrée into a home? Figaro is your man, he tells the audience directly. Everyone calls him, everyone needs him, Figaro here, Figaro there. What a din! But he thrives on being essential. When a strapping baritone with a strong voice and good diction tosses off the aria, Figaro should command the stage.

The really broad moments of comedy are almost always based on musical humor, for example, the scene in act 2 when Almaviva and Figaro have rescued Rosina from her imprisonment in Dr. Bartolo's house and are trying to make a quick getaway. Figaro can't get the eager young couple to hurry up because they keep taking time to deliver lyrical expressions of their devotion, decorated with elaborate coloratura roulades.

I love the moment in act 2, during Rosina's music lesson, when Dr. Bartolo, who does not like the new trends in music, sits at the fortepiano and plays a little song in the old manner he favors, a gentle little rococo-styled air in a lilting triple meter. Suddenly Rossini lets you see another side to Dr. Bartolo, who is an old softie for tried-and-true music. He really is not a bad guy. Why shouldn't he want to marry his ward? He thinks she'll have a nice life with him. Besides, it turns out that he was right to be suspicious of the count. In the next part of the Beaumarchais trilogy, *The Marriage of Figaro*, some years have gone by and the count has grown tired of the countess, Rosina, and started philandering.

Rosina was conceived as a role for a lustrous mezzo-soprano, not a perky lyric soprano. Yet for generations the role was appropriated by sopranos who simply had Rosina's music transposed to higher keys. During the late nineteenth and early twentieth centuries the entire opera was routinely tampered with and altered. In 1972 the insightful conductor Claudio Abbado made an important contribution to opera by recording *Il Barbiere* with a splendid cast using the most scholarly critical sources available. That Deutsche Grammophon recording remains a classic.

The mezzo-soprano Teresa Berganza is a rich-voiced, technically agile, and completely beguiling Rosina, a vulnerable portrayal of a plucky yet poignantly trusting young woman. The fine tenor Luigi Alva makes a sweet-toned and vibrant Almaviva. The baritone Hermann Prey as Figaro may not have the most nimble coloratura technique, but his suave, clever, and robustly sung portrayal offers ample rewards. Abbado conducts with palpable respect for the score, eliciting plenty of madcap energy from the cast and the London Symphony Orchestra, but leaving room for the music to breathe and the comic subtleties to register.

The other essential recording is EMI's 1958 account with Maria Callas as Rosina. In earlier years Callas, like many sopranos of the day, had sung the role with the music transposed higher. But for this recording she adhered to almost all of the original mezzo-soprano keys. She gives a remarkable performance, tossing off the coloratura with aplomb and dipping easily into the dusky lower range of her voice. This Rosina knows that she is smarter than any of the men she encounters, but being a woman she must rely on ploys and manipulation to get her way.

There is a renowned moment in Callas's account of Rosina's introductory aria, "Una voce poco fa." Explaining that, yes, of course, she can be docile and obedient when need be, Callas prolongs the final note of the melodic line and slides up to end the phrase on a single clipped word, "ma," the Italian for "but." But, she says, when she is crossed she can be a viper. The way Callas exudes innocence, then turns it all around on that one word, "ma," and continues with a determination you don't want to mess with, was such a brilliant interpretive stroke that countless Rosinas since have stolen the idea.

Luigi Alva is again Almaviva, captured here when younger and his voice was fresher than in the Abbado recording. Tito Gobbi makes a blustery and idiomatically Italian Figaro. Alceo Galliera conducts a sprightly and lithe performance. I'd be hard-pressed to pick one of these recordings over the other. But perhaps I'd give the edge to Abbado's informed and authoritative account.

Deutsche Grammophon (two CDs) 457733

Claudio Abbado (conductor), London Symphony Orchestra; Prey, Berganza, Alva, Dara, Montarsolo

EMI Classics (two CDs) 56310

Alceo Galliera (conductor), Philharmonia Orchestra and Chorus; Gobbi, Callas, Alva, Rossi-Lemeni

63. GIOACCHINO ROSSINI (1792–1868)

La Cenerentola (Cinderella)

Jacopo Ferretti, librettist

First performance: Rome, Teatro Valle, January 25, 1817

Rossini composed *La Cenerentola* in the first twenty-two days of 1817, which even for this prolific creator of assembly-line operas was fast work. Naturally, he had to take his typical shortcuts. Instead of writing an overture he recycled one from *La Gazzetta,* a recent opera buffa. According to the scholar Richard Osborne, some stretches of recitatives and three of the sixteen number arias performed at the premiere were actually composed by an associate, Luca Agolini (though modern research suggests that these arias were added as concessions to specific singers in Rome and omitted by Rossini whenever he was involved in subsequent productions). To conclude the opera Rossini adapted a bravura aria for Count Almaviva from the final scene of *Il Barbiere di Siviglia,* turning it into the brilliant rondo "Nacqui all'affanno" for Angelina, the Cenerentola of the title.

Sounds like a hodgepodge method of composition, right? In some ways it was. But Rossini lived at a time when the demand for opera was insatiable, much like the decades of the 1920s and 1930s when Broadway audiences hungered for musicals and composer/lyricist teams like the Gershwin brothers would sometimes turn out two or three a season. In both cases working fast and sticking to convention was not necessarily a hindrance to creativity and inspiration.

In a good performance *La Cenerentola* comes across as an utterly assured and consistently rich comic opera. Actually, Rossini describes the work as a "dramma giocoso," the same designation Mozart used for *Don Giovanni,* which provides a clue to its essence. *La Cenerentola* was based on the French version of the Cinderella fairy tale by Charles Perrault. But Rossini's librettist, Jacopo Ferretti, eliminated most of the supernatural elements of the tale so as to transform it into a realistically human comedy. Rossini had an unsentimental insight into the morbid, venal, and cruel aspects of human nature. For all its buffa qualities *La Cenerentola* is not all that funny.

In the opening scene, we see the sisters Clorinda and Tisbe engaged in one of their daily tussles over fashion and finery. Yet, as presented by Rossini, their snippy exchanges, while amusing, are quite nasty. Meanwhile, Angelina, their stepsister, whom everyone calls Cinderella (Cenerentola), sings her favorite song, a forlorn folk ballad, as she glumly does the housework and fans the cinders in the fire with a bellows. This simple, minor-mode song, which tells of a lonely king searching for a wife, poignantly captures Cinderella's solitary and affectionless life.

Rossini makes Don Magnifico, the indulgent father to Clorinda and Tisbe and the abusive stepfather to Cinderella, a laughably pompous buffa figure. Yet even his inner life comes through when he describes an extraordinary dream he had in which a magical donkey sprouted wings and flew to the top of a steeple. The Don takes the dream to mean that his family will make a societal leap and acquire royal connections. While bumptious, the aria projects a quality of amazement. More than eighty years before Freud published *The Interpretation of Dreams,* Rossini was fascinated by this character's attempt to account for his subconscious.

In a later scene Don Magnifico shows himself capable of psychological cruelty. Alidoro, an angel who appears in several guises (the opera's equivalent of Cinderella's fairy godmother), arrives at the house dressed as a palace official. He carries a census list indicating that the Don has not just two daughters, as he claims, but three. With tearful relief Cinderella lurches for the book. Could this be official proof that she is not just some ragtag nobody? But in one of the most horrible moments in all of opera the Don lies to Alidoro, saying that his third daughter has died. Later, alone with her, the Don rips the page into shreds, leaving Cinderella to pick up the pieces of her elusive identity from the floor.

With her phenomenal popularity the mezzo-soprano Cecilia Bartoli has brought new attention to *La Cenerentola* in recent years. The title role remains one of her finest achievements and her 1993 Decca recording has much to recommend it. She sings with impeccable coloratura technique, engaging spunk, and, where called for, melancholic beauty. Cenerentola is revealed as an oppressed working girl, someone modern audiences can relate to. Riccardo Chailly, conducting the orchestra and chorus of the Teatro Comunale di Bologna, presides over an ebullient performance with an impressive cast, including the tenor William Matteuzzi as the prince Don Ramiro, the baritone Enzo Dara as Don Magnifico, and the baritone Alessandro Corbelli as Dandini, the prince's enterprising valet, who spends half the opera disguised as his boss. The prince has enlisted his valet into a scheme to discover the true natures of the women he is considering as his potential princess.

The recording I cherish, though, is Deutsche Grammophon's 1972 account with Claudio Abbado conducting the London Symphony Orchestra and a splendid cast headed by Teresa Berganza. This recording was the culmination of scholarly work that finally assembled an authoritative performing edition of the score. But there is nothing academic about this buoyant, genial, and musically distinguished performance, which captures both the work's somberness and whimsy. The rich-voiced Berganza, a consummate Rossinian, is an alternatively feisty and tender Cenerentola. The tenor Luigi Alva as the most elegantly lyrical Don Ramiro, the robust baritone Renato Capecchi as Dandini, and the blustery baritone Paolo Montarsolo as Don Magnifico are other standouts among the cast.

La Cenerentola is Rossini's three-week wonder.

Decca (two CDs) 436 902-2
Riccardo Chailly (conductor), Orchestra and Chorus of the Teatro Comunale di Bologna; Bartoli, Matteuzzi, Dara, Corbelli, Pertusi

Deutsche Grammophon (two CDs) 423 861-2

Claudio Abbado (conductor), London Symphony Orchestra, Scottish Opera Chorus; Berganza, Alva, Capecchi, Montarsolo

64. GIOACCHINO ROSSINI (1792–1868)

Semiramide

Gaetano Rossi, librettist, after Voltaire's *Sémiramis*

First performance: Venice, Teatro La Fenice, February 3, 1823

In 1823 when Rossini's *Semiramide,* a tragic melodrama in three acts, was presented in Vienna fresh from its triumphant premiere in Venice, the young Rossini, arguably the most popular and prolific composer of the day, met Beethoven. From all reports Beethoven advised Rossini to write more *Barber of Sevilles.* In other words, he told Rossini to stick to comedy. Later generations of opera impresarios and historians would use Beethoven's comment to buttress the general opinion that Rossini's serious operas are ineffective, lacking in substance, and at times downright silly.

Today, thanks to fifty years of scholarship and championing by important singers and conductors, the opera world knows better. Those who patronize *Semiramide* are missing out on a stirring, grand, and affecting opera. If Beethoven didn't get it, the French novelist Stendhal certainly did, who wrote: "The glory of the man is only limited by the limits of civilization itself, and he is not yet 32." *Semiramide* was the last work Rossini wrote for an Italian theater, before ending his career prematurely in Paris, where he wrote his five last operas.

A 1962 revival at La Scala in Milan starring Joan Sutherland and Giulietta Simionato dramatically changed opinion about the work. Even more, an extraordinary 1965 recording featuring Sutherland in the title role and the mezzo-soprano Marilyn Horne as Arsace, with Richard Bonynge conducting, marked a turning point in the

---

appreciation of *Semiramide*. Horne's performance was a particular revelation. She seemed born to the role, an ideal Rossini singer whose accomplishment has yet to be equaled.

The story, based on Voltaire, which could be viewed as a clunky melodrama, in Rossini's hands becomes a compelling tale of generational intrigue with an oedipal resonance. Semiramide, the Queen of Babylon in the eighth century B.C., is the widow of King Nino. But we soon discover that fifteen years earlier the queen, in league with Prince Assur, who claims to be descended from Baal, murdered the king and attempted to murder her son, also called Nino, and claimed the throne for herself. Now Assur hopes to succeed to the throne by marrying Princess Azema, also descended from Baal.

But the queen's son, called Arsace, escaped long ago and knows nothing of his true identity. He now serves as the valiant commander of Semiramide's forces in an outer region of the kingdom. Arsace has been mysteriously summoned to court, and the tensions mount when Assur fears that Oroe, a high priest, knows too much about the past. Meanwhile Semiramide finds herself powerfully drawn to the young Arsace, who is attracted to Princess Azema and confounded by the romantic feelings of the queen.

Rossini gives his characters rich, elaborate, and emotionally complex arias. In keeping with the reigning style of Italian opera, the vocal lines abound with virtuosic passagework and ornamental filigree that can sometimes obscure the music's lyrical elegance and noble expressivity. As the opera develops, Arsace and Semiramide come to realize their true relationship. Rossini creates a portrait of a ruthless queen finally overcome by motherly love and forced to confront her horrific ambition, and a son who, despite his heroic exploits, has lived with a painful core of longing for his unknown mother. He is so overcome at finding her that he cannot help forgiving Semiramide, a sentiment you share during their ennobled and poignant duet. Working at the height of his powers, Rossini folds the sensational arias, mellifluous duets, and gripping choral scenes into musical and dramatic structure of architectonic genius.

The way Horne combines husky power and breathtaking agility in her singing of Arsace seems miraculous. Though there is womanly beauty in her sound, the sheer virility and fervor of her singing, the fearless leaps, the incisive attacks, all combine to make her completely plausible as Rossini's tormented hero. Sutherland, always a superb vocalist, could sometimes be dramatically dull. But she is inspired here, singing with radiance, vocal charisma, volatility, and, of course, flawless coloratura technique. The rest of the cast—the bass Joseph Rouleau as Assur, the soprano Patricia Clark as Azema, the bass Spiro Malas as Oroe—is quite strong, with the small exception of the tight-voiced tenor John Serge as Idreno, an Indian king. Bonynge conducts a tellingly paced and stylish performance. But Sutherland and Horne are in a class of their own. Decca knows better than to let this recording slip from the catalog.

The Paris period of Rossini's career ended splendidly with *Guillaume Tell* in 1829. But after this, though only thirty-seven, Rossini retired from the opera business, having composed over three dozen works in seventeen years. Why did he stop? There was a new generation of composers to carry on his innovations and new currents stirring. Perhaps he did not want to adapt, or felt he had already said what he had to say, or was exhausted, or just not that ambitious. He lived another thirty-nine years, composing a few works, living to see the breakthroughs of Verdi and Wagner, enjoying himself immensely despite long bouts of poor health, eating very well and growing quite portly.

Decca (three CDs) 425 481-2
Richard Bonynge (conductor), London Symphony Orchestra, Ambrosian Opera Chorus; Sutherland, Horne, Rouleau, Serge, Clark, Malas

65. POUL RUDERS (b. 1949)

Tjenerindens Fortaelling (The Handmaid's Tale)

Paul Bentley, librettist, after a novel by Margaret Atwood

First performance: Copenhagen, Royal Danish Opera, March 6, 2000

It's the early twenty-first century, and a tremor at the San Andreas fault has devastated nuclear power plants in California. War and environmental havoc have caused famine and infertility throughout the United States. Right-wing Christian fanatics have assassinated the president and the Congress, reconstituting the nation as a male-controlled totalitarian state called Gilead in which women are deprived of all rights. Some of those still able to breed are enslaved as handmaids, after the biblical story of Jacob and Rachel, and forced to copulate with high-ranking commanders in degrading threesomes involving the commanders' barren wives.

Margaret Atwood fans will recognize the plot of her apocalyptic novel, *The Handmaid's Tale,* a book both derided as a preposterous polemic and devoured as a chilling fantasy that explored the implications of fundamentalism from the Moral Majority to the Taliban.

The story may seem a bit much to pack into an evening at the opera, but the ingenious Danish composer Poul Ruders thought otherwise. *The Handmaid's Tale,* his second opera, received its premiere at the Royal Danish Opera in 2000. Too many new operas in recent years have been well conceived but musically negligible. *The Handmaid's Tale* may be dramatically bewildering, no argument there. But it is so musically inventive that you get pulled in anyway.

The story is told in flashbacks. At an international video conference in 2195 a professor is giving a lecture on two monotheocratic states in the early twenty-first century: Iran and Gilead. A newly discovered audiocassette diary recorded by a handmaid from the long-gone Christian republic is played for the conference participants.

So the opera unfolds as disconnected scenes from the life of Offred, who, as all handmaids must, takes her name from that of her commander: she is "of Fred." The narrative device keeps the focus on Offred, who is given several halting, poignant monologues that may find their ways to the recital stage.

In addition Ruders and his British librettist, Paul Bentley, whose original English text was translated into Danish for the Copenhagen premiere, invent a character called Offred's Double, who portrays her in earlier times when she had a husband and a daughter. The result is deliberately cinematic, as the opera crosscuts between the handmaid's life before and after the revolution.

Offred and her double engage each other musically, climaxing when the two voices converge in an unconventional duet. Their elegiac melody, sung in unison, is enshrined in Ruders's hazy orchestral harmonies spiked with quizzical dissonances and spectral colors.

In places Ruders ironically adapts older musical idioms, as in his bizarre settings of "Amazing Grace," associated with Serena Joy, a former gospel singer, now the wife of Offred's commander. The familiar hymn is undercut by gloppy chromatic chords and piercing discordant notes, like some futuristic facsimile of angelic music. Relentless minimalistic riffs agitate a chorus of Gilead's class of frenetic aunts, who impart dogma to the handmaids and enforce the procreative regimen.

Yet for long stretches the score just breathes and sighs in shimmering, quasi-atonal harmonies, enriched by an array of electronic instruments, while the characters converse in singable vocal lines that somehow sound elusive. The striking exception is the role of the maniacal Aunt Lydia, whose jagged coloratura flights make her seem a sci-fi cousin of Mozart's avenging Queen of the Night.

The story may sound convoluted, but this audacious opera is an enthralling and important work, as well as a potential plaything for an imaginative director. As of this writing there has only been one U.S. production, a compelling staging by the Minnesota Opera in 2003, performed in Bentley's original English text. As adventurous American opera buffs await additional productions, they thankfully can enjoy the Dacapo recording drawn from the world premiere performances at the Royal Danish Opera, with Marianne Rorholm and

Hanne Fischer as Offred and Offred's Double, Susanne Resmark as Serena Joy, and other excellent singers. Michael Schonwandt conducts a glittering, inexorable, and enthralling performance.

Dacapo (two CDs) 8.224165-66
Michael Schonwandt (conductor), Royal Danish Opera Chorus, Royal Danish Orchestra; Rorholm, Fischer, Elming, Dahl, Resmark

66. ARNOLD SCHOENBERG (1874–1951)

Moses und Aron

Arnold Schoenberg, librettist

First performance (staged): Zurich, State Theater, June 6, 1957

For many mainstream opera buffs just the idea of Arnold Schoenberg's *Moses und Aron* is off-putting. It's assumed to be a grimly serious didactic work with a formidably complex, dissonance-saturated score. Fortunately, opera companies are beginning at last to mount the work so that audiences can experience the real thing. The Metropolitan Opera presented its first *Moses und Aron* in 1999, a boldly modern production by the director Graham Vick, conducted with palpable excitement by James Levine. To the Met's great surprise the production was a solid success with the public. You don't have to know twelve-tone technique from a Viennese torte to be engrossed by this volatile, haunting, and powerfully ambiguous music.

Everything Schoenberg believed about Jewish history and religion, the persecution that prophets in all realms of life inevitably encounter, and the aesthetics of modern art found expression in this ambitious opera. Schoenberg wrote his own three-act libretto, using the story of the wary relationship between the biblical brothers Moses and Aaron to explore conflicting modes of spiritual revelation. Schoenberg finished composing the music for the first two acts in 1932, a year before he reconverted to Judaism, fled Nazi Germany, and immigrated to the United States, eventually settling in Los Angeles. Though Schoenberg lived another eighteen years he never composed the final act. He complained constantly that teaching obligations, a forced retirement on an inadequate pension, and the financial burdens of supporting a young family made finishing the work impossible. But the issues raised in the opera have no resolution. So you can imagine Schoenberg thinking that by completing *Moses und Aron* he would somehow negate it.

The opera tells the brothers' story at the most crucial juncture of their lives. Moses has been charged by the invisible voice of God to lead the Israelites, the chosen people. Feeling inarticulate, he doubts his suitability for the task. Moreover, his people are dubious over the whole notion of an intangible and unknowable deity. The charismatic Aron, a smooth talker, is a big help to Moses at first. But Moses rightly worries that Aron is too sympathetic to the craving of the Israelites for a concrete image of god.

Schoenberg boldly distinguishes the vocal styles of the two characters: Moses, a bass, sings in Sprechtstimme, a mixture of speech and song that when performed by a powerful vocalist can poignantly convey the character's halting humanity; Aron, a tenor, sings curvaceous vocal lines in full voice. An ideal Aron should ooze slickly tenorial tones.

The third major character of the opera is the chorus, which sings the various roles of the frightened, contentious, and malleable Israelites. An imaginative director can really go to town with this work. The libretto calls for Moses to encounter the burning bush, for jugs of water from the Nile to be turned into blood and back again. Following the Old Testament story, Moses leaves his people for forty days as he travels to the summit of the mountain of revelation. As the days wear on a chorus of seventy Jewish elders warn Aron that the Israelites are growing mutinous. So Aron fashions a tangible object of worship, the Golden Calf, and the people break into an orgy of dancing and sex. If a company presented this scene according to Schoenberg's stage directions, the local vice squad would close down the performance. But what's going on is explicitly clear from Schoenberg's orgiastic music for the frenzied chorus and orchestra.

The nearly two-hour score continually shifts in mood to convey states of prophetic rigor, wistful resignation, terrifying rebellion, and more. It takes a conductor with an innate sympathy for Schoenberg's style and resourceful technique to bring off an effective performance. Pierre Boulez masters the challenge in his 1995 recording with the Royal Concertgebouw Orchestra and the Chorus of the Netherlands Opera. The bass David Pittman-Jennings is a stentorian and pitiable Moses; the husky-voiced dramatic tenor Chris Merritt is an alluring and unusually powerful Aron. The chorus throws itself with abandon into the opera's fitful crowd scenes. And Boulez draws a luminous, lucid, and arresting performance from the great Concertgebouw Orchestra and the robust choristers.

Act 2 ends with Moses utterly dispirited by the fickleness of his people, whose faith has been rekindled by the latest concrete sign: a pillar of fire. Alone onstage, he ponders whether his own idealism is just another attempt to capture in verbal imagery an idea that cannot and must not be expressed. *Moses und Aron* just breaks off at this point with nothing resolved. Yet very few operas end more movingly.

Deutsche Grammophon (two CDs) 449 174-2

Pierre Boulez (conductor), Royal Concertgebouw Orchestra, Chorus of the Netherlands Opera; Pittman-Jennings, Merritt

67. DMITRI SHOSTAKOVICH (1906–1975)

Lady Macbeth of the Mtsensk District

Dmitri Shostakovich and Alexander Preys, librettists, after a short story by Nikolay Leskov

First performance: Leningrad, Malïy Opera Theatre, January 22, 1934

In late January 1934 Dmitri Shostakovich's second opera, *Lady Macbeth of the Mtsensk District,* had dual premieres, one could say dueling premieres, in separate productions by rival companies in

Leningrad and Moscow. Though the first production, in Leningrad, was the official premiere, each company offered a slightly different version of the opera. Both had instantaneous impacts. The opera, which tells of the passions, frustrations, and murderous brutality of a bored young wife of a wealthy merchant in a provincial region of mid-nineteenth-century Russia, stunned audiences and impressed critics with its graphic rendering of sex and violence, its grotesquely satirical portrayal of Russian authority figures, especially the police force, and the sheer power and brash modernism of its music.

Over the next two years the opera received some two hundred productions. In her article for the *New Grove Dictionary of Opera,* the Shostakovich scholar Laurel Fay notes that for a brief period in January 1936, three productions of *Lady Macbeth* were playing simultaneously in Moscow, two from resident companies, the third from the touring Maliy Opera Theatre of Leningrad.

But on the twenty-sixth of that month, Joseph Stalin took a delegation of Soviet officials to the Bolshoi production of the opera. Deeply shocked, the party left before the fourth and final act. Two days later a scathing review, unsigned but indisputably dictated by Stalin, appeared in *Pravda* under the title "Muddle Instead of Music."

The article condemned the work for its "deliberately dissonant and confused stream of sounds," for replacing "singing with screaming," for resorting to "quacks, hoots, pants and gasps" to depict the love scenes with demeaning naturalism. The review ridiculed the opera for its pretensions as social satire. With this act Stalin instigated a repressive cultural policy: all artistic works would now be expected to conform to the aesthetic doctrine of socialist realism.

As is well known, the decree resulted in the production of a lot of timid and provincial Soviet art. One specific result for Shostakovich, who was still under thirty at the time, is that he never wrote another opera, even though *Lady Macbeth* was meant as the first in a tetralogy of operas about women. Instead, Shostakovich channeled his genius primarily into the creation of symphonies, string quartets, and other instrumental work where his message, however ironic, resigned, or defiant, could be better hidden. While instrumentalists, especially string quartets, are the richer for his shift, his withdrawal from opera was an incalculable loss.

After Stalin's death Shostakovich made revisions to *Lady Macbeth,* sanitizing some aspects of the story and softening the edge of the gnarly music. That version, called *Katerina Ismailova,* was finally approved for a production in Moscow in 1963. But the original version of this towering work has been the standard ever since it was recorded definitively in 1978 by EMI in a performance starring the soprano Galina Vishnevskaya in the title role with Mstislav Rostropovich conducting the London Symphony Orchestra.

Shostakovich adapted the opera from a short story by Nikolay Leskov, though he made the central character more sympathetic. The alluring Katerina, the wife of the merchant Zinoviy Borisovich Ismailov, is an idle and bored young woman, unhappy in her marriage, childless, even unable to read. One of the workers in her husband's factory, Sergey, who has a well-earned reputation as a seducer, sweeps Katerina into his arms one day when she is defending her plump servant woman against the pawing and ridicule of a group of workers. Lonely and vulnerable, Katerina succumbs to Sergey's forceful embraces.

Katerina's father-in-law, a cranky and demanding old codger chronically upset with his daughter-in-law, turns apoplectic when he sees Sergey leaving her bedroom. So Katerina mixes poison into the mushrooms he demands for a meal, and seized with spasms of pain he dies. When her husband returns from a business voyage, demands to know what happened, and starts to slap her, Katerina and Sergey strangle him.

They bury the body in the basement, but a shabby peasant discovers it and alerts the police, who show up in the midst of the wedding festivities for Katerina and Sergey. No longer caring, she confesses all. The couple is sent to a Siberian prison camp. There Sergey is enticed by a pretty young convict. Together they taunt the distraught Katerina, who, recalling what it was once like to be honored and respected, drowns herself in a lake. The opera ends with the queries of an old convict about why life is so dark and horrifying.

The story's appeal to Shostakovich is not hard to fathom: it can be seen as a metaphor for life in the dogmatic, repressive, and mind-numbing Soviet state. As the scholar Solomon Volkov points out in his liner notes to the EMI recording, even at this early stage of his career Shostakovich had observed firsthand how a bureaucratic apparatus, with increasing cruelty, could curtail "any attempts at a different trend of thought." And that a bright and outstanding personality could as easily be crushed by the "eternal stupefying Russian boredom" as by direct totalitarian oppression.

Even though Katerina acts monstrously, Shostakovich invites us to admire her willpower and vitality, her open flouting of authority, her refusal to deny herself. Musically he wins sympathy for his heroine by giving her the opera's only stretches of poignantly lyrical and emotionally full-fleshed music. All the other characters are made to seem grim parodies: her husband and father-in-law, the workers, and, in an especially brassy, hypercharged, and bitingly sarcastic scene, the police officers.

Rostropovich, who was an intimate friend of Shostakovich, brings cultural, musical, emotional, and psychological authority to his riveting performance. Though Vishnevskaya, Rostropovich's wife, does not try to disguise Katerina's horridness, her plaintive, warm, and radiant singing makes the character's lyrical effusions and isolated ruminations real and pitiable. With his bright and ringing tenor voice, Nicolai Gedda lends Sergey a convincingly seductive and dangerous dimension. The bass-baritone Dimiter Petkov as Boris, Katerina's husband, and tenor Werner Krenn as the father-in-law both give chilling performances. Even small roles are well cast, like the shabby peasant of the fine tenor Robert Tear.

Listening to this impressive recording of Shostakovich's arresting work, you cannot but wonder what he might have accomplished in opera had Stalin not decided to become a music critic.

EMI (two CDs) 7 499552
Mstislav Rostropovich (conductor), Ambrosian Opera Chorus, London Philharmonic Orchestra; Vishnevskaya, Gedda, Petkov, Krenn, Tear

68. STEPHEN SONDHEIM (b. 1930)

Sweeney Todd: The Demon Barber of Fleet Street

Hugh Wheeler, librettist; lyrics by Stephen Sondheim

First performance: New York, Uris Theatre (now the Gershwin), March 1, 1979

To say that Stephen Sondheim has a love/hate attitude toward opera is close to the truth but not quite right. He doesn't hate opera. Aspects of it interest him. But he cares too much about words and the art of mingling words with music to have patience for opera, which to him is so often musically grandiose and dramatically long-winded. He considers *Sweeney Todd: The Demon Barber of Fleet Street,* which opened on Broadway in 1979, a musical, not an opera.

Of course, the distinctions between the two are not always so clear. But you can tell a great deal by where a work winds up being performed. Since the original production of *Sweeney Todd,* directed by Harold Prince, closed in late 1980, there has not been a full-scale revival on Broadway. (There was a pared-down version that some critics found fascinating and others dubbed *Teeny Todd.*) But the work has fared well in opera houses. As I write this, a production is running at the New York City Opera, another is coming up at the Royal Opera at Covent Garden in London, and in 2002 it played at the Lyric Opera of Chicago with the bass-baritone Bryn Terfel, a reigning opera star, in the title role.

Sondheim may have conceived *Sweeney Todd* for a Broadway stage and had musical theater voices in mind, like the two incomparable stars who created the leading roles: Len Cariou as Sweeney and Angela Lansbury as Mrs. Lovett. Still, in terms of musical sophistication, harmonic daring, effective writing for the voice, skill at handling large ensembles and chorus, and a deftness for mixing literate and clever words with music that makes those words soar and sing,

Sweeney Todd is a more important and accomplished work than the majority of operas written in Sondheim's lifetime.

The score is almost continuous music. Though Hugh Wheeler's brilliant book is essential to the work's success, there is not much spoken dialogue in this musical. The reason for this, Sondheim has said, is not that he was trying to write an opera. Rather, he was paying homage to nineteenth-century British melodramas, which had instrumental music churning away in the orchestra pit almost nonstop.

Few of those scary melodramas, though, were as gruesome as *Sweeney Todd*. The musical tells the tale of the return to London of a downtrodden and avenging barber who had been sentenced by a corrupt judge to a prison work camp on trumped-up charges. That judge, we learn, had coveted Todd's attractive wife, Lucy. With Todd put away, the judge abused and discarded Lucy, then adopted her pretty young daughter, Todd's only child, as his ward. Now back in London, Todd meets Mrs. Lovett, whose meat-pie business is languishing due to the prohibitive price of meat. She entices Todd to go back into the barbering business, but his all-consuming quest for revenge leads him into a mutually beneficial enterprise with Mrs. Lovett: many of Todd's customers never return from their trip to the barber chair; meanwhile, Mrs. Lovett suddenly seems to have a fresh and free supply of meat.

From the start of the score Sondheim lures you into this story with his beguiling and ingenious music. In act 1, as we learn more about the true natures of the two main characters, our growing sense of shock is undermined by the increasingly charming music. The final scene of the first act, when Mrs. Lovett explains her plan to Todd and he immediately embraces the idea as inspired and just (for once, "those above will serve those down below"), they sing "A Little Priest," an evocation of a snappy vaudeville number, complete with traded quips and bad puns. But in act 2, as the story turns horrific, Sondheim's music, as it must, becomes bleaker and invites you to condemn the pair. Still, it's all very subtly done. For example, early in act 2, young Toby, the innocent and dim-witted boy Mrs. Lovett has taken in, sings to her the kindly song "Not While I'm Around," a pledge to protect her from harm. He has grown suspicious of Mr. Todd. Genuinely touched, Mrs. Lovett sings a refrain to the song back to the boy. So it's utterly chilling when late in that act she sings the refrain again as she searches frantically for Toby, who has discovered what is going on and must be taken care of.

Though I'm glad that *Sweeney Todd* and several other essential Sondheim musicals have found continued life in the opera house, I tend to find operatic productions disappointing. The score wants real actors, performers who can project words and attitude, not singers in love with their voices, a failing of many artists in opera. A performance must be fleet and incisive, with clarity of musical textures as well as text.

Therefore, the recording to have is the 1979 original cast version, with Lansbury and Cariou (who won Tony Awards for their work), Victor Garber as Anthony Hope, Merle Louise as the beggar woman (who turns out to be Todd's half-crazed and abandoned wife), Sarah Rice as Johanna, and Ken Jennings as Tobias. Most essential of all is the conductor Paul Gemignani. (The orchestrations are by the prodigiously skilled Jonathan Tunick.) Gemignani, who has been the musical director for most of Sondheim's musicals, understands this style better than any other conductor of my experience.

RCA Red Seal (two CDs) 3379-2-RC
Paul Gemignani (conductor); Lansbury, Cariou, Garber, Louise

69. RICHARD STRAUSS (1864–1949)

Salome

Richard Strauss, librettist, from Hedwig Lachmann's German translation of the play by Oscar Wilde

First performance: Dresden, Hofoper, December 9, 1905

In the last dozen years of the nineteenth century Richard Strauss won international acclaim for his trailblazing orchestral tone poems,

"Don Juan" and "Death and Transfiguration" among them. But his work in opera at that point was marginal: an ill-conceived first opera, *Guntram,* a medieval drama; and a ribald, one-act lyrical epigram, as he called it, *Feuersnot,* which enjoyed a somewhat scandalous success in 1901. With the 1905 premiere of *Salome,* though, Strauss announced himself as a formidable opera composer. Opera would dominate his work and his life for almost the entire first half of the new century.

One key to the success of *Salome* was that the work already existed as a stage play of proven effectiveness by Oscar Wilde, written in French for Sarah Bernhardt, though she never performed it. Strauss attended a production of the play, slightly abridged and translated into German by Hedwig Lachmann, in Berlin in 1903 and decided on the spot to make it into an opera, hewing closely to the Lachmann/Wilde text though he made some prudent cuts.

Yet, Wilde's *Salome,* with its ornately poetic language and lyrical effusions, was an arch take on the shocking biblical tale. That Wilde, for titillation, posed in drag as Salome for a now-famous photograph suggests what his attitude toward his own work really was.

Strauss treated the sensational story seriously. He was relatively unconcerned with its psychological undercurrents. Instead he turned *Salome* into an onrushing, tellingly structured, one-act, hundred-minute operatic tone poem. The idea that Jokanaan (John the Baptist) first sings while imprisoned below stage in a cistern fired Strauss's dramatic imagination. Even Salome's necrophilia, when she hungrily kisses the lips of Jokanaan's severed head, is depicted as a stunning musicodramatic effect, not as an entry into the mind of a morbidly disturbed young woman.

At its premiere in Dresden, Strauss and the cast received thirty-eight curtain calls. Still, it was considered a bristling, raw, vehement shocker, filled with "cruel dissonances" which defy explanation, in the words of Fauré, who admired the work. Today the dissonances may seem less cruel, more familiar, but the opera is still a shocker. Strauss contrasts Salome's music—boldly chromatic, harmonically unstable, constantly flitting from key to key—with Jokanaan's— prophetic, tonally grounded, full of rectitude, and intentionally stiff.

For the title role Strauss said his ideal soprano would be a

Conductor Georg Solti

"16-year-old princess with the voice of an Isolde." Wagnerian sopra-nos, like Birgit Nilsson, Astrid Varnay, and Leonie Rysanek, have excelled in the role. Yet singers with lighter voices, like Mary Garden, Teresa Stratas, and Phyllis Curtin, have brought out alluring lyrical aspects of the vocal writing. Ideally, of course, the role wants a singer who can look convincing while gyrating through the "Dance of the Seven Veils," though the large-framed Nilsson learned to convey the character's seductive sensuality with a minimum of strategic movements, confident that her vocal prowess would wow listeners into accepting her portrayal. Believe me, it did.

Birgit Nilsson's classic 1961 recording with Georg Solti conducting the Vienna Philharmonic Orchestra remains the best overall choice. While bringing her cool Nordic voice to the music, nailing the top notes with chilling power, she also managed to inflect Strauss's phrases where called for with a supple pliancy that many lyric sopranos would covet. Solti conducts an intense and simmering account of the score, without ever slipping into hyperdrive, a tendency of his later years. The baritone Eberhard Wächter as Jokanaan, the mezzo-soprano Grace Hoffman as Herodias, and the tenor Gerhard Stolze as Herod are also impressive.

Herbert von Karajan's 1978 recording with the Vienna Philharmonic and Hildegard Behrens in the title role offers another excellent choice and a different approach to the work. Karajan achieves intensity with haunting restraint and ravishing orchestra colors. And he milks the music for its touches of Germanic decadence: just listen to the way he shapes the fleeting bits of Viennese waltzes. Behrens may not be born to the role vocally, but she makes it her own, singing with tremulous excitement and dusky richness. If Strauss does not plumb the underside of Salome's character, Behrens certainly does in this volatile and unhinged portrayal. Agnes Baltsa as an earthy Herodias and José van Dam as an unflappable Jokanaan are also excellent.

Decca (two CDs) 414 414-2
Georg Solti (conductor), Vienna Philharmonic; Nilsson, Wächter, Stolze, Hoffman

EMI Classics (two CDs) 5 67159 2
Herbert von Karajan (conductor), Vienna Philharmonic; Behrens, van Dam, Baltsa

70. RICHARD STRAUSS (1864–1949)

Elektra

Hugo von Hofmannsthal, librettist, based on a play by Sophocles

First performance: Dresden, Hofoper, January 25, 1909

In 1903, a year after Strauss saw Wilde's *Salome,* performed in German translation, at Max Reinhardt's Kleines Theater in Berlin, he attended at the same theater with the same leading actress a new German version of Sophocles' *Electra* by Hugo von Hofmannsthal. Strauss was struck by the similarly raw tone and compact structure of the two plays, each moving in one dramatic arc of action. In 1906, with the premiere of *Salome* behind him, Strauss approached Hofmannsthal with the idea of turning *Elektra* (to conform to the German spelling) into an opera. So began one of the most productive and contentious collaborations in opera history.

Though ten years Strauss's junior, Hofmannsthal considered himself socially and intellectually the composer's superior. Born into an extremely cultured Viennese banking family of Austrian, Italian, and Jewish lineage, Hofmannsthal was an acknowledged poet and playwright when Strauss and he began working together.

Strauss's background was more complicated. Franz Strauss, Richard's father, was an illegitimate-born musician who became one of Germany's notable horn players. After the death of his first wife, Franz married the daughter of a prosperous family of Bavarian brewers. So when Richard was born the couple could provide him with an excellent education.

As is well known, the collaboration between composer and librettist took place mostly through an extensive correspondence, since they often resided in different cities and tended to rattle each other in person. Also, Hofmannsthal could not abide Strauss's intrusive and opinionated wife, Pauline. But the letters document in detail a landmark working relationship. Whatever their interpersonal tensions,

Strauss and Hofmannsthal elicited the best from each other and they knew it.

With *Elektra,* as with *Salome,* Strauss was again drawn to an existing stage play with a proven impact. Understanding the prehistory of the story, drawn from Greek mythology, is essential to entering into the opera. Agamemnon, the king of Argos and the commander of the Greek forces in the Trojan War, had left his wife, Klytämnestra, to rule in his absence. With Agamemnon away, Klytämnestra took a lover, Aegisth, her husband's bitter enemy. Together, they ruthlessly murdered the king when he returned to Greece from Troy.

When the opera begins, we learn that Elektra, Agamemnon's devoted older daughter, is consumed with hatred of her mother, anguish over the loss of her father, and a steely determination to avenge his murder. Elektra's obsession has taken over her life. She lives like a wild woman and is treated by the household servants like an animal. She and her weak-willed, terrified, but good-hearted sister Chrysothemis yearn for the return of their exiled brother, Orest, from whom they have had no word in years.

On the day the opera takes place Orest returns, unrecognizable at first to Elektra. Shocked by his sister's ravaged state and goaded by her into action, he ensnares and stabs to death first his mother and then her paramour.

Strauss's taut, inexorable, 110-minute score was audaciously dissonant and harmonically radical for its day. Many conductors drive the music hard, exaggerating its brutality and its barbaric outbursts. Yet, the more sensitive conductors are attuned to the music's fleeting and subdued moments of lyricism, as in the wrenching scene between the two sisters. Though also horrified by her murderous mother, Chrysothemis finds Elektra's self-consuming anger equally terrifying. She pleads with her sister to relent, to let go, so that the two women might actually experience a few moments of pleasure and affection in their lives. Strauss cushions Chrysothemis's pleas in music of consoling sadness and bittersweet lyricism. To me, the message of the opera is that by clinging to hatred and revenge you can destroy yourself. In the final scene, elated that she has brought about the retribution she had longed for, Elektra dances herself into a wild and ecstatic fit, finally collapsing lifeless on the ground.

I prefer performances of *Elektra* that allow the opera's stunning power to come through, but not at the expense of its poignancy. Georg Solti excels at this balance in his classic 1967 recording with Birgit Nilsson in the title role. He conveys the score's surging power and rippling tension, eliciting vibrantly colored and dynamically characterized playing from the incomparable Vienna Philharmonic. But he treats every lyrical turn in the score as an opportunity for repose, a time-out from the anxiety. In the opening scene, when five servant women jabber about the wild behavior of the unkempt Elektra, Solti revels in the bizarre comic quality of their music, not far removed in tone from the sardonic humor that would later permeate *Der Rosenkavalier*.

The luminous soprano Marie Collier as Chrysothemis, the earthy mezzo-soprano Regina Resnik as Klytämnestra, the robust baritone Tom Krause as Orest, and the nasal-toned tenor Gerhard Stolze as the sniveling Aegisth are all excellent. Nilsson, in one of her best roles, sings with cool radiance, abundant power, alluring subtlety, and, in the final scene, riveting abandon.

Another choice is the recording taken from a live concert performance in November 1988 with Seiji Ozawa conducting the Boston Symphony Orchestra. Ozawa's long tenure with the Boston Symphony produced exasperatingly uneven results, but this *Elektra* was among his finest achievements. The orchestra playing is dynamic, incisive, and palpably inspired. By this point in her career, the voice of Hildegard Behrens, who sings the title role, had started sounding rough-edged and unsteady. But she still gives an intense, insightful, and arresting performance, supported by Christa Ludwig's chilling Klytämnestra, Nadine Secunde's vulnerable Chrysothemis, and Jorma Hynninen's sturdy Orest.

Both recordings reveal *Elektra* as one of the most assured and original operas of the twentieth century.

Decca (two CDs) 417 345-2
Georg Solti (conductor), Vienna Philharmonic; Nilsson, Resnik, Collier, Krause

Philips (two CDs) 422 574-2
Seiji Ozawa (conductor), Boston Symphony Orchestra; Behrens, Ludwig, Secunde, Hynninen, Ulfung

---

Richard Strauss

71. RICHARD STRAUSS (1864–1949)

Der Rosenkavalier

Hugo von Hofmannsthal, librettist

First performance: Dresden, Königliches Opera House, January 26, 1911

After the stunning one-two punch of *Salome* and *Elektra*, Strauss decided that he should next give opera audiences something light, perhaps akin to a Mozart comedy. Hugo von Hofmannsthal felt similarly. Just weeks after the 1909 premiere of *Elektra* he wrote to Strauss to say that he was already at work on a scenario for an entertaining opera set in Vienna at the time of the Empress Maria Teresa.

There would be two main characters: an adolescent nobleman flush with romantic fervor, played by a woman in the tradition of Mozart's Cherubino; and a bass-baritone role, a blustery, self-important aristocrat, who would arrange to marry the comely daughter of a rich and ambitious commoner only to have the plan sabotaged when the two young people meet and fall in love.

The young nobleman and the aristocrat would become, respectively, the characters of Count Octavian and Baron Ochs. We would first encounter Octavian in the midst of an impulsive affair with an older woman, the Princess of Werdenberg, the wife of the Field Marshall of the Austrian army, hence called the Marschallin. But as Hofmannsthal and Strauss immersed themselves in the creative process they became more and more enamored of the Marschallin. Soon Strauss saw her as the emotional focal point of the opera, a direction that Hofmannsthal obligingly followed.

The Marschallin is surely one of the most believable and beloved characters in all of opera. Educated at a convent school, married young with no say in the matter to a prince, she seems to be undergoing a midlife crisis. But in often-quoted comments Strauss warned against casting the role with too old a soprano and playing the character as a resigned middle-aged woman. The Marschallin must be still beautiful, Strauss wrote, a woman of no more than thirty-two who in a sullen mood may think herself a has-been and fear that the best of life has already happened. Still, she is adored, however exaggeratedly, by a seventeen-year-old boy. And, as Strauss emphasized in oft-quoted recollections, Octavian "is neither the first nor the last lover of the beautiful Marschallin, nor must the latter play the end of the first act sentimentally, as a tragic farewell to life, but with Viennese grace and lightness, half weeping, half smiling."

Despite Strauss's words numerous sopranos have played the scene as a tragic farewell to at least a younger phase of life, and it's easy to understand why. After all, a woman of thirty-two in eighteenth-century Vienna was considered middle-aged. Moreover, Hofmannsthal gives the Marschallin such sadly wise things to say about the passage of time and the entry into later life. Today or tomorrow you will leave me for a younger and prettier woman, she tells the over-eager Octavian, who is still in the throes of puppy love. When he protests that she is heartless, the Marschallin counsels him that one must take life—and love—lightly, with light heart and light hands, hold and take, hold and let go ("halten und nehmen, halten und lassen"). Those who do not, she adds, will be punished by life and by God. Strauss sets these sentiments to the most wistfully lyrical music imaginable.

Yet, as *Der Rosenkavalier* evolved from a mere burlesque in the spirit of eighteenth-century opera and took on the dimensions of a ruminative music drama, Strauss lost his sense of how to balance its comic and tragic elements. Some of my favorite moments from all of opera are in this waltzing and bittersweet score. I adore the entire last third of the first act beginning with the Marschallin's monologue as she speaks to herself in her mirror, sees little signs of aging, then tries to have a sober chat with the love-struck boy. The "Presentation of the Rose" scene in act 2 is another of the opera's glories. Octavian, dressed like a young cavalier, presents a silver rose to Sophie Faninal, a token from the Baron to the young woman he has arranged to marry. Of course, the two adolescents fall in love at first sight. Strauss conveys the sense of magic hovering in the air by punctuating the beautifully restrained lyrical exchanges of Octavian and Sophie with soft, strange, seemingly random, off-key parallel chords in the orchestra, a touch that injects a "What's going on here?" quality into what should be an elegant but formal ceremony. And then, of course, there is the sublime final trio in which the Marschallin, seeing Octavian and Sophie, instantly figures out what has happened. She knows that a lovely episode in her life has ended. Now she will move on and literally cede the stage to the young lovers, which is as things should be.

Still, in many performances the long stretches of broad comedy can seem like intrusive, heavy-handed comic bits. You need a deft actor in the role of Baron Ochs to not make this character come off like a dumb parody of the oafish aristocrat. *Der Rosenkavalier* could easily lose a good half hour of its stock comic scenes and be better for the trimming.

So I prefer performances that don't overplay the comic elements, while bringing wistful elegance to the score's disarmingly lovely passages. Herbert von Karajan accomplishes this masterfully in his renowned 1956 recording with the Philharmonia Orchestra. That landmark recording has long been a subject of debate because of Elisabeth Schwarzkopf's Marschallin, which, like much of this German soprano's work, has divided listeners. Some find her the paragon of vocal artistry; others find her singing overinterpreted and mannered. I understand what Schwarzkopf's detractors object to. Still, to me her portrayal is vocally exquisite and psychologically penetrating. The entire cast is extraordinary, with the mezzo-soprano Christa Ludwig at her youthful and rich-voiced best as Octavian, the sweet-toned lyric soprano Teresa Stich-Randall as Sophie, and, crucially, the robust bass Otto Edelmann, a refined comic actor, as the Baron. Also, the recording was reissued in 1996 in a pressing that was reedited, with Schwarzkopf's guidance, from the original monaural master tapes, and the sound quality is warm, clear, and honest.

I may be in a minority on this one, but I cherish the 1971 recording with Leonard Bernstein conducting the Vienna Philharmonic and a splendid cast. The recording grew from a 1968 production at the Vienna State Opera, Bernstein's first time conducting the work. Like the composer and probing musician he was, Bernstein approached the score fresh, refusing to simply accept so-called performance traditions that had accrued to the work. To him these traditions were just excuses for lax rhythmic tension and too much Viennese easygoingness.

Bernstein's tempos, even when slow, are steady and clear; the orchestra textures are lucid. There is plenty of spacious and shimmering lyricism in this performance but also, where called for, a bracing intensity. And the Vienna Philharmonic, which could have probably played this score from memory, sounds reanimated and excited.

The mezzo-soprano Christa Ludwig, who had been an acclaimed Octavian, moves up here to the soprano role of the Marschallin and gives a distinguished and vocally rich performance. As Octavian, the soprano Gwyneth Jones sometimes sounds tremulous. Still, she makes an impassioned and vulnerable young count. The radiant soprano Lucia Popp is quite simply the best Sophie on record. You cannot believe the effortless, soaring, and angelic beauty of her singing. Walter Berry, the bass-baritone, is a dramatically savvy and vocally solid Ochs.

I couldn't choose between these two favorite recordings. Each one honors Strauss's most popular opera, a flawed but remarkable work.

EMI Classics (three CDs) 5 56113 2
Herbert von Karajan (conductor), Philharmonia Chorus and Orchestra; Schwarzkopf, Ludwig, Stich-Randall, Edelmann

Sony Classical (three CDs) 3 42564
Leonard Bernstein (conductor), Vienna Philharmonic, Chorus of the Vienna State Opera; Ludwig, Jones, Popp, Berry

72. RICHARD STRAUSS (1864–1949)

Ariadne auf Naxos

Hugo von Hofmannsthal, librettist

First performance of final version: Vienna, Hofoper, October 4, 1916

Ariadne auf Naxos went through several incarnations before it became the opera known today. Initially, Hugo von Hofmannsthal persuaded Strauss to collaborate on a short divertissement on the Ariadne myth, which was paired in performance with Hofmannsthal's German translation of Molière's play *Le Bourgeois gentilhomme*. This unwieldy confabulation never took hold with audiences. So Strauss and Hofmannsthal reconceived it as a two-act opera, before dropping the Molière element entirely and shaping the work into the familiar one-act opera with a prologue. Of course, some would charge that the final version is as much of a hodgepodge as that initial hybrid.

Through all the changes, the original idea of using low comedy to debunk the pretensions of serious opera remained intact. The Prologue tells a backstage drama about the preparations for a grand dinner party at the home of the richest man in eighteenth-century Vienna, whom we never meet. The host has arranged some entertainment for his guests. First will be the premiere of "Ariadne auf Naxos," a tragic opera by a serious-minded young composer. Following this will be an amusing show by a troupe of dancers and minstrels.

But the dinner has run late, so the Major-Domo of the house tells the assembled artists and entertainers that the host has changed his mind: to ensure that the guests will have time to get to a scheduled fireworks display that evening, the opera and the minstrel show will have to be performed simultaneously.

The composer, called, simply, the Composer, flies into an indignant rage. He will never survive the next hour, surely the most miserable of his life. But Zerbinetta, the coquettish star of the minstrel troupe, tries to calm down the hotheaded young man. "Oh, you'll survive a lot worse," she says. The Composer finds himself smitten with the young girl, who professes to have deeper complexities than her perky manner suggests. Perhaps the next hour will not be such a horror after all, the Composer thinks, before ending the Prologue with an impassioned paean to the uplifting power of music.

The opera that follows the intermission is meant to be the composer's work, "Ariadne auf Naxos," interspersed with the songs and dances of the minstrels. So as Ariadne, in her mythic desolation, alone on the Isle of Naxos, deserted by her beloved Theseus, sings of her wish to travel to the realm of death, the minstrels stroll in and try to cheer her up with some jolly songs and dances.

When performed and produced with sensitivity and wit, *Ariadne auf Naxos* can seem a miraculous work in which sadness and silliness blithely mingle. But performers must be able to convey the tenderness that underlies the comic bits and the whimsy that runs through the heroic flights. For me no recording does this better than Herbert von Karajan's 1954 account with the Philharmonia Orchestra. Elisabeth Schwarzkopf sings Ariadne, or, more precisely, the Prima Donna of the Prologue who portrays Ariadne in the "opera." Schwarzkopf's voice may be somewhat lighter than what Strauss had in mind, but Schwarzkopf gives one of her finest performances on record, shaping the phrases with unmannered directness and poignancy. The agile coloratura soprano Rita Streich as Zerbinetta and the dusky-toned soprano Irmgard Seefried as the Composer are also splendid.

Most impressive, though, is Karajan's work. For a conductor who took himself so seriously, he shows a surprisingly lighthearted touch in the comic scenes. For example, under Karajan's genial guidance the Harlekin's song in verse, sung with aching simplicity by the elegant baritone Hermann Prey, emerges as a sweetly forlorn little love ode.

To hear the title role sung gloriously by a Wagnerian soprano you'll want the 2000 recording featuring Deborah Voigt, with Giuseppe Sinopoli conducting the orchestra of the Staatskapelle Dresden. This role has become so important to Voigt that she has dubbed her career "Ariadne, Inc." You will never hear the music sung with such a wondrous combination of gleaming power and beguiling beauty. Yet, there is a wonderfully self-effacing, even self-debunking quality to

Voigt's portrayal, which lets the music's fancifulness come through along with its majesty.

The petite French coloratura Natalie Dessay makes an ideal Zerbinetta. Often, the elaborate scene and aria in which Zerbinetta explains herself to the mournful Ariadne (and, more important, to the audience) can seem like a tasteless, overwritten, even vulgar showpiece. But Dessay turns all the endless roulades, runs, and ornamental phrases into fine-spun streams of radiant singing. For once Zerbinetta's inner nature comes through. How can she not be fickle about men, Dessay's Zerbinetta asks with utter earnestness, when God created them in so many interesting varieties? The mezzo-soprano Anne Sofie von Otter is an impassioned and rich-voiced Composer.

Though Strauss was the ultimate pragmatist of opera, he miscalculated badly in composing the role of the Tenor who sings Bacchus, the god who comes to rescue Ariadne from her depression and distract her with the promise of new love, enhanced by a mystical love potion more commonly known as wine. The tessitura of the role sits uncomfortably high in the tenor voice; the long final duet, as daunting as any in Wagner, demands sustained and athletic singing from the tenor. Rudolf Schock sings it admirably on the Karajan recording, but Ben Heppner does even better paired with Voigt on Sinopoli's.

My only reservation concerns Sinopoli's conducting on what turned out to be his final recording before he collapsed of a heart attack onstage during a performance of *Aida* in Berlin in 2001, dead at fifty-four. Though Sinopoli elicits a dynamic and detailed account of the score from the orchestra, he fusses too much with the music, stretching this phrase, compressing that one. Still, you can't call his conducting dull. And you will seldom hear a stronger cast in this elusive yet enchanting work.

EMI (two CDs) 5 55176 2
Herbert von Karajan (conductor), Philharmonia Orchestra; Schwarzkopf, Streich, Seefried, Schock, Prey

Deutsche Grammophon (two CDs) 289 471 323-2
Giuseppe Sinopoli (conductor), Staatskapelle Dresden; Voigt, von Otter, Dessay, Heppner, Genz

---

73. RICHARD STRAUSS (1864–1949)

Die Frau ohne Schatten

Hugo von Hofmannsthal, librettist

First performance: Vienna, State Opera, October 10, 1919

As Richard Strauss once wrote to Hugo von Hofmannsthal, in picking opera subjects his strong inclination was for "realistic comedy with really interesting people." So he was rather wary when Hofmannsthal suggested that they make an opera based on a fairy tale. But Hofmannsthal adapted the story in ways that wound up enticing Strauss. Though *Die Frau ohne Schatten* (*The Woman without a Shadow*) has unwieldy elements and almost buckles under the weight of its metaphysical trappings, the opera is arguably their masterpiece.

Set in the mythical past, *Die Frau ohne Schatten* takes place in three spheres of existence. The spirit world is ruled by the god Keikobad, whom we never meet. The world of man is represented by Barak, a good-hearted but dull-witted Dyer whose shrewish wife is miserable over the grueling routine of their life and her childless state after nearly three years of marriage. There is also a middle world, half spiritual, half earthly, in which dwell the Emperor and Empress (Der Kaiser and Die Kaiserin in the opera). The daughter of Keikobad, the Empress has forsaken her godliness by marrying a quasi-mortal. She has no shadow, symbolizing her ethereal essence. Keikobad, dismayed by his daughter's impulsive marriage, has given her one year to become fully mortal by gaining a shadow, or else her husband will be turned to stone and she will be recalled to the spirit world.

That year is almost up. So the Empress's dour and mysterious nurse, whose main allegiance seems to be with Keikobad, proposes that she and her mistress descend to the home of the Dyer's Wife and persuade the unhappy woman to relinquish her shadow (in essence, her fertility) in exchange for riches, servants, young lovers, and whatever worldly pleasures she desires.

Strauss fretted to Hofmannsthal that the characters as conceived were too fantastical, that they could never be "filled with red corpuscles" in the same way as a Marschallin or an Octavian. He need not have worried, for his music invests them with a bittersweet humanity that turns the opera into a morality tale about the process of becoming human. When she meets Barak and his wife, the Empress is deeply touched to observe a married couple trying to sort through their contrary feelings and cope with constant deprivation. She cannot bear to go through with the bargain; nor, finally, can the Dyer's Wife give up her shadow. In the end both are rewarded for choosing compassion over selfishness. Keikobad's spell is broken and the couples reunite with newfound tenderness. You imagine that the longed-for babies will come along in no time.

More than any other of Strauss's mature scores, this one offers a rebuttal to the criticism that after the radicalism of *Salome* and *Elektra* he became increasingly conservative, retreating opera by opera into an obstinately tonal harmonic language. It's true that Strauss could never go along with Schoenberg's complete break with tonality. Still, in *Die Frau ohne Schatten* he rekindled tonality through some of his most excitingly restless, harmonically unstable, and continually inventive music. This score sounds too fresh, startling, and magical to label it conservative.

In any event, the opera's warmth and beauty are what ultimately make it great. The score abounds with amazing musical and dramatic strokes: the offstage chorus of unborn children who yearn for the Dyer and his wife to reconcile and procreate; the fearsome bellowing in the orchestra that conjures up the invisible presence of Keikobad; the wondrous music that accompanies the Empress's entrance, with its high-range vocal flights and shimmering harmonic radiance, identifying her as a creature of light and air.

The decent and befuddled Barak, one of Strauss's great characters, wins your heart as he tries to placate his bitter wife and recalls with wistfulness his own youth as part of a large and boisterously happy though struggling family. Strauss gives Barak music to match his hardy, self-effacing nature, including a theme of love for his wife—

my favorite melody in all of Strauss. Significantly, Barak is the only major character with a name. The others are identified only by their title or position.

The Vienna State Opera presented the famed 1919 premiere of *Die Frau ohne Schatten* with Lotte Lehmann as the Dyer's Wife, Richard Mayr as Barak, and Maria Jeritza as the Empress. The recording of choice was also made at the Vienna State Opera, a live recording from 1977 with the masterful Straussian Karl Böhm conducting and a cast that has never been topped. Birgit Nilsson's portrayal of the Dyer's Wife was a landmark in her career. She sings with cool radiance and steely power, but also, when called for, tremulous fragility. She has seldom sounded as touchingly vulnerable. Leonie Rysanek, another formidable dramatic soprano, brings a disarming combination of molten power and delicacy to the role of the Empress. The great bass-baritone Walter Berry as Barak and the robust heldentenor James King as the Emperor are matchless. Böhm conducts with such inexorable pacing you lose all sense of a pace-keeper at work. He captures the music's shifting moods and surging beauties. The orchestra plays with verve, richness, and glittering nuance.

Today's reigning Empress, Deborah Voigt, sang the role superbly for a recording taken from live performances at the Dresden State Opera in 1996, vibrantly conducted by Giuseppe Sinopoli. Some Strauss buffs think the tenor Ben Heppner's Emperor, sung with ringing tone and unforced power, the best on record. The baritone Franz Grundheber brings an unusual refinement to Barak, and Sabine Hass makes a dusky-toned and affecting though somewhat wobbly-voiced Dyer's Wife. Hanna Schwarz's strident Nurse gets tiring. Overall, much recommends this fine recording. But the Böhm version is legendary.

Deutsche Grammophon (three CDs) 415 472-2
Karl Böhm (conductor), Chorus and Orchestra of the Vienna State Opera; Rysanek, King, Nilsson, Berry, Hesse

Teldec (three CDs) 0630-13156-2
Giuseppe Sinopoli (conductor), Chorus and Orchestra of the Dresden State Opera; Voigt, Heppner, Hass, Grundheber, Schwarz

74. IGOR STRAVINSKY (1882–1971)

The Rake's Progress

W. H. Auden and Chester Kallman, librettists, after a series of etchings by William Hogarth

First performance: Venice, Teatro La Fenice, September 11, 1951

Igor Stravinsky was a slow worker. He produced, on average, one major composition per year. Of course, he lived many years and produced many works, about one hundred, though only a handful run longer than a half hour. The longest by far is his only full-length opera, *The Rake's Progress*. Each of its three acts took a year to compose.

By the time of the opera's premiere, in 1951 in Venice, with a luminous cast including Elisabeth Schwarzkopf, Robert Rounseville, and Jennie Tourel, the musical world was immensely curious. What had the most important living composer been up to?

Many of the cutting-edge modernists who attended, or heard reports, were baffled. For twenty years Stravinsky had been immersed in neoclassicism, his breathtaking effort to reanimate classical genres and forms through reinvented tonal procedures and complex shifting meters. To the modernists *The Rake's Progress* seemed a virtual pastiche of Mozartean opera, complete with numbered arias and harpsichord-accompanied recitatives. The negative reaction must have rattled Stravinsky, though, for he soon gave up neoclassicism and began exploring twelve-tone techniques.

But Stravinsky's neoclassicism was not merely an attempt to reinvent the past. In a way, his neoclassical works are music about other music. In *The Rake's Progress* you hear one of the greatest composers in history grappling with music he loves, questioning, wondering: "What is it about the Mozart operas with all their conventional forms and protocols that engages me? Why do I react the way I do?"

Composer Igor Stravinsky

Composing this beguiling and ingenious opera was Stravinsky's way of answering those questions.

The inspiration for the opera came in 1947 when Stravinsky saw an exhibit in Chicago of Hogarth's *Rake's Progress,* a series of eight engravings depicting the ruination of a young English gentleman. In one stroke Stravinsky got an idea for an opera, a title, and the gist of a story: an Englishman of no means and less discipline comes into an inheritance, wastes his money on gambling, needless luxuries, and whores, and winds up in a madhouse, where he is faithfully visited by the forgiving woman to whom he had been engaged. As many commentators have noted, the libretto, by W. H. Auden and Chester Kallman, evokes with fondness but also satire the ornate poetry of Pope and Congreve. The text is archly British and at times floridly poetic. Yet Stravinsky sets the words with clipped rhythms and fractured phrase lengths. Though some consider the text setting flawed, the irregularities seem a deliberate attempt to lend the poetry a contemporary edge.

If you read the libretto, the main characters might seem only emblematic: Tom Rakewell, the strapping, eager, but weak and improvident protagonist; Anne Trulove, the guileless, good-hearted daughter of a country widower; and the Devil in the guise of Nick Shadow, who becomes Tom's valet and tempts him into a life of extravagance and debauchery. Yet Stravinsky's precise, lucid, emotionally restrained music endows the characters with complexity and humanity.

Again and again in this score Stravinsky comes up with an idea that powerfully conveys the dramatic point. In the penultimate scene when Nick Shadow, having lost his wager and hence his claim to Tom's soul, starts back to the underworld, he chillingly announces that he still has the power to extract some revenge. So he turns Tom insane. The music that Tom then sings, accompanied by high-pitched and reedy woodwinds, sounds like some English pastoral air gone all jagged, off-kilter, and out of focus. And few arias in all of opera are more consolingly beautiful than the lullaby that Anne sings in the final scene to comfort Tom (who of course doesn't recognize her) and the other tormented inmates at the asylum.

There are two available recordings of Stravinsky conducting the opera, one documenting the Venice premiere at the Teatro La Fenice in 1951. Yet, the sound quality on this historic recording is only passable and there are some first-night jitters in the performance. The Stravinsky performance to have is his 1964 studio recording made in London for Columbia Records (now Sony) with the Royal Philharmonic Orchestra. The splendid cast includes the tenor Alexander Young as Tom, the soprano Judith Raskin as Anne, and the baritone John Reardon as Shadow. The performance is not flawless. Details in the orchestra are not always clear; Stravinsky sometimes fails to highlight arresting inner lines and pungent harmonies in the score that he may take for granted. Yet the conception has an organic rightness, the tempos work perfectly, and the performers sound understandably inspired.

Some first-rate recordings have come out in recent years, including the conductor John Eliot Gardiner's lithe performance with the

London Symphony Orchestra that gives the work the British flavor Stravinsky had in mind, thanks in part to two British artists, the tenor Ian Bostridge as Tom and the soprano Deborah York as Anne, and the Welshman Bryn Terfel as Shadow. The contrast between Bostridge's lyric tenor with its choirboy purity and Terfel's malevolently booming bass-baritone ignites the contest of wills between their characters.

Another excellent choice would be the 1995 recording with Seiji Ozawa conducting the Saito Kinen Orchestra, whose players come from the festival in Japan named in honor of Ozawa's beloved teacher. The respect these young musicians have for Ozawa comes through in their precise and vibrant playing. The excellent cast includes Anthony Rolfe-Johnson as Tom, Sylvia McNair as Anne, and Paul Plishka as Nick Shadow. It's fun to imagine how Auden and Kallman would react to hearing their archly British words sung with quite clear but hardly idiomatic diction by the well-drilled members of the Tokyo Opera Singers. Ozawa's fine recording suggests how important *The Rake's Progress* has become to the world of international opera.

Sony (two CDs) SM2K 46299
Igor Stravinsky (conductor), Sadler's Wells Opera Chorus, Royal Philharmonic Orchestra; Young, Raskin, Reardon

Deutsche Grammophon (two CDs) 289 459 648-2
John Eliot Gardiner (conductor), Monteverdi Choir, London Symphony Orchestra; Bostridge, York, Terfel, von Otter

Philips (two CDs) 454 431-2
Seiji Ozawa (conductor), Tokyo Opera Singers, Saito Kinen Orchestra; Rolfe-Johnson, McNair, Plishka, Bunnell

75. PETER ILYICH TCHAIKOVSKY

(1840–1893)

Eugene Onegin

Konstantin Stepanovich Shilovsky, librettist, after Pushkin's novel

First performance: Moscow, Malïy Opera Theatre, March 17 and 29, 1879, by students of the Moscow Conservatory

Like many composers drawn to opera, Tchaikovsky complained all the time about the difficulty of finding suitable subjects. After disappointing early efforts that included a historical costume drama and a folk comedy, he was more frustrated than ever.

Then, in the spring of 1877, during a social call, the contralto Yelizaveta Lavrovskaya, an acquaintance of Tchaikovsky, suggested that he make an opera of Pushkin's *Eugene Onegin*. As the composer later wrote to his younger brother and closest confidant, Modest, at first he dismissed Lavrovskaya's idea as "wild."

Pushkin's novel in verse was the most beloved work of Russian literature, widely admired for its all-knowing narrative tone, its irony, and its keen commentary on class-conscious Russian mores. Yet the story was almost deliberately uneventful.

In the opera, as in Pushkin, a landowner in the country has two impressionable daughters of marriageable age: Olga, who is cheerful by nature, and Tatyana, who is shy and pensive and filled with notions about love she has garnered from romantic novels. Olga is engaged to Lensky, an impetuous young man and aspiring poet of, it becomes clear, no appreciable talent. One day Lensky arrives with his friend from the big city, the dashing, cultivated, and privileged Eugene Onegin. Though he is quite aloof and somewhat dandyish, Tatyana immediately sees Onegin as a soul mate. That night she writes him a boldly impassioned letter. The next day he coolly but politely explains that he has no intention of forming an attachment just now.

Some time later, during a birthday dance for Tatyana, Onegin, bored as usual with the rituals of country life, overhears some gossip about himself: he is a drunkard and, even more shocking, a Freemason. To provoke the guests he dances flirtatiously with Olga. Deeply offended, Lensky challenges Onegin to a duel and when the former friends meet the next day, Lensky is killed.

Some years have passed before the third act begins. Onegin, now chastened by his haughty disregard of Tatyana and yearning for something meaningful in his life, visits her in St. Petersburg. She is now married to a kindly and older prince. Onegin admits to his longings and Tatyana concedes that she too still loves him. But she will not abandon her husband. Left alone, Onegin sinks into despair.

As we know from a letter Tchaikovsky wrote to Modest, after dismissing the suggestion of an opera based on *Eugene Onegin,* Tchaikovsky spent a sleepless night consumed by the idea. By the next day he had written a scenario that proved to be an effective basis for the libretto by Shilovsky. To make clear that he was not attempting a comprehensive adaptation of Pushkin's complex novel, Tchaikovsky fashioned his opera as a series of seven "lyric scenes" taken from the story.

That he was drawn to a main character so initially devoid of emotions might seem curious. It was during the composition of this opera that Tchaikovsky, a tormented and secret homosexual, endured his brief and disastrous marriage to a smitten student from the conservatory. Tchaikovsky was acquainted with hidden passion, longing, anxiety, guilt and shame, and depression. But the opera can be seen as a cautionary tale about the tragic results of being aloof from one's own feelings.

He brought to the task his illimitable melodic gift and profound ability to convey character through music. Tatyana's "Letter Scene" is an achingly true depiction of a bookish yet impetuous young woman whose meeting with a man who practically ignores her unleashes years of pent-up longings. Pushkin makes clear the inelegance of Lensky's hapless poetry by giving readers some sample verses. Tchaikovsky accomplishes the same through slyly musical means: Lensky declares his love for Olga in a "charmingly conventional melody," to quote the scholar John Warrack.

Tchaikovsky found other musical ways to match the subtleties of this sacrosanct literary work. He vividly depicts local color and sketches the social backgrounds of his characters through his deft use of folk music and dance, not real folk themes lifted from an anthology but his own earthy evocations, as in the rustic yet beautifully wistful chorus and dance for the peasants in the opening scene. Also, he provides a musical counterpart to Pushkin's irony. For example, in the last scene, when Onegin effusively professes his love for the married Tatyana and castigates his earlier obliviousness, we hear a fleeing recollection of the music with which he rejected her.

Tchaikovsky was so determined that *Eugene Onegin* seem believable that he insisted the 1879 world premiere be presented by the students of the Moscow Conservatory, a cast of fledgling singers who looked and acted like the characters they portrayed. That performance was only marginally successful. The work did not catch on until after the professional premiere two years later at the Bolshoi Opera.

But the qualities of youthful urgency that Tchaikovsky imagined come through in the 1992 Philips recording, with the dynamic Russian conductor Semyon Bychkov leading the Orchestre de Paris and an impressive cast. The Siberian-born baritone Dmitri Hvorostovsky makes an ideal Onegin. Hvorostovsky's refinement conveys Onegin's cultivation, just as his restrained delivery suggests Onegin's hauteur. Yet the poignant richness and sheer charisma of Hvorostovsky's singing make clear that Onegin has teeming inner emotions he works hard to ignore. Lensky's emotions are right on the surface in the vivid portrayal by the clarion-voiced tenor Neil Shicoff. Though the soprano Nuccia Focile has a somewhat earthy sound for Tatyana, she gives a deeply expressive and handsomely vocalized performance. The mezzo-soprano Olga Borodina brings touching warmth to Olga, a character who can sometimes seem too chirpy. The stentorian bass Alexander Anisimov as Prince Gremin offers an affecting account of the noble last act aria in which this husband's decency and genuine regard for his young wife are made manifest. Bychkov conducts a radiant, subtly nuanced, and aptly rhapsodic account of Tchaikovsky's deservedly popular opera.

Philips (three CDs) 438 235-2
Semyon Bychkov (conductor), Orchestre de Paris, St. Petersburg Chamber Choir; Hvorostovsky, Focile, Shicoff, Borodina, Anisimov

76. PETER ILYICH TCHAIKOVSKY

(1840–1893)

Pique Dame (The Queen of Spades)

Modest Ilyich Tchaikovsky and the composer, librettists, after Pushkin's novella of 1833

First performance: St. Petersburg, Mariinsky Theatre, December 7 (19), 1890

As well as I know the music, whenever I hear the opening of act 2, scene 2 from *Pique Dame* I am stunned again by the dramatic nuance, psychological insight, and musical inspiration Tchaikovsky demonstrates as an opera composer.

Herman, a brooding and frustrated soldier in late-eighteenth-century St. Petersburg, has fallen helplessly in love with a woman far above his station, Lisa, the granddaughter of a bitter old countess. But Herman's romantic feelings are trumped by his obsession with gambling. He has heard stories that, as a young woman in Paris known throughout aristocratic circles as "The Venus of Moscow," the countess lost her fortune at the gambling table, but won it back when, in exchange for her sexual favors, she was given a secret winning combination of three cards by a French count. Since then she has revealed the secret only twice. As we learn, the countess, who believes in such things, has heard a prophecy that she would die at the hands of the third person were she to impart the winning combination again, which is what happens in this act 2 scene.

The tormented Herman is driven to learn the secret, win a fortune, pay off his debts, and claim Lisa, who has been promised to someone else. He skulks into the countess's empty bedroom late one night after a masquerade ball she has attended. As an ominous orchestral ostinato quietly drones on, the violins play a yearning melody in broken phrases, juxtaposed with a suspenseful motif in pizzicato basses.

Then, as the orchestra music continues, Herman sings a halting solil-oquy affirming his scheme, pausing only to view an enormous full-length portrait of the countess in the glory of her youth, "la Venus muscovite," he says sarcastically.

Hearing the countess and her retinue of women attendants com-ing into the room, Herman hides himself. The servants sing a fasci-natingly ambiguous chorus to the countess. It sounds like some wistful old folk song with a gently insistent gait, a tune that seems uplifting on the surface, yet weighted with regret. They flatter the old woman. "How did our noble benefactress enjoy herself?" they ask, calling her "the light of our eyes." They compliment her for putting on a brave show and assure her that though some at the ball may have been younger, "none were fairer." Naturally, the jaded old woman, who sinks into an armchair, does not believe them. Still, it's a ritual she has come to expect; and a remarkable operatic stroke.

Like *Eugene Onegin, Pique Dame* was also adapted from Pushkin—a short and grim novella that another opera composer might have deemed suitable only for a one-act shocker. But working with a libretto by his brother, Modest, Tchaikovsky boldly expanded the story and pushed back the setting from the time of Alexander I to the reign of Catherine the Great (1762–1796). This allowed him to evoke the era of his beloved Mozart. Indeed, the act 2 ball scene includes a Mozartean pastiche when the guests are entertained by a divertissement: "The Faithful Shepherdess," complete with a pas-toral dance, a lyrical love duet, and a gentle parody of the peasant chorus from *Don Giovanni*. The episodes of the pastiche might at first seem incongruous with the gruesome story. It ends with the dis-traught Lisa, shaken by Herman's gambling obsession, drowning herself in a river. Herman stabs himself to death at the card table when the secret combination he extracted from the countess before she died of fright turns out to be a sham. Yet Tchaikovsky knew that the lighter music could both evoke the era and provide a context for Herman's addiction.

And, as presented by Tchaikovsky, Herman does suffer from an addiction that utterly claims him. Tchaikovsky, a tormented and secret homosexual, knew something of illicit obsessions. In a way, like Her-man, he felt that life had dealt him a bad hand, that the cards were stacked against him. Tchaikovsky's Herman is as deluded, aggrieved, fitful, and menacing as Verdi's Otello. And for a tenor the role is just as challenging.

As with so many other Russian operas, the conductor Valery Gergiev's recording, taken from live performances in May 1992 by the Kirov Opera at the Mariinsky Theatre in St. Petersburg, is, all in all, the one to have. This was the company that presented the 1890 premiere of the opera. Gergiev draws a rich, resonant, moody, and tellingly detailed performance from the Kirov Orchestra, and his fine cast brings a palpable understanding of the Russian style to its work. As Herman, the tenor Gegam Gregorian is a volatile and frightening force. Every time he starts to win your sympathy with some baffled and poignant reflection, he erupts with unhinged anger. The soprano Maria Guleghina brings lustrous sound and lyrical intensity to the role of Lisa, recorded in the years before she turned herself, with mixed results, into a vocal powerhouse. The plush-voiced mezzo-soprano Olga Borodina gives a beguiling performance as Pauline, Lisa's confidante. The baritone Vladimir Chernov is a distinguished and aptly melancholic Yeletsky, the patient prince to whom Lisa is betrothed before she gets swept away by Herman's aggressive passion. And the veteran Irina Arkhipova makes a riveting countess, a role that demands almost nothing vocally but occupies the dramatic core of the opera.

Philips (three CDs) 438 141-2
Valery Gergiev (conductor), Kirov Opera and Orchestra, Mariinsky Theatre, St. Petersburg; Gregorian, Guleghina, Borodina, Chernov, Arkhipova

77. VIRGIL THOMSON (1896–1989)

Four Saints in Three Acts

Gertrude Stein, librettist

First performance: Hartford, Connecticut, Avery Memorial Theatre, Wadsworth Atheneum, February 8, 1934

Despite a twenty-two-year age difference, from the moment Virgil Thomson and Gertrude Stein met in Paris in late 1925, they "got along like a couple of Harvard boys," as Thomson would later write. One important thing they had in common was a devotion to her writing. Thomson had been drawn to Stein's famously hermetic prose since college. His longed-for meeting with Stein prodded him finally to set her words to music.

As he would later write in his autobiography, Thomson's hope in putting Stein to music was "to break, crack open, and solve for all time anything still waiting to be solved, which was almost everything, about English musical declamation." His theory was that if a text were "set correctly for the sound of it," then the meaning would take care of itself. To this end, Stein's texts, with their meanings already abstracted, or even absent, were "manna," he wrote. There was no temptation toward "tonal illustration, say, of birdie babbling by the brook or heavy heavy hangs the heart." You could make a setting "for sound and syntax only."

The first text Thomson set was a wonderfully rich yet seemingly hermetic portrait called "Susie Asado." Stein was delighted with the result, and so was Thomson. So after a while the idea naturally sprang up of collaborating on an opera.

Both agreed that they wanted something startling, wondrous, and radical. Nothing realistic. They settled on a metaphorical idea in which the lives of a community of sixteenth-century Spanish saints would represent the working artist's life, that is, the very life that Thomson and Stein and their artist friends were living in 1920s Paris.

The two main characters would be based on historical figures: St. Teresa of Avila and St. Ignatius of Loyola. But Stein wound up filling her libretto with made-up saints, far more than the "four" of the title. The saints would be shown living as a community amid pleasantries while devoted to something larger than themselves, God, just as the Parisian artists in the Stein circle were devoted to something larger than themselves, art.

Stein embraced the idea and was soon afire with inspiration, though in letters to Thomson she spoke of the "struggle" she had in getting the words to take shape as an opera. You might wonder what the struggle involved when you read the text. Consider the opening lines:

> To know to know to love her so.
> Four saints prepare for saints.
> It makes it well fish.

Or, this typical line: "Believe two three. What could be sad beside beside very attentively intentionally and bright."

Thomson adored the text and set every word of it, including, such as they are, the stage directions. Naturally, he had scant idea of what the words meant and no idea of what was going on. Stein offered only vague suggestions as to what might be happening. In one scene, she said, the saints have a vision of a heavenly mansion and speculate about it: "How many doors how many floors and how many windows are there in it." One scene was clearly a type of funeral procession with incantatory repetitions: "in said led wed dead wed dead said led led said wed dead wed dead led." There was also St. Ignatius's wondrous vision of the Holy Ghost: "Pigeons on the grass alas." Among the characters are a Compère and a Commère who serve as the host and hostess for the evening, welcoming the audience, introducing new scenes, and commenting on the opera as it goes along.

The text invited Thomson to create a musical pageant, a latter-day, recitative-driven opera seria, something elegant and noble, not without whimsy and wit, but a thoroughly fresh, delightfully disorienting, and vibrant spectacle. Thomson sets the words with syntactical clarity and the natural rhythms of speech. In a good performance

Stein's words should bound from the stage. His music evokes hymns both of the ancient and Southern Baptist variety, marches, ditties, Spanish dances, children's play songs. Long stretches of the words are set in an arioso-type of vocal writing that Thomson came to call his "Missouri plainchant." The simplicity of the score is deceptive. With a special kind of sophistication, Thomson makes familiar musical materials sound discombobulating. The score is rich with subtle harmony and lucid contrapuntal writing, and imaginatively conceived writing for an orchestra that includes an accordion and a harmonium.

Still, what is the opera about? When Thomson finished composing it, he turned the whole work over to his close friend and on-and-off lover, the painter Maurice Grosser, who devised a scenario in which a succession of scenes show the saints in their daily routines, exchanging courtesies, being entertained by a roster of dancers, tending to daily tasks like the mending of fishnets, and, in the brief final act (and there are four not three acts, despite the title), enjoying their heavenly reward in the afterlife.

It took six years for a production to come about, during which time Thomson and Stein had a nearly four-year-long spat. That original production in February 1934 has joined the annals of American avant-garde history. *Four Saints in Three Acts* inaugurated a theater in a new wing for modern art at the Wadsworth Atheneum in Hartford, Connecticut. The elegant costumes and fanciful cellophane sets were by the artist Florine Stettheimer. The choreographer was the young Frederick Ashton. John Houseman, embarking on his first work in the theater, served as a creative producer/director. The conductor was Alexander Smallens, who would the next year preside over the premiere of *Porgy and Bess*. And, at Thomson's insistence, the entire cast, singers and dancers alike, were black. After the Hartford premiere the production played on Broadway for six weeks, eliciting equal measures of rapture and ridicule from audiences and critics, which pretty much remains the reaction. But in a sensitive performance *Four Saints in Three Acts* is a bold, disarming, humanely amusing, and deeply spiritual work.

The only available full-length recording, on the Nonesuch label, though not ideal, offers an honorable account of the work, recorded shortly after a live performance at Carnegie Hall in 1981 to celebrate Thomson's eighty-fifth birthday. Joel Thome, an able conductor with palpable respect for the work, directs the Orchestra of Our Time and a fine cast including the splendid mezzo-soprano Betty Allen (a lifelong friend of Thomson's) as the Commère, the stentorian bass Benjamin Matthews as the Compère, the hardy baritone Arthur Thompson as St. Ignatius, and the distinguished duo of soprano Clamma Dale and mezzo-soprano Florence Quivar as St. Teresa I and II. (After receiving Stein's completed libretto Thomson decided to divide the long role of St. Teresa in two. He thought the idea of having the strong-willed saint sing duets with herself would be modernistic and charming.) I admire this recording and recommend it.

The truly glorious recording of the work is, unfortunately, incomplete. In 1947 Thomson conducted a performance of the opera on the radio with several members of the original 1934 cast. Alas, as Stein might say, due to time constraints he was compelled to abridge the score by half. Still, the performance is a miracle. The original Commère and Compère—Altonell Hines and Abner Dorsey—could not be more elegant. The original St. Teresa I, Beatrice Robinson-Wayne, a soprano who might have had a major career had the world of opera in the 1930s not been closed to black artists, brings warmth, tenderness, and charisma to her affecting performance. The suave baritone Edward Matthews as St. Ignatius makes the visions of "pigeons on the grass alas" truly seem a revelation. But it's Thomson's conducting, at once incisive and exuberant, and the spirited singing of the chorus that make even this abbreviated *Four Saints in Three Acts* essential.

Nonesuch (two CDs) 9 79035-2
Joel Thome (conductor), Orchestra of Our Time; Allen, Matthews, Thompson, Dale, Quivar

RCA Victor Red Seal (one CD) 09026-68163-2
Virgil Thomson (conductor), Chorus and Orchestra assembled by Thomson; Robinson-Wayne, Greene, Matthews, Hines, Dorsey

78. VIRGIL THOMSON (1896–1989)

The Mother of Us All

Gertrude Stein, librettist

First performance: New York, Brander Matthews Theatre, Columbia University, May 7, 1947

In 1984 the erudite music critic Andrew Porter wrote that every time he hears *The Mother of Us All* he is "tempted to consider it the best of all American operas" and, on calm reflection, would "hardly modify that beyond 'one of the three best.'" If Thomson's second and final collaboration with Gertrude Stein is better known, more widely appreciated, and far more often produced than the first, it's probably because *The Mother of Us All* more or less tells a story and has a plot, fractured and nonsensical, perhaps, but still a plot.

The opera presents the story of Susan B. Anthony and the campaign for women's suffrage. We meet Susan B., as she is called throughout the opera, in a domestic scene sitting at home with her devoted companion Anne, probably meant to be Anna Howard Shaw, a young suffragette who lived with Anthony toward the end of her life. We see Susan B. in a great public debate with a political antagonist, Daniel Webster. There are scenes of Susan B. reflecting on the progress of her cause, questioning a character called Negro Man about his views on equality for women, presiding over a wedding, and suffering a bitter setback when politicians after the Civil War grant freed male slaves the right to vote while women are still denied. In a mystical epilogue, a statue of Susan B. Anthony, who has died before seeing her dream realized, is unveiled. Left alone, Susan B. reflects on "all my long life" of "effort and strife."

Of course, this being an opera by Stein the story is filled with a menagerie of characters—some made up, some based on historical figures, including real friends and colleagues of the two creators—who never could have interacted as they do here. Jo the Loiterer and

Chris the Citizen are recently discharged Civil War veterans, Jo being a stand-in for Stein's friend Joseph Barry, an American soldier she met during World War II who became a journalist and author and was actually charged with loitering during his days as a student picketer. We meet John Adams (probably John Quincy Adams), who spends most of his stage time courting a woman unfortunately beneath his lofty station, Constance Fletcher. A gruff Ulysses S. Grant, the alluring actress Lillian Russell, and Donald Gallup (another one of Stein's beloved American soldiers, who would later become a librarian at Yale University and the curator of the Stein Collection) interact with each other along with Andrew Johnson, Thaddeus Stevens, and other historical figures.

Thomson was able to shape the libretto to his purposes because it turned out to be Stein's last completed work. With a commission in hand from Columbia University, supported by the Alice M. Ditson Fund, Thomson began working on the opera with Stein in 1945. By the next year she had died of cancer, before Thomson had written a note. He again called upon Maurice Grosser, who had devised a scenario for *Four Saints in Three Acts,* to help make *The Mother* more explicit in its dramaturgy. They cut some scenes, switched the order of others, and restored an idea Stein had considered and rejected of having a character named Virgil T. appear in the opera. Thomson took some of Virgil T.'s lines and gave them to a character named Gertrude S. So, like the Commère and Compère in *Four Saints in Three Acts,* Gertrude S. and Virgil T. serve as our hosts for the evening, introducing characters and scenes and commenting on the opera as it progresses. During the great debate, Virgil T. gets the crowd going with some nonsensical rabble-rousing.

In creating the opera Thomson and Stein were inspired by a shared passion for nineteenth-century political oratory, the era when grandiloquent speeches captured the lifeblood of the nation and citizens of every station would travel long distances to hear Lincoln, Douglas, or whomever, debate the issues of the day for hours at a time. Though, as in *Four Saints,* Thomson sets whole stretches of dialogue with his self-styled "Missouri plainchant," the score vividly evokes sounds that would have been familiar to all Americans in the 1940s: concert bands playing waltzes in the park; military marching bands on the Fourth of July; church organs; parlor songs sung around the piano; schoolyard ditties; Negro gospel choirs. Though bugle calls and fanfares are built right into the contours of the vocal lines, a continuous and beguiling lyrical thread runs through the entire score and binds this story together. Susan B. ponders her life and work in wistfully melodic ruminations. Yet astringent bouts of bi-tonality and dissonant harmonies accompany cold weather, pre-monitions of defeat for the cause, General Grant's bluster, and patri-archal prejudices against women.

As of this writing there is only one full-length recording of the work. Fortunately it's a good performance that documents a produc-tion at the Santa Fe Opera in 1976 to mark the American Bicenten-nial. Raymond Leppard, at the time best known for his work in early music, conducts a lively, clear-textured, and sensitive account of a score he obviously admires. The cast enters into the joyous and won-derfully disorienting spirit of the work. Thomson was not pleased that Mignon Dunn, a thick-voiced mezzo-soprano, was chosen to sing Susan B., a role he had conceived for a strong and high soprano: "They got the wrong girl!" he told me. Dunn may not be ideal, but the more I listen to this recording the more I admire the earthy vigor and sheer charisma she brings to her portrayal. For the most part the other cast members do admirable work, especially Batyah Godfrey as Anne, Philip Booth as Daniel Webster, James Atherton as Jo the Loi-terer, Linn Maxwell as his spunky bride Indiana Elliot, William Lewis as John Adams, and Helen Vanni as Constance Fletcher.

In 1940 Thomson became the chief music critic at the *New York Herald Tribune*. So he saw Stein infrequently during the last six years of her life. He used to say that it never occurred to him or Gertrude that either of them would die. "Otherwise," he would say, "we would have written an opera every year." If only!

New World Records (two CDs) 288/289-2
Raymond Leppard (conductor), Santa Fe Opera Orchestra and Chorus; Dunn, Godfrey, Booth, Atherton, Maxwell, Lewis, Vanni

79. GIUSEPPE VERDI (1813–1901)

Macbeth

Francesco Maria Piave, librettist, with additional material by Andrea Maffei, after Shakespeare

First performance: Florence, Teatro della Pergola, March 14, 1847; revised version: Paris, Théâtre-Lyrique, April 21, 1865

Verdi was a devoted and perceptive reader of Shakespeare. But he wrote nine operas before he finally took on a Shakespeare play, *Macbeth*. It was partly the generous circumstances of the commission from a fine theater in Florence that convinced him to adapt a play he called "one of the greatest creations of man." "If we can't do something great with it," he said in a letter to his librettist, Piave, quoted in the *New Grove Dictionary of Opera*, "let us at least try to do something out of the ordinary."

The commission allowed him all the input into the production that he could possibly want. Though he was generally pleased with Piave's libretto, he kept insisting on changes and, when still not satisfied, turned to his colleague Andrea Maffei for further retouches. Verdi was a constant presence at the rehearsals where he coerced the production team into complying with his wishes and extensively coached the handpicked cast. The 1847 premiere was a triumph. But even then he was unhappy. So when a Paris production was proposed in 1865, he took the opportunity to revise the score some more. Most productions today use the revised version.

The role of Macbeth is a superb creation. Verdi conveys the character's tragic passivity in music that strives to be regal but is undercut by halting complexity, as in "Mi si affaccia un pugnal?" ("Is this a dagger I see before me?") This arioso begins the Grand Scene and Duet of act 1, when Macbeth sees a horrific vision of a dagger and bolsters himself to murder King Duncan. In the final scene, Macbeth's confessional aria "Pieta, rispetto, amore" ("Compassion, honor, love") achieves tragic grandeur as the poignant phrases are rattled by restless harmonic modulations driven by the orchestra.

The main difference that lovers of Shakespeare will discern in Verdi's operatic adaptation, though, is the increased presence, indeed, almost the dominance, of Lady Macbeth. Her introductory scene, when performed effectively, should be a riveting tour de force. It begins with Lady Macbeth reading aloud the letter she has received from her husband describing the predictions of the witches. Then she sings a chilling double aria, first "Vieni! t'affretta!" in which, through steely, soaring vocal lines supported by the coolly urgent chordal accompaniment of the orchestra, she bids Macbeth to come home quickly so together they can make the predictions come true. When she learns from a messenger that Duncan is to visit that very night, Lady Macbeth sings a ferocious cabaletta, a quick-paced aria of resolution, "Or tutti sorgete," in which bravura bel canto vocal flights are reined in by the aria's formal structure and relentless accompaniment. It's as if the orchestra, acting as a commentator, can barely control the woman's bloody ambition.

Verdi once wrote that Lady Macbeth's voice should be "hard, stifled and dark," the voice of a "devil." Surely he exaggerated to make the point that some generically beautiful soprano voice would be all wrong. One Lady Macbeth managed to convey the hard-edged, dark, and devilish qualities that Verdi had in mind, yet also sing with vocal culture, chilling authority, and a visceral beauty that is anything but pretty: Shirley Verrett on the 1975 recording with Claudio Abbado conducting the forces of La Scala. Paradoxically, at the time Verrett was still considered a mezzo-soprano. But any doubts that she had the voice to sing this demanding, weighty soprano role were expelled by the reaction to her performance in the La Scala production that led to this studio recording. Such performances led the Milanese fans to dub Verrett "La Negra Callas" (The Black Callas). Because she was a mezzo-soprano, the dusky and deep colorings of her voice lend her singing the quality Verdi was after. Yet in the eerie sleepwalking scene she sings the aching lines with poignant lyricism and caps the aria with a pianissimo high D-flat that many a full-time soprano would covet. The burnished power, clarion top notes, devilishly agile execution of the coloratura embellishments, dramatic insight, and coolly sensual allure of her performance make it one of the classics of the Verdi discography.

And the entire performance is excellent. Abbado's work is vibrant, supple, and sensitive. The baritone Piero Cappuccilli, a great Verdian, brings idiomatic phrasing and, as the king is forced to face his villainy, pitiable anguish to his portrayal of Macbeth. Plácido Domingo sounds fresh-voiced and fearless as the determined Macduff. The bass Nicolai Ghiaurov is a gravelly Banco (Banquo).

Fortunately, Deutsche Grammophon has reissued this recording on its prestigious Originals series, so it should be readily available.

Deutsche Grammophon (two CDs) 449 732-2
Claudio Abbado (conductor), Orchestra and Chorus of the Teatro alla Scala; Verrett, Cappuccilli, Domingo, Ghiaurov

80. GIUSEPPE VERDI (1813–1901)

Rigoletto

Francesco Maria Piave, librettist, after a tragedy by Victor Hugo

First performance: Venice, Teatro La Fenice, March 11, 1851

Often when a production updates the story of an opera to a contemporary setting the concept just seems a self-conscious attempt to make an old work newly relevant. But the director Jonathan Miller's updated production of *Rigoletto,* introduced at the English National Opera in 1982, provided some revelatory insights into Verdi's work.

Miller zapped the story from sixteenth-century Mantua to Manhattan's Little Italy in the 1950s. The rapacious Duke of Mantua becomes the Duke, a dashing and fearsome local mafia boss. And in an inspired imaginative leap, the hunchback jester becomes Rigoletto, the bartender at the restaurant where the Duke and his men hang out. Though on the job Rigoletto must let himself be the butt of everyone's jokes, he is also expected to keep everyone entertained, which he typically does by mimicking the men who cower in the Duke's presence. He has kept the existence of his daughter, Gilda, secret by sending her away to school, though when the opera opens, as in the original setting, she has just returned home.

In any setting *Rigoletto,* adapted from a Victor Hugo play, is a disturbing tale of power relationships. The jester defends himself against the pity and contempt of the Duke's courtiers by laughing at himself first and then turning the jokes back on them.

Yet to me Verdi's *Rigoletto* is also an insightful exploration of the catastrophes that can result by keeping secrets. Rigoletto thinks he can protect his innocent daughter by keeping her in the dark about their family background and isolating her from the cutthroat outside world. He tells her nothing of his origins and little about her dead mother, except to say that she was an angel from heaven. Fear that the courtiers would think it a lark to seduce the daughter of a hunchback jester drives him to be an overbearing and paranoid parent. But his secrecy just makes Gilda more curious about the outside world. So it's not surprising that on walks to church with the family maid, Gilda has been smitten with the dashing Duke, disguised as a poor student.

The story inspired Verdi to one of his most assured and multi-textured scores. It opens not with an overture but with an orchestral prelude that encapsulates the opera's bleak mood and essential themes. *Rigoletto* marks Verdi's passage from early striving to midcareer maturity. There are ingenious strokes, as when the hired assassin, Sparafucile, encounters Rigoletto on the street at night and offers his services, should they ever be needed. As the two men converse in almost naturalistic vocal lines, a deceptively innocuous theme is played by a solo cello and bass, accompanied eerily by low strings. Horrified, Rigoletto shoos him away. But their exchange leads Rigoletto into an impassioned Verdian soliloquy ("Pari siamo") in which he bitterly reflects that he and the assassin are not really so different: Sparafucile wounds with daggers, Rigoletto with words.

Yet, this haunting score also contains some arias that were cleverly crafted to be big hits, notably the Duke's cavalier ode to the lovable fickleness of women, "La donna e mobile." And the act 4

Composer Giuseppe Verdi

quartet in which the Duke and his latest interest, the assassin's sister Maddalena, cavort in a remote lodge by a riverbank as Rigoletto and Gilda watch with dismay from outside is a classic example of what makes opera opera: four characters at odds with one another expressing themselves simultaneously in deliriously engaging music. This is what opera can do that stage drama can't.

Rigoletto has fared well on recordings, so let me recommend three worthy choices. I still love my first recording, the 1950 RCA album with the incomparable Verdi baritone Leonard Warren in the title role, the coloratura soprano Erna Berger as pristine-voiced Gilda, and the Duke of the beloved American tenor Jan Peerce, who may not have had a glorious voice, but sings with Verdian flair and intelligence. Renato Cellini draws a dynamic performance from the RCA Victor Orchestra. For sheer vocal splendor you can't go wrong with the 1971 Decca recording featuring the virile baritone Sherrill Milnes as Rigoletto, Luciano Pavarotti in radiant voice as a stylish but slightly scene-stealing Duke, and Joan Sutherland as a Gilda who is a little too vocally resplendent to come across as innocent, but is certainly a treat to hear. Richard Bonynge conducts the London Symphony Orchestra in a historically informed and surely paced performance. The recording I most tend to reach for, though, is the 1955 La Scala performance with the great Italian stylist Tito Gobbi as Rigoletto, the great but inconsistent tenor Giuseppe di Stefano, who is in radiant voice as the Duke, and Maria Callas as Gilda. Callas gave only two stage performances of this role, in 1952. But on this recording she sings with an affecting blend of insight, passion, and heart-melting fragility. Tullio Serafin conducts with dramatic sweep and sure understanding.

Preiser Records (two CDs) 90452
Renato Cellini (conductor), RCA Victor Orchestra; Warren, Berger, Peerce, Merriman

Decca (two CDs) 414 269-2
Richard Bonynge (conductor), London Symphony Orchestra; Milnes, Sutherland, Pavarotti, Talvela

EMI Classics (two CDs) 5 56327 2
Tullio Serafin (conductor), Orchestra and Chorus of Teatro alla Scala, Milan; Gobbi, Callas, di Stefano, Zaccaria

81. GIUSEPPE VERDI (1813–1901)

Il Trovatore (The Troubadour)

Salvatore Cammarano and Leone Emanuele Bardare, librettists, after a play by Antonio Garcia Gutiérrez

First performance: Rome, Teatro Apollo, January 19, 1853

From Gilbert and Sullivan to the Marx Brothers, humorists of all stripes have reveled in poking fun at *Il Trovatore*. Even Plácido Domingo and Luciano Pavarotti concluded the opening night gala program they shared at the Metropolitan Opera in 1993 with a *Trovatore* spoof: two sword-wielding Manricos, costumed exactly alike, show up onstage at the same time to their mutual dismay.

Lovers of this seminal Verdi work have to admit that it invites kidding, what with its story of a distraught gypsy who throws the wrong baby, her own, into a pyre, and its clunky operatic conventions. Manrico, upon learning that his gypsy mother is about to be burned at the stake, rushes off frantically to save her, but not before declaring his intentions and rousing his troops with two verses of the tenor showpiece aria "Di quella pira," topped off with the requisite high C.

The plot may be hokey. Yet Verdi, great psychologist that he was, penetrates the story line to reveal the complex human dilemma that lurks beneath. In fifteenth-century Spain, a band of gypsies lives in uneasy proximity to the house and lands of the powerful Count di Luna. Of course, the Count could easily subjugate the gypsies. Yet he and his soldiers know that the gypsies have a fearsome power of their own, a connection to the dark side.

At its core, *Il Trovatore* is a story of a daughter, the wizened gypsy woman Azucena, who is haunted by the last command of her mother as she burned at the stake: "Avenge me." When Azucena, transfixed by a campfire in the gypsy compound, sings her first aria, "Stride la Vampa," her state of mind as reflected in the haunting music might today be diagnosed as post-traumatic stress disorder. Watching those flames, she relives the horror of her mother's death and confronts again her powerlessness to avenge it. Manrico, who is the gypsy woman's adopted son, and the Count are brothers, though only Azucena knows this. Yet in the depiction of the relationship, Verdi uncannily captures the almost psychic connection that these two enemies, who have no idea of their biological kinship, feel for each other.

If the achievement of *Il Trovatore* is not fully appreciated, it may be due less to its convoluted plot than its musical difficulty. All it takes to perform *Il Trovatore,* Enrico Caruso once said, is the four greatest singers in the world. And he knew what he was talking about. Stylistically the opera hovers on the border between the bel canto heyday and the new venture into romanticism that Verdi was exploring. The four leading roles—Leonora (soprano), Manrico (tenor), Count di Luna (baritone), and Azucena (mezzo-soprano)— require singers who can spin and sustain long, arching, ornamented bel canto lines, often in quite exposed arias where the voices are accompanied only by those trademark Verdian oom-pah-pahs. Yet these are full-bodied vocal roles that require weighty tone and carrying power. Leonora may be the most classic example in opera of a lirico spinto role, which demands a deft combination of lyric and dramatic vocal qualities.

Leontyne Price was best known for her Aida. But the role of her 1961 Met debut, the role that ideally captured the glories of her singing, was Leonora in *Il Trovatore.* She was the Leonora (and the Verdi soprano) of my youth, which may still influence my preference for her two complete recordings of this work from 1959 and 1970 on RCA. But by any estimation, each account offers utterly exquisite singing. The earlier version, with Richard Tucker, Leonard Warren, and Rosalind Elias, conducted by Arturo Basile, is hard to find. But I'd wager that RCA Red Seal will never let the 1970 version slip out of the catalog. Though her voice is perhaps not quite as fresh in the latter account, her singing is richer, more mature, and achingly beautiful. The fine cast includes Plácido Domingo at his youthful best as Manrico, the great Sherrill Milnes as the Count, and the veteran Italian mezzo-soprano Fiorenza Cossotto as Azucena. Zubin Mehta, who doesn't exactly leap to mind as a classic Verdi stylist, leads a surprisingly pliant, sensitive, and tellingly paced performance with the New Philharmonia Orchestra.

As with almost every role she took on, Maria Callas brings insight and intensity to Leonora in the 1957 EMI Classics recording with the forces of La Scala conducted with affecting restraint by Herbert von Karajan. The stellar cast includes Giuseppe di Stefano at his best as Manrico and Fedora Barbieri as an unforgettable Azucena. The 1956 Decca recording, if you can track it down, is also fine, with Renata Tebaldi, Mario Del Monaco, and Giulietta Simionato heading the cast. But if I could only have one, I'd choose the 1970 RCA recording with the incomparable Leontyne Price.

RCA Red Seal (two CDs) 74321-39504-2
Zubin Mehta (conductor), New Philharmonia Orchestra; Price, Domingo, Milnes, Cossotto

EMI Classics (two CDs) 5 56777 2
Herbert von Karajan (conductor), Orchestra and Chorus of Teatro alla Scala, Milan; Callas, di Stefano, Barbieri, Panerai

82. GIUSEPPE VERDI (1813–1901)

La Traviata

Francesco Maria Piave, librettist, after a play by Alexandre Dumas

First performance: Venice, Teatro La Fenice, March 6, 1853

Translated into Italian, the title of the younger Alexandre Dumas's popular play *La dame aux camelias* (*The Lady of the Camellias*) would have made an evocative title for Verdi's operatic adaptation. But Verdi and his librettist, Piave, called their opera *La Traviata*, in English *The Fallen Woman*. You have to think that Verdi meant the title as bitterly ironic, for the music he composed to tell her story makes clear how deeply he admired Violetta Valéry.

The opera explores the dilemma of a charming, lovely, and independent-minded courtesan in Parisian society who has no inherited wealth and is barred from using her intelligence to make her own way in a profession. But how different is she, Violetta thinks, from upper-class women who sell themselves into loveless social marriages? Verdi identified with his strong-willed heroine who flouted morality. After the death of his young wife and two children, he lived for nearly fifteen years in an open relationship with the soprano Giuseppina Strepponi before they quietly married in 1859. Fiercely anticlerical, contemptuous of convention, Verdi had a built-in hypocrisy detector. He wanted to set *La Traviata* in modern dress to underline the point. Of course the administrators of La Fenice in Venice, where the opera was to be given its premiere, would not even consider such a thing. Today the opera is usually set in the mid-nineteenth century, as Verdi intended.

The role of Violetta is famously challenging, for Verdi reflects her psychological evolution in music that changes vocal character from act to act. At first we see Violetta as an unabashedly vivacious hostess, charmed by the attentions of the smitten young Alfredo but determined to resist them. She already suspects that she is mortally ill. Her high spirits are conveyed through the brilliant coloratura flights in the cabaletta "Sempre libera," in which she vows to keep herself unentangled.

In act 2, now contentedly living with Alfredo in a house outside Paris that she is paying for by secretly selling her possessions, Violetta is confronted by Alfredo's father, Giorgio Germont, a man of stern rectitude. Here her music requires the weightier sound and carrying power of a classic lirico spinto soprano. And in the final act, when she is frail and dying, a soprano must be able to float the ethereal phrases of Violetta's farewell to the world, "Addio, del passato," yet summon power for her anguished outbursts.

There are several classic recordings of *La Traviata,* including Toscanini's live 1946 performance with the NBC Symphony and Licia Albanese as Violetta. But the version I'd recommend is an impressive ensemble effort by great artists: the 1977 Deutsche Grammophon recording with Carlos Kleiber conducting the orchestra and chorus of the Bavarian State Opera and featuring the superb Romanian soprano Ileana Cotrubas as Violetta. Her creamy and affecting voice was ideally suited to conveying pathos. Though coloratura singing was not her strong suit, she delivers a technically able account of "Sempre libera," while managing to project Violetta's inner doubts and emotional frailty. And she is heartbreaking in the act 2 scene with Germont, here sung by the great Verdi baritone Sherrill Milnes with a gratifying blend of gravity and charisma. Those who know Plácido Domingo only from the latter phase of his career when he turned his attention to more heavy-duty dramatic tenor roles may be surprised by the younger Domingo's elegantly lyrical yet impassioned account of Alfredo.

Except for two extended scenes with the full chorus, including a masquerade party at a Paris salon complete with dancers dressed as gypsies and toreadors, *La Traviata* is mostly an intimate drama with long scenes for one, two, or three characters. Kleiber understands this. For all its sweep and urgency, he captures the chamber opera qualities of the work.

Another fine recording that has been overlooked is the 1971 account on EMI Classics with Beverly Sills as Violetta. Sills, who has seldom sounded better on recordings, gives a keenly intelligent, technically accomplished, and involving performance. The exquisite tenor Nicolai Gedda brings gorgeous sound and great refinement to the role of Alfredo. Rolando Panerai is a solid Germont. Aldo Ceccato conducts the Royal Philharmonic Orchestra in a supple performance that includes sections of the opera that are often omitted, like the second verse of Violetta's aria "Ah, fors'e lui."

Deutsche Grammophon (two CDs) 415 132-2
Carlos Kleiber (conductor), Orchestra and Chorus of the Bavarian State Opera; Cotrubas, Domingo, Milnes

EMI Classics (two CDs) CMS 7 69827 2
Aldo Ceccato (conductor), Royal Philharmonic Orchestra; Sills, Gedda, Panerai

83. GIUSEPPE VERDI (1813–1901)

Simon Boccanegra

1857 version, Francesco Maria Piave, librettist; 1881 revision, Francesco Maria Piave, librettist, with additions and alterations by Arrigo Boito

First performance: original version, Venice, Teatro La Fenice, March 12, 1857; revised version, Milan, Teatro alla Scala, March 24, 1881

Verdi's *Simon Boccanegra* is the Bermuda Triangle of opera plots: enter and you may never get out. Surely Verdi realized how baffling the story was. But to him the characters and situations of Antonio Garcia Gutiérrez's play were deeply resonant and powerfully suitable for musical enrichment. Simon Boccanegra is a corsair in the service of the Genoese Republic in the mid-fourteenth century, a willful and impetuous man whose secret affair with Maria Fiesco, the daughter of a city nobleman, has resulted in an illegitimate baby daughter.

In the opera's prologue Boccanegra is devastated to learn that Maria, whom we never meet, has died. Her father will forgive Boccanegra only if he promises to relinquish all claims to Maria's daughter. Meanwhile, the townspeople, looking for stability at a time of political strife, press the stalwart Boccanegra to accept an appointment as the new Doge of Genoa. Act 1 takes up the tale twenty-five years later, and that timeless cliché "the plot thickens" hardly suffices to describe the resulting entanglements.

But the story gave Verdi a chance to bring to life flawed, lost, and fatalistic human beings with whom he no doubt identified. Boccanegra covets power and acclaim yet feels inwardly unworthy, given his mangled relationship with Maria, which haunts him. He is also a guilty father, yearning to know his daughter but paralyzed by the fear of facing her. The opera is like a bleak morality tale about the ways in which acts taken as a young person set the course of your life for good or ill.

At its 1857 premiere in Venice, *Simon Boccanegra* was a dismal failure. Verdi blamed the response on the work's pervasively dark tone. Surely another reason was its convoluted story. But he so loved the score, with good reason, that he revised it extensively later in life. His play-doctor was the composer and librettist Arrigo Boito, and in asking him for help Verdi was testing Boito out as a potential collaborator. Boito passed the test, for he went on to write the librettos to *Otello* and *Falstaff* for the aging composer. The revised version, first performed at La Scala in 1881, is almost always the version performed today. It's one of Verdi's most assured and stunning scores, and the story at least has dramatic thrust and gripping moments.

Once in a while everything about a recording project works out ideally. That's what happened when Deutsche Grammophon brought together the conductor Claudio Abbado, a stellar cast, and the orchestra and chorus of La Scala to record *Simon Boccanegra* in 1977. Under Abbado the pacing, textures, gravity, and grandeur of the work come through affectingly. In the title role Piero Cappuccilli gives a demonstration of what it means to be a Verdi baritone. He sings with elegant lyricism, unforced power, vivid diction, and stylistic authority. Mirella Freni as Maria, the grown-up daughter whom Boccanegra discovers in act 1, is at her radiant best. You will not believe the lush beauty and supple phrasing she brings to the French-style aria that opens act 1, "Come in quest'ora bruna," in which she greets the rising dawn. And Abbado makes magic of the innovative orchestra accompaniment, which in the aria's opening section is scored for winds alone. The tenor José Carreras sang unevenly in his career even before he battled leukemia, but this recording captures him in his prime as Gabriele Adorno, young Maria's love interest. His singing is marked by ardent phrasing, clarion tone, and real charisma.

The robust bass Nicolai Ghiaurov is Jacopo Fiesco, young Maria's grandfather. And the elegant bass-baritone José van Dam is Paolo Albiani. Who is Paolo? Hmm. No one has ever been quite sure. I'll just pass on advice from my *Times* colleague Bernard Holland, who in writing about the plot of *Simon Boccanegra* said all you need remember is that "Paolo is a bad man."

Deutsche Grammophon (two CDs) 415 692-2
Claudio Abbado (conductor), Orchestra and Chorus of Teatro alla Scala, Milan; Cappuccilli, Freni, Ghiaurov, Carreras, van Dam

84. GIUSEPPE VERDI (1813–1901)

La Forza del Destino (The Force of Destiny)

Francesco Maria Piave, librettist, based on a drama by Angel de Saavedra

First performance: St. Petersburg, Imperial Theatre, October 29 (November 10), 1862; revised version, with additional text by Antonio Ghislanzoni: Milan, Teatro alla Scala, February 27, 1869

La Forza del Destino abounds with Verdian musical riches. But if you approach the opera expecting to find strong narrative continuity or even a consistent musical-dramatic tone you will be disappointed. Verdi was drawn to the subject matter because it offered him a chance to depict life in all its multiplicity—the tragic, the comic, and the pictorial thrown together into a sprawling musical drama. Yet, the patchwork quality for which the opera has often been criticized can also be seen as its defining achievement.

In eighteenth-century Seville, fate, or "the force of destiny," looms over the lives of the Marquis of Calatrava and his children, Don Carlo di Vargas and the lovely Leonora. The Marquis has proper plans for his daughter's future, but Leonora is about to elope with her clandestine lover, Don Alvaro, a nobleman of Incan descent. When late at night the Marquis overhears the young lovers talking in a courtyard, he rushes in, sword drawn. Alvaro throws his pistol to the floor and, alas, it goes off, killing the Marquis instantly.

From this point on the lives of all the characters are driven by forces that seem beyond their control. Don Carlo commits himself to finding and punishing his sister, who has left the family disguised as a young man, and to seeking revenge on his father's murderer. But *La Forza* is an opera where two strangers who meet on the battlefield and swear eternal allegiance to each other turn out to be sworn enemies, Carlo and Alvaro. And Leonora, convinced that her father's death was not an accident but some godly retribution for their forbidden love, seeks refuge in a monastery. A benevolent friar provides Leonora an isolated mountain cave where she lives disguised as a monkish hermit, until, by chance, of course, Alvaro and Carlo, whom fate has brought together, burst upon the scene in the midst of a ferocious duel. You get the idea?

Yet, in *La Forza* the juxtaposition of different moods and styles can be more rattling than the plot. Act 2 begins with a boisterous scene at an inn, where a gypsy girl, Preziosilla, tells fortunes amid a group of rowdy peasants and mule drivers. Suddenly the mood—and the music—completely changes character and a chorus of pilgrims en route to Holy Week services appear, inspiring the entire ensemble to sing an ethereal prayer.

Given the shifts and disparities in the music and the drama, a conductor must convey that the overall quality of the work is dark and somber. Even during fleeting moments of comedy, or impulsive expressions of desire, or impassioned outbursts of hatred, a performance should have gravity and restraint.

The recording that accomplishes this best is the one to own: James Levine's 1976 account with the London Symphony Orchestra, the John Alldis Choir, and a cast headed by Leontyne Price, Plácido Domingo, and Sherrill Milnes. Levine's performance is vigorous yet never hard-pressed, incisive yet never rigid, lyrically supple yet never saggy. If you want to understand what opera buffs mean when they talk about "a Verdian lirico spinto soprano," listen to Price's performance here. Her voice is throbbing and vibrant, yet cultured and elegant. She brings an affecting mix of passion and dignity to her portrayal. And her exquisite performance of the great act 4 aria "Pace, pace, mio Dio" is a model of how to spin a Verdian melodic line.

Domingo sounds youthful, ardent, and charismatic. Milnes sings with husky power and plangent lyricism. The baritonal colorings of Domingo's low register and the tenorial ping of Milnes's top notes make their voices blend alluringly in the solemn duet "Solenne in quest'ora." The distinguished cast includes the mezzo-soprano Fiorenza Cossotto as Preziosilla, the bass Bonaldo Giaiotti as Padre Guardiano, and the baritone Gabriel Bacquier as Fra Melitone.

Another choice would be the 1954 recording with Tullio Serafin conducting the forces of the La Scala Opera. Its main interest is the volatile Leonora of Maria Callas, and the burnished Alvaro of Richard Tucker. With Serafin emphasizing the opera's impetuosity, this is, overall, a wilder and more unsettled performance. The opera seems more like a series of gripping and sometimes incongruous scenes. This is a valid and fascinating approach to the work. Overall, though, I prefer the cooler beauty of the Levine recording.

RCA Victor Red Seal (three CDs) 74321-39502-2
James Levine (conductor), London Symphony Orchestra; Price, Domingo, Milnes, Cossotto

EMI Classics (three CDs) 5 56323 2
Tullio Serafin (conductor), Orchestra and Chorus of Teatro alla Scala, Milan; Callas, Tucker, Tagliabue, Rossi-Lemeni, Nicolai

85. GIUSEPPE VERDI (1813–1901)

Don Carlos

Joseph Méry and Camille Du Locle, librettists, after Schiller's poem

First performance: Paris, Opéra, March 11, 1867; revised version in four acts, French text revised by Camille Du Locle and translated into Italian, Milan, Teatro alla Scala, January 10, 1884

Verdi's *Don Carlos,* some three and a half hours of music, is a dramatically unwieldy opera. It is also arguably Verdi's most profound work.

When he received a commission in 1865 from the Paris Opera to compose a full-scale grand opera, Verdi again considered Shakespeare's *King Lear* as a subject, a lifelong temptation, but rejected the idea, deeming it too lacking in spectacle. He settled on an adaptation of Schiller's dramatic poem, *Don Carlos,* a tragic personal drama that would also provide, he thought, the requisite grandeur and pageantry.

Thankfully, the personal trumped the pageantry in the completed work. In the description of the critic Andrew Porter, six "interesting and complicated characters are enmeshed in a web of Church and State where their actions affect not only one another, but the fate of two nations." In the opening act in a forest at Fontainebleau in France, Don Carlos, the infante of Spain and heir to the throne, who is in disguise, approaches the young princess he has been commanded to marry, Elisabeth de Valois, the daughter of Henry II. To his delight he finds himself swept away by the lovely, kindly young woman. When Elisabeth realizes who Carlos really is, she too is excited by the prospect of their life together, all of which is expressed in a serenely beautiful duet. But their joy is short-lived, for word comes from Henry II that to finally end the war between France and Spain, Elisabeth has now been pledged to Carlos's father, the aged King Philip II. A sense of duty and well-founded fear lead them both to miserably accept the inevitable.

The central moment of the opera comes much later, in act 4, when Philip, alone in his study, having discovered his young wife's affections for his son, sings the most searching and psychologically complex soliloquy in all of Verdi. Was it simply foolish of him to think that Elisabeth might actually love him?, he wonders. Is there no one he can trust, not even his son? He has always tried to convince himself that maintaining a mistress, the swarthy and alluring Princess Eboli, has nothing to do with the rest of his life. But at this moment of torment and self-doubt Philip knows better. He is a ruler, yes, but completely beholden to the dictates and pronouncements of the Grand Inquisitor, who appears before Philip as an old, blind, and unyielding monk.

Eboli, a richly drawn character, has used her beauty as a source of power in a world where even princesses must abide by the wishes of men. She has two scene-stealing moments: the vocally brilliant "Veil Song" in act 2, when, spinning an exotic melody over an undulant Spanish rhythm, she tells the tale of a Moorish king who mistakenly wooed his own disguised wife one night; and "O don fatal," the volatile two-part aria in which she laments her fatal beauty and then vows to save Carlos after having caused the bitter rupture between him and his father.

The Marquis of Posa, Rodrigo, torn between devotion to King Philip and a fraternal bond with Carlos, is perhaps a more two-dimensional character. Indeed, his music seems a throwback to a more traditional operatic era. But the music fits with his nature. That Carlos is thought by some commentators to be inadequately fleshed out poses a bigger problem. Yet, looked at another way, Carlos's conflicted emotions, so well depicted in Verdi's ambiguous music, make him seem a Hamlet-like hero.

The main problem in presenting *Don Carlos* is that there is no definitive version of the score. At its 1867 premiere the five-act French grand opera proved too long and bafflingly complex for the audience, and Verdi agreed. Over the next twenty years he tinkered with the work, eventually cutting it down to four acts for an Italian version presented at La Scala in 1884. Paradoxically, removing large stretches of music, including almost the entire original first act, just made the opera seem more unwieldy. The most successful versions, devotees tend to agree, are the five-act Italian version (basically the original French work but pruned and translated into Italian), which was first tried out at Modena in 1867, or, for ambitious companies, the original French version.

Fortunately, there are remarkable recordings of each. Carlo Maria Giulini conducted the five-act Italian version with the forces of the Royal Opera at Covent Garden in London, and the 1971 EMI recording of that production is a landmark of the opera discography. Giulini miraculously balances urgency and spaciousness in this performance. His ideal cast is headed by the tenor Plácido Domingo in one of his great recorded portrayals. Domingo fills the phrases with heroic Verdian heft while conveying Don Carlos's inner doubts and anguish at every turn. For all the sumptuous beauty of her voice, the soprano Montserrat Caballé could sometimes be a stolid singer. Her portrayal of Elisabeth, though, is disarmingly tender and surprisingly ardent. The mezzo-soprano Shirley Verrett's Eboli, sung with a deep, dusky tone and gleaming power, is the best performance of the role on record. The baritone Sherrill Milnes is in robust voice as Rodrigo and the distinguished bass Ruggero Raimondi makes a grave and pitiable King Philip.

When it was announced that the tenor Roberto Alagna would sing the title role for a production of the original five-act French *Don Carlos* at the Théâtre de Châtelet in Paris in 1996, skeptical critics and buffs thought that surely his voice was too light and lyrical for the role. Alagna proved everyone wrong. His performance revealed a French lyrical elegance in the vocal writing that many tenors miss. Yet when called for he sang with plenty of ardor and power.

The production was no star vehicle but a team effort, and the conductor Antonio Pappano assembled quite a team: Karita Mattila as Elisabeth, Thomas Hampson as Rodrigo, José van Dam as Philip II, and Waltraud Meier as Eboli. Under Pappano, the Orchestre de Paris gives a lucid and incisive account of this ennobled score.

Which one to buy? If I could only have one I'd go with Giulini. But get to know this opera and you will want them both.

EMI Classics (three CDs) 7 47701 2

Carlo Maria Giulini (conductor), Orchestra of the Royal Opera House, Covent Garden, Ambrosian Opera Chorus; Domingo, Caballé, Verrett, Raimondi, Milnes

EMI Classics (three CDs) 56152

Antonio Pappano (conductor), Orchestre de Paris, Chorus of the Théâtre de Châtelet; Alagna, Mattila, Meier, Hampson, van Dam

86. GIUSEPPE VERDI (1813–1901)

Aida

Antonio Ghislanzoni, librettist

First performance: Cairo, Opera House, December 24, 1871

Aida has long been famous, laughably so, some would say, for its grand spectacle. Opera companies try to outdo one another in staging the "Triumphal Scene." Typically, a row of Egyptian heralds trumpet the victory of their army over their Ethiopian enemies as the conquering soldiers march past the cheering throngs trailed by carriages full of war booty and exotic dancers. For years a tourist must in Rome used to be the annual summer production of *Aida* in the outdoor Baths of Caracalla involving hundreds of supernumeraries and real elephants.

Actually, except for the "Triumphal Scene" in act 2 and one earlier scene—when Radames, the captain of the guards, is proclaimed leader of the Egyptian army and is sent off to battle by the king—*Aida* is an intimate drama dominated by extended scenes for one, two, or three characters. Verdi's score, composed in his full maturity (of new works, only the Requiem, *Otello,* and *Falstaff* were to follow), is sometimes faulted as a throwback to an earlier style of Italian opera. The criticism is valid in that Verdi reembraces traditional forms of aria, duet, and ensemble. Yet, in attempting to evoke the world of ancient North Africa, however inauthentically, Verdi fashioned a harmonically daring musical language rich with exotic melodic turns. Perhaps the structural formality of the score was meant to compensate for the experimentation.

The challenging title role is among the greatest creations in Italian opera. *Aida* was one of the first operas I attended in my early teens during the waning days of the old Metropolitan Opera House. The soprano was Leontyne Price. Seated in the stratosphere of the upper balcony, I had only the vaguest notion of what was going on in the plot. Yet I will never forget the almost physical sensation of being enveloped by Price's singing. The ethereally soft and sustained high notes, the sudden bursts of smoky power, the sheer beauty of her plaintive voice—everything about the performance seemed miraculous.

How deeply Price identified with Aida, a woman torn between duty to her oppressed nation and an illicit love for her nation's conqueror, became poignantly clear to me when I wrote about a visit she made to a group of schoolchildren in Harlem in the spring of 2000. Price went there to read a children's book adaptation of the *Aida* story that she had written, and also to sing for and take questions from an assembly of youngsters. Asked why Aida was her favorite role, she answered: "When I sang Aida, I used the most important plus I have. You have it; I have it: this beautiful skin. When I sang Aida, my skin was my costume."

Soprano Leontyne Price as Aida

When we meet Aida she has been forced into slavery as a servant to Amneris, the Egyptian princess. In secret, Aida has been carrying on a love affair with Radames, who is promised to Amneris. Her captors do not know that Aida is herself a princess, the daughter of the Ethiopian king, Amonasro. But Aida knows it, something Price never forgot when she portrayed the character. Price's identification with a dark-skinned race of people who were suffering oppression lent aching sadness to her singing. But her sense of pride and self-confidence—as a Southern black woman, as an artist, as a diva—lent her portrayal of Aida an affecting nobility.

Price recorded the role twice and each recording is a classic. She preferred the latter version, from 1970, with Erich Leinsdorf conducting the London Symphony Orchestra. But I particularly admire her 1962 recording with Sir Georg Solti conducting the orchestra and chorus of the Rome Opera, mostly because of the company she keeps. The tenor Jon Vickers may not be a classically Italianate Radames, but he tames his powerhouse dramatic tenor voice just enough to shape the Verdian lines lyrically, conveys the character's aching confusion, and still manages to sound like a force of nature. The baritone Robert Merrill is a burly yet elegant Amonasro. The mezzo-soprano Rita Gorr brings throbbing intensity to the role of Amneris. Solti's performance is excitingly volatile, by turns spacious and sizzling.

In the Leinsdorf recording the starry cast offers Plácido Domingo as Radames, Sherrill Milnes as Amonasro, and Grace Bumbry as Amneris. All do distinguished work. Leinsdorf conducts an expert performance. But Solti achieves greatness.

Another excellent choice, though, is the 1959 recording with Herbert von Karajan conducting the Vienna Philharmonic and Renata Tebaldi in the title role. Those who associate Tebaldi with sumptuously beautiful singing may be surprised at how impassioned she sounds as Aida, surely the result of good chemistry with Karajan. Carlo Bergonzi, who knows everything about the Verdi style, is Radames. The impressive Giulietta Simionato sings Amneris and the robust baritone Cornell MacNeil is Amonasro.

But every opera collector should have at least one of Price's *Aida* recordings on the shelf.

Decca (three CDs) 417 416-2
Sir George Solti (conductor), Chorus and Orchestra of the Rome Opera; Price, Vickers, Gorr, Merrill

RCA Red Seal (three CDs) 74321-39498-2
Erich Leinsdorf (conductor), London Symphony Orchestra; Price, Domingo, Bumbry, Milnes

Decca (two CDs) 289 460 978-2

Herbert von Karajan (conductor), Vienna Philharmonic; Tebaldi, Bergonzi, Simionato, MacNeil

87. GIUSEPPE VERDI (1813–1901)

Otello

Arrigo Boito, librettist, after Shakespeare

First performance: Milan, Teatro alla Scala, February, 5, 1887

By the late 1870s Verdi considered himself all but officially retired. He felt cut off from the new developments in Italian opera. Young composers had long been looking outside Italy for models, especially to Germany and to Wagner. So opera lovers can only be grateful that the composer and librettist Arrigo Boito lured Verdi, then in his late sixties, out of his self-imposed isolation.

Just a decade earlier Boito was a firebrand who considered Verdi old hat and urged the new generation to radicalize Italian opera. As he matured, though, Boito grew to appreciate the immensity of Verdi's accomplishments. You might have expected the thin-skinned elder composer to resist Boito's come-lately importuning. But knowing of Verdi's lifelong reverence for Shakespeare, Boito proposed a subject that he thought might hook the old man: *Othello*. It worked. When Verdi saw the drafts of Boito's libretto, he committed himself to the project, which took years to complete. At the time of the 1887 premiere Verdi was seventy-three.

Boito hoped that by working with Verdi he could both learn from the master and prod him into innovation. He was right on both counts. In a departure for Verdi, the musical drama sweeps along inexorably, stopping only occasionally for a set-piece aria or stand-and-sing ensemble. Still, Verdi's great achievement here was to figure out how music could enhance a play that was already iconic. Nothing in Shakespeare matches the ferocious, overpowering, and harmonically radical storm scene that opens the opera, with the chorus of Cyprian citizens voicing their terror as they watch Otello's ship being battered by the raging storm as it tries to dock.

Verdi understood the ability of music to reveal the psychological subtext of the story. For example, there is the scene when young Cassio, Otello's loyal platoon leader, having disgraced himself by getting drunk and provoking a duel, egged on, of course, by the scheming Iago, goes to the good-hearted Desdemona to confess his shame and ask advice. By this point in the opera Otello's belief in his wife's virtue has been undermined by Iago's lies. When Desdemona pleads with her husband to forgive Cassio and give him another chance, the plaintive music she sings is so lush and romantic that subliminally you wonder whether there isn't some truth to Iago's charge that Desdemona secretly loves handsome young Cassio.

Iago's account of Cassio's dream is another instance of Verdi's music taking us even deeper into the twisted psychology of the character than Shakespeare's verse. While sleeping next to Cassio one night (and what were they doing sleeping together?), Iago explains to Otello, Cassio started moaning Desdemona's name in his sleep and grabbing Iago as if to kiss him. Verdi's music, so deceptively diaphanous and eerily strange, taps into what would seem to be Iago's deeply buried, homoerotic drives.

To turn the play into an opera, Verdi made some brutal cuts. A whole soliloquy of Otello's is replaced, in the opera's second act, by a seemingly superfluous scene: a delegation of townspeople and children bearing flowers come to serenade and honor their new first lady with songs and mandolins. Yet Verdi and Boito knew just what they were doing by making the substitution. The action of act 2 moves with onrushing tension, much more quickly and viscerally than in the play. Verdi knew that his audience needed an emotional time-out, which the serenade provides. When it ends, the crucial scene between Otello and Iago picks up and builds to the menacing duet that concludes act 2, "Si, pel ciel," in which Otello swears bloody vengeance on his wife and Iago duplicitously vows to help.

Were it not for the punishing difficulty of the title role, which ideally needs a tenor who has both Wagnerian lungs and Verdian lyricism, and for the demands placed on the orchestra, *Otello* would be performed as often as *La Traviata*. Completely first-rate live performances do not happen so often. But you can choose among several classic recordings.

One of the great events of my early teenage years was hearing Renata Tebaldi sing Desdemona twice at the old Metropolitan Opera House in late 1964. During the final act, in the bedroom scene, Desdemona sings the mournful "Willow Song," then the wistful "Ave Maria," then retires to bed, until Otello, with murder on his mind, enters over the ominous stirrings in the lowest strings of the orchestra. Tebaldi's sublimely luminous and gently floated singing enveloped me in a way I will never forget. On one of those nights the ovations for her went on so long that she finally appeared in her coat, to signal that it was time for her to leave.

So, I have always had a fondness for the 1961 London recording with Tebaldi, Mario Del Monaco as Otello, and Aldo Protti as Iago, conducted by Herbert von Karajan. Del Monaco, with his powerhouse voice and assured mastery of Verdian style, is a phenomenal Otello. Protti sings with husky sound and suavity, never indulging in stereotypical villainous bluster. Some opera buffs prefer the 1954 recording these same three artists made with Alberto Erede conducting the Academy of Saint Cecilia in Rome. Tebaldi sounds fresher on the earlier recording. But her singing is more poignantly expressive in the 1961 version, which also offers Karajan's mesmerizing account of the score and the great Vienna Philharmonic.

The tenor Jon Vickers was a force of nature in the title role, and the 1960 RCA recording, with the elegant Leonie Rysanek as Desdemona and the charismatic Tito Gobbi as Iago, with Tullio Serafin conducting, is also excellent. Then there is the 1978 RCA recording with Plácido Domingo in what would become arguably his greatest role, Sherrill Milnes as Iago, and Renata Scotto as Desdemona, conducted by James Levine. This taut, incisive, and exciting performance, recorded in London with the National Philharmonic Orchestra, captures Domingo in clarion voice. Milnes too is superb. Scotto's performance is the drawback. Though intelligent and passionate, she lacks the subtlety and tenderness Desdemona should also ideally have.

I could not be without all three of these recordings, not to mention

Soprano Renata Tebaldi

Toscanini's historic 1947 live performance with the NBC Symphony, and a few other versions as well. But if I could have only one, I'd go with the 1961 Karajan account, with my beloved Tebaldi.

Decca (two CDs) 411 618-2
Herbert von Karajan (conductor), Vienna Philharmonic Orchestra and Vienna State Opera Chorus; Tebaldi, Del Monaco, Protti

Giuseppe Verdi   263

RCA Victor (two CDs) 09026-63180-2
Tullio Serafin (conductor), Rome Opera Chorus and Orchestra; Vickers, Rysanek, Gobbi

RCA Red Seal (two CDs) RCD2-2951
James Levine (conductor), National Philharmonic Orchestra; Domingo, Scotto, Milnes

88. GIUSEPPE VERDI (1813–1901)
Falstaff

Arrigo Boito, librettist, after Shakespeare's plays *The Merry Wives of Windsor* and *Henry IV*

First performance: Milan, Teatro alla Scala, February 9, 1893

The 1887 premiere of *Otello* was such a triumph that frenzied Milanese opera lovers unhitched the horses from Verdi's carriage and dragged it from the theater of La Scala to the hotel where the seventy-three-year-old composer was staying. Throngs milled all night outside his window shouting "Viva Verdi!" Surely now, the composer thought, he could return to his retirement.

But Boito, the composer and librettist who had enticed him into collaborating on *Otello,* staunchly backed by the directors of La Scala, implored Verdi to write one more work, perhaps a comedy, an intriguing idea, the composer thought. His only other comedy was *Un Giorno di Regno,* his second opera and a dismal failure. When Boito proposed another subject from Verdi's beloved Shakespeare and sketched out a scenario drawn from *The Merry Wives of Windsor* and *Henry IV* that would focus on Falstaff, the composer was hooked.

The composition process was difficult and slow. Verdi worked in spurts, slowed down, the scholar Roger Parker suggests in the *New Grove Dictionary of Opera,* by the deaths of several friends. Still, its

1893 La Scala premiere was another triumph for the composer, now seventy-nine. Surely, though, another reason Verdi's work was arduous was that he was breaking new ground.

With *Falstaff* you sense Verdi thinking: "I don't care what opera is supposed to be, or what audiences expect. This time I'm finally going to indulge myself." Inspired by Boito's snappy adaptation of Shakespeare's comic verse, Verdi crafted music that responded minutely to the verbal patterns of the text. This miraculous score is a gossamer-like fabric stitched together from hundreds of musical snippets, any one of which might have been the basis for an entire aria or scene in earlier Verdi works. The closest the opera has to a complete aria is Fenton's "Dal labbro il canto" in act 3, when the young man sings a love sonnet in the Windsor forest at night addressed to his awaiting Nannetta, the winsome daughter of Alice Ford. Yet even this short aria merges into a duet as Nannetta arrives, and the duet is stopped cold before it gets going by the appearance of Alice. Later in the act comes Nannetta's lovely quasi-aria, really an extended scene for soprano and chorus, when, disguised as the queen of the fairies, she gathers the townspeople in the forest where they intend to teach the rotund knight a lesson. Essentially, *Falstaff* is one continuous ensemble, teaming with vitality and prone, like people, to quick shifts of mood.

When you think about it this comedy is not all that funny. The merry wives play some downright mean tricks on tubby old Sir John, whose bloated ego is easy to prick. True, he's a moocher and a loudmouth. Yet he has done nothing worse than send the same preposterous love letter to two married women. Why don't the ladies just laugh him off?

Because he's asking for it. The opera only works on the resonant level Verdi intended if Falstaff is portrayed as more than some risible has-been. Long the butt of jokes, he carries around a bellyful of resentments. A great Falstaff must dare to convey the character's darkness and simmering anger, while still making him the kind of irascible charmer you'd like to have a beer with.

The Welsh baritone Geraint Evans accomplished this exceedingly well on the 1963 Decca recording conducted by Sir Georg Solti, my favorite of the many fine recordings of Verdi's final masterpiece. Though Evans's voice was not that large, his warm sound, clear diction, and lively dramatic sense make his Falstaff a comic hero worthy of both Verdi and Shakespeare.

The cast is incomparable. I doubt the lovers Fenton and Nannetta will ever be as beautifully sung as here, by the tenor Alfredo Kraus and the soprano Mirella Freni, both captured at their fresh-voiced, youthful best. Ilva Ligabue as Alice Ford, Giulietta Simionato as Mistress Quickly, and Rosalind Elias as Mistress Meg Page are wonderful merry wives. Robert Merrill makes a vibrant Ford, Alice's jealous husband, who gets his comeuppance along with Sir John. Solti, as you might expect, conducts a fleet and vigorous performance. Yet seldom has he brought such silken delicacy and sweet lyricism to his work as here.

Another classic is EMI's 1956 recording with Herbert von Karajan conducting the Philharmonia Orchestra and Chorus. What, you say? The stern Teutonic Karajan conducting such an ebullient Italian opera? You won't believe the lightness and transparency of the orchestra, the geniality of the singing Karajan elicits from this fine cast. Tito Gobbi is a husky-voiced, Italianate Falstaff. Luigi Alva and Anna Moffo are disarming as the young lovers. The top-notch trio of merry wives offers, no less, Elisabeth Schwarzkopf as Alice, Nan Merriman as Meg, and Fedora Barbieri as Quickly. Overall, this is a warm and nimble ensemble effort under Karajan, available on EMI's Great Recordings of the Century series.

Verdi concludes *Falstaff* with an everyone-on-stage final fugue: "Tutto nel mondo e burla" ("The whole world's a jest"), a wryly satirical and ingenious send-up of this most learned of musical forms. Like *Otello*, *Falstaff* explores the effect of jealousy, thwarted desire, and scapegoating. But this great fugue teaches us that the only answer is to laugh at ourselves.

Decca (two CDs) 417 168-2
Sir Georg Solti (conductor), RCA Italiana Opera Orchestra and Chorus; Evans, Ligabue, Freni, Kraus, Merrill, Elias, Simionato

EMI Classics (two CDs) 5 67162 2
Herbert von Karajan (conductor), Philharmonia Orchestra and Chorus; Gobbi, Schwarzkopf, Alva, Moffo, Merriman, Barbieri, Panerai

89. RICHARD WAGNER (1813–1883)

Der Fliegende Holländer (The Flying Dutchman)

Richard Wagner, librettist, after Heinrich Heine

First performance: Dresden, Hoftheater, January 2, 1843

With his penchant for enshrouding his life in myth, Richard Wagner wrote in his autobiography that the inspiration for *Der Fliegende Holländer* (*The Flying Dutchman*) came from his experience crossing the Baltic Sea and the Straits of Kattegatt en route to London. It's true, as historians have noted, that in the summer of 1838 Wagner and his wife, Minna, heavily in debt, their passports having been confiscated, set sail clandestinely at night on a small merchant ship that encountered a terrifying storm and nearly met with disaster. But, as the Wagner scholar Barry Millington reports, there is no evidence that he set down any musical sketches of that experience. Indeed, he didn't begin the composition of the opera until two years later.

Still, it's a great story, and the opening of *The Flying Dutchman* certainly conjures up the scene he described—so vividly that listening to a recording at home or sitting at the opera, you may just sense the rainy squalls and choppy seas. The shouts of the crew echoing off the stony bluffs of a Norwegian fjord, the heaving hulk of the ship as it sways, the demonic intensity of the accursed Dutchman—it's all there.

The story comes from Heinrich Heine's retelling of a renowned nautical legend about a defiant Dutch sea captain who one day swore that despite the devil himself he would undertake to sail around the Cape of Good Hope, even if it took him forever. For his brashness the Dutchman is condemned (by the heavens, the fates, the devil?) to roam the seas endlessly, allowed ashore just once every seven years to seek redemption, if he can, through a woman's love. In Wagner's operatic version the Dutchman docks in a Norwegian harbor where he encounters Senta, the daughter of a hardy sea captain, Daland.

Senta is a winsome yet distracted young woman who has become obsessed with a picture of the Dutchman and the legend the towns-folk tell of him. She imagines herself the chosen woman who can rescue the Dutchman by pledging devotion to him unto death.

With *The Flying Dutchman,* Wagner's fourth opera but his first great one, he tried to realize his goal of creating musical drama in which words, music, and stage action combine to make an organic and continuous entity. He wanted to sweep away all the tired oper-atic conventions: the clear divisions between set-piece arias, ensembles, and recitative; the requisite spectacle. He didn't yet have the courage of his convictions because the opera still contains a song for the Steersman, several distinct arias, a rousing Sailors' Chorus, and a "Spinning Chorus" for the women who spend their days together mending sails and making cord for their men.

But there are long episodes of daringly innovative music, like the duet for Senta and Erik, the eager young sailor who has been court-ing her with no luck, and the highly charged duet between Senta and the Dutchman in act 2. In these scenes Wagner composed music that ebbs and flows with the contours and pacing of the words and begins to achieve the inexorable continuity that would characterize his later works. The long, brooding, and fearsome monologue for the Dutch-man when he first steps haltingly ashore is a remarkable scene that anticipates Wotan's anguished narrative in *Die Walküre.*

Wagner originally composed the work as one continuous swath of musical drama lasting about two hours and twenty minutes. This was the version he conducted at the opera's 1843 premiere. But later, for pragmatic reasons, he divided the score into three acts, and this version became the standard, though more recently many companies, including the Metropolitan Opera under James Levine, have gone back to the original.

Of the many great singers who have assayed the opera's two lead-ing roles, few have surpassed the bass-baritone George London as the Dutchman and the soprano Leonie Rysanek as Senta. In a perfor-mance together at the Metropolitan Opera in 1960 the ovation after act 2 was so ecstatic that many in the audience stayed in the house and kept applauding through the entire intermission until Thomas Shippers, who was conducting, returned to the pit to begin act 3.

Following that triumph, London and Rysanek sang their roles for a 1961 recording made in England, with Antal Dorati conducting the Orchestra and Chorus of the Royal Opera House, Covent Garden, and a superb supporting cast, including the bass Giorgio Tozzi as Daland, the tenor Karl Liebl as Erik, the mezzo-soprano Rosalind Elias as Mary (Senta's nurse), and the lyric tenor Richard Lewis as the Steersman.

There is also a renowned recording from 1968 with the great Otto Klemperer conducting the New Philharmonia Orchestra and the BBC Chorus and an impressive cast headed by the distinguished Theo Adam as the Dutchman and the impassioned Anja Silja as Senta. And, though I am in something of a minority about this, I also admire James Levine's 1994 recording with the orchestra and chorus of the Metropolitan Opera. Some object to his slowish tempos, but I find them fascinating. And the cast is excellent with James Morris, a renowned Dutchman, past his prime but still riveting, and the radiant dramatic soprano Deborah Voigt as Senta. The Wagnerian tenor Ben Heppner as Erik represents luxury casting of a supporting role.

Decca (two CDs) 417 319-2
Antal Dorati (conductor), Orchestra and Chorus of the Royal Opera House, Covent Garden; London, Rysanek, Tozzi, Liebl, Elias, Lewis

EMI Classics, Great Recordings of the Century series (two CDs) 5 67405 2
Otto Klemperer (conductor), New Philharmonia Orchestra, BBC Chorus; Adam, Silja, Talvela, Kozub

Sony Classical (two CDs) S2K 66342
James Levine (conductor), Metropolitan Opera Orchestra and Chorus; Morris, Voigt, Heppner, Rootering

90. RICHARD WAGNER (1813–1883)

Tannhäuser

Richard Wagner, librettist

First performance: Dresden, Hoftheater, October 19, 1845

To appreciate *Tannhäuser* you have to accept the heavy-handed way Wagner presents a dichotomy between spiritual and profane love. Wagner fashioned the story from two unrelated medieval legends. There was the tale of Tannhäuser, a knight crusader from Franconia, who becomes a courtier of Venus, the goddess of love. Into this story Wagner wove a tale of the song contests on the Wartburg, in which knights and minstrels competed for prizes that sometimes included the hands of marriageable young ladies.

In exploring the differences between spiritual and profane love Wagner creates two realms of life, two sets of characters, and two types of music. As the opera begins Tannhäuser is in the midst of a bacchanal in the Venusberg, the hideaway of Venus, where bathing naiads, reclining sirens, and dancing nymphs reach a peak of orgiastic abandon. The frenzy is even more intense in the subsequent Paris version of the opera (more on that later), where wild satyrs and fauns enter the scene and cause a riot by chasing the nymphs.

Eventually the bacchanal simmers down and we see Venus, reclining on a couch with Tannhäuser half-kneeling at her side, his head resting in her lap—staging details carefully specified by Wagner. The music is voluptuous and harmonically unhinged. But Tannhäuser, surfeited by sensual delight, pines for the simple, goodly qualities of his earthly life as a knight. When he speaks to Venus of his nostalgia and invokes the Virgin Mary, the goddess, infuriated, releases him and ruefully predicts that he will return to her one day in desperation.

The earthly realm is represented in act 2 in the Hall of Song in the Wartburg, where Elisabeth, the young niece of the Landgrave of

Thuringia, sings a joyous greeting to the hall itself, "Dich, teure Halle," a compact, set-piece aria that has become a favorite of sopranos in concert. Elisabeth fell in love with Tannhäuser when she heard him compete in an earlier song contest. As she returns to the site of that meeting she anticipates his arrival and imagines their blissful future.

The world of the Wartburg is conveyed by Wagner through much more conventional music: arias and duets structured in regular eight-bar phrases, songs, and marches, lofty four-squared hymns for the pilgrims who pass by. The most famous moment of the opera, the "Hymn to the Evening Star," sung by the noble knight Wolfram, with its symmetrical phrase lengths and singable melody, sounds like Wagner's homage to Schubert lieder.

During the song contest the two realms collide. Wolfram, the first contender, sings a paean to pure love, a stiff and formal song. Scoffing, Tannhäuser answers with a song about love as a burning desire, a sensual ecstasy, the qualities he has come to know firsthand. The entire assembly is shocked, Elisabeth especially.

There is no real synthesis between the two realms of the story or the two styles of music. The spiritual wins. Elisabeth, again abandoned by Tannhäuser, withers away. But her sacrificial death sanctifies Tannhäuser, whose calls for salvation in the opera's final moments are answered as he falls lifeless to the ground.

The score does not represent a leap forward in Wagner's quest to create continuous musical drama, with the exception of the innovative monologue known as the "Rome narrative." Here, in music that boldly follows the contours and flow of the text, Tannhäuser tells the story of his despairing pilgrimage to Rome, from which he returned unrepentant and yearning for the Venusberg. Still, in this work Wagner made some enormous strides, especially in the increasingly sophisticated use of the orchestra and the chromatic richness of his harmonic language.

There are Wagnerian tenors who would rather take on Parsifal or even Tristan than the daunting role of Tannhäuser, with its high tessitura (vocal range) and continual shifts between long spans of arioso-like dialogue and vigorously lyrical, hypercharged outbursts. The tenor Wolfgang Windgassen brings distinction as well as vocal heroics to his performance on a live recording from the 1962 Bayreuth

Festival. With this historic production, the American mezzo-soprano Grace Bumbry, singing Venus, broke the color barrier at Bayreuth, becoming the first black artist to appear there. Her singing is impressive for its rich colorings, unforced power, and seductive phrasing. The great Anja Silja, sometimes dubbed the Callas of the German repertory, is in radiant voice as Elisabeth. The baritone Eberhard Wächter as Wolfram is also excellent. Wolfgang Sawallisch conducts a sweeping and rhapsodic performance.

Almost sixteen years after the opera's 1845 premiere at Dresden, Wagner presented a new version of the score prepared for the Paris Opera. The main change involved greatly extending the bacchanal scene, in accord with the Parisian demand for ballet in opera, though there are other changes and alterations throughout the score. With *Tristan und Isolde* behind him, Wagner brought a new level of sensual intensity to the Venusberg scenes. The Paris version would eventually become the preferred one. But some companies combine the two, incorporating the ballet music but then switching, essentially, to the Dresden version. This option, sanctioned by Wagner, is followed on the Bayreuth recording.

Georg Solti's exciting 1971 recording with the Vienna State Opera essentially follows the Paris version. The tenor René Kollo makes a youthful and impulsive Tannhäuser, Helga Dernesch is a beguiling Elisabeth, and Christa Ludwig a smoldering yet cagey Venus. And Solti, as always, brings dynamic energy to the score even in its moments of restraint.

Philips (three CDs) 434 607-2
Wolfgang Sawallisch (conductor), Chorus and Orchestra of the Bayreuth Festival; Windgassen, Silja, Bumbry, Wächter, Stolze

Decca (three CDs) 470 810-2
Georg Solti (conductor), Vienna State Opera Chorus and the Vienna Philharmonic; Kollo, Dernesch, Ludwig, Braun

91–94. RICHARD WAGNER (1813–1883)

Der Ring des Nibelungen

Richard Wagner, librettist

First performance as a cycle: Bayreuth, Festspielhaus, August 13, 14, 16, 17, 1876

Prologue: Das Rheingold

First performance: Munich, Royal Court and National Theatre, September 22, 1869

First day: Die Walküre

First performance: Munich, Royal Court and National Theatre, June 26, 1870

Second day: Siegfried

First performance: Bayreuth, Festspielhaus, August 16, 1876

Third day: Götterdämmerung

First performance: Bayreuth, Festspielhaus, August 17, 1876

You have to look to Michelangelo's Sistine Chapel murals or Proust's cyclic novel *In Search of Lost Time* to find a work in any field as ambitious as Wagner's operatic tetralogy *Der Ring des Nibelungen*. Also called a "stage festival play," the *Ring* consists of a prologue lasting two and a half uninterrupted hours and three full-evening operas, all thematically linked. Typically, to attend a complete performance of the cycle you must commit to roughly eighteen hours at the opera house within a six-day period.

The *Ring* is far from flawless. For one, the story, adapted by Wagner from Norse mythology, is full of narrative holes. Moreover, Wagner worked on the *Ring* over a span of twenty-five years, writing the librettos of the four works in reverse order and then composing the scores from first to last. Two-thirds of the way through *Siegfried,* the third work, he set aside the project for over eleven years, composing *Tristan und Isolde* and *Die Meistersinger* in the interim. Wagner's compositional style changed markedly over that quarter century and the *Ring* can be faulted for its stylistic inconsistencies.

And yet the cycle is one of the most colossal works ever created, not just in opera but in all of art. Here Wagner finally fulfills his aesthetic ideal of *Gesamtkunstwerk,* a dramatic form in which all the arts—poetry, drama, music, song, scenic design, visual imagery—are united to form a new and heightened art form. Wagner found this mythic tale ideal for that end. And what a tale! The best way to help newcomers into the world of the *Ring* is to tell some of the story in context, to suggest how Wagner's music powerfully explores the subliminal themes of the complex story.

The title, which translates as *The Ring of the Nibelungen,* refers to Alberich, a smithy of the downtrodden race of Nibelungen dwarfs, who is seething with resentments and frustrated ambitions. In the subaquatic opening of *Das Rheingold,* the first opera, called a prologue, we meet three Rhinemaidens who guard an enchanted magical lump of gold near the bed of the river. Anyone who will renounce love and fashion that magic gold into a ring, the legend holds, can become master of the universe.

Alberich comes upon the Rhinemaidens and, randy as usual, flirts with them. Naturally, they mock and rebuff him, but in doing so let slip the secret of the gold. So Alberich, who has never had much luck with love, renounces it, steals the gold, and flees.

In the next scene the god Wotan and his wife, Fricka, are seen arising at daybreak atop a high mountain plateau. The entire *Ring* can be taken as the story of a battle for world dominance between the lordly Wotan and the lowly Alberich, continued over generations. Wotan, one of the most complex characters in opera, should be recognizable to anyone who follows politics. He is the head god of a family of gods. But his power is reined in by an elaborate system of checks and balances and a cabinet of subgods, each with his or her function. Wotan can't even keep himself eternal without the goddess Freia, who tends the golden apples that give the gods immortality. His main responsibility involves enforcing the rules and covenants, engraved in ancient German runes upon the spear he carries with him always.

But Wotan has gotten greedy for power. We soon learn that some time ago he hired the giants Fasolt and Fafner to build the castle Valhalla. If he can just get all the gods under one roof, he thinks, he might better control them. Valhalla will become like an imperial White House.

In payment for the construction job Wotan promised the giants something he cannot deliver: Freia. When the time came, Wotan figured, he would just finagle this. But Valhalla is finished and the payment is due. Suddenly Wotan understands the arrogance of his rash promise.

Loge, a demigod of fire and trickery, tells Wotan about what Alberich has done. Down in Nibelheim the dwarf has fashioned a ring from the stolen Rhine gold and is using its power to brutally force the Nibelungen workers into mining more gold, hoards of it. Loge leads Wotan to Alberich, and together they hoodwink the dwarf and steal the amassed gold, hoping that the giants will accept it in lieu of Freia. They also steal the ring, but not before Alberich places a chilling curse on it, a motif ominously doubled in the orchestra by the blaring brass.

Though the giants accept the substitute payment, they demand the ring as part of it, something Wotan refuses to relinquish until, in perhaps the most crucial scene of the entire cycle, the earth goddess Erda ascends from the underworld with a prophecy. Intoning her lines over the mysteriously beautiful music of the orchestra (a subtle transformation of the motif associated with the swirling currents of the Rhine), Erda warns Wotan that by stealing the ring he has broken the covenants he swore to uphold, that he has no choice but to give it up, that his authority has been shaken, and that the ring carries a curse.

To me, the *Ring* is about the relationship between power and love. You can have one, but it's nearly impossible to have both. Love, real love, not just lust or sex, but love, requires you to surrender power. Few people bent on acquiring power make room in their lives for mutual, self-effacing love. Wotan has grown bored in his marriage and distracted himself with affairs, but even these did not stem his restlessness and hunger for power.

What Wotan learns from Erda is that real power involves much more than erecting castles and asserting control. Knowledge is power, and Erda is the source of all knowledge. So, despondently, Wotan relinquishes the ring. But the ring's curse kicks in immediately. The giants squabble over it until Fafner kills Fasolt, then disappears with his booty as the gods, having barely escaped this crisis, ascend the rainbow staircase to Valhalla. But Wotan has been hooked by Erda's prophecies and vows to return to her and find out more.

In the time lag between *Das Rheingold* and *Die Walküre* Wotan has done more than find out things from Erda. He has fathered nine warrior daughters with her, the Walküre maidens, godly tomboys whose job it is to protect Valhalla by bringing the bodies of fallen heroes to the castle where they are revived and conscripted as palace guards to the gods. He has also fathered two children from a mortal woman, the twins Siegmund and Sieglinde, his idea being that perhaps they, especially Siegmund, might carry out the deed he cannot do himself and return the ring to the Rhine. This may be the only way the gods will survive.

At first, we learn, Wotan raised the twins in the forest with their mortal mother. One day when he was off hunting with the young boy, a brutal clan of warriors attacked the house, killed the mother, and captured Sieglinde. Soon afterward Siegmund and Wotan were separated as well and the young boy was left to grow up alone, unsure of his identity or even his name.

As *Die Walküre* begins, a raging storm is evoked by demonically driven music that crests and swells. As it settles down Siegmund, injured and exhausted, finds his way to the door of an isolated house in the forest where he is greeted warily by a scared young woman, Sieglinde, of course, whose husband, Hunding, is about to arrive home.

An affecting demonstration of how emotionally resonant Wagner's use of leitmotifs can be comes early in this act. Terrified of her abusive husband, Sieglinde boldly adds a sleeping drug to his nightly drink, so that she can talk more with this stranger. Something compels her to open up to the young man, to tell him of the way she was forced by her captors into marriage. On her awful wedding day, she continues, her husband's coarse friends came over to congratulate

Richard Wagner

him and get drunk as she sat in a corner, miserable. But then a mysterious man in a gray cloak with a hat pulled over one eye just showed up and silently glowered at the guests. Sieglinde thought the ominous visitor had a look of sadness and longing. Though she did not recognize him, she intuitively knew who he was.

The man was Wotan, which anyone who has just heard *Das Rheingold* would know, because as Sieglinde tells her story in forlorn melodic lines the orchestra plays the subdued yet magisterial motif of Valhalla and the gods. The theme is prolonged and transformed into a wistfully comforting passage, music that reminds the audience of something even Sieglinde does not know: that her father is a god, that she too is godly, not the rootless nobody everyone treats her like, and that the beautiful young stranger hearing her story is her long-lost brother.

It's paradoxical and somehow touching that in the *Ring* operas, where all the marriages and couplings seem to result from pacts, bargains between clans, or even magic potions, the one relationship of uncontrollable and somehow pure love is the incestuous relationship between Siegmund and Sieglinde. When Siegmund finally bursts into a love song, the rhapsodic "Winterstürme," in which he describes the yielding of winter to spring, the music seems like Wagner's benediction on their love.

Wotan blesses their relationship, too. But not Fricka, whose responsibilities include protecting the sanctity of marriage. In act 2 she confronts her husband and demands that the twins, guilty of both adultery and incest, be punished. Hunding is in furious pursuit of the fleeing couple, but Wotan must not assist Siegmund in the fight that is certain to result, Fricka insists. Wotan's wish to somehow indirectly lead Siegmund into regaining the ring and returning it to the Rhine is futile, as Fricka rightly points out, because his controlling hands would be all over the deed. Wotan realizes that the cause is lost and the curse prevails. He must let his beloved son face Hunding unprotected.

The problem is Brünnhilde, Wotan's favorite Walküre daughter, who knows his heart and reveres him, despite his bluster and temper. Wotan has instructed Brünnhilde to empower Siegmund in the coming fight. Now he must change his instruction. You will know you have become a true Wagner devotee when the long monologue called

"Wotan's Narrative," which many operagoers consider deadly dull, seems the emotional core of the entire *Ring*. In this deliberate, slow, halting scene, Wotan tells Brünnhilde the whole sorry story of his restless wanderings, his theft of the ring from Alberich, and of Erda's prophecies. Though she is confused and troubled by her father's distress, Brünnhilde agrees to obey.

But when she sees Siegmund and Sieglinde together, as they flee from Hunding, she is deeply moved. Brünnhilde has never seen two people in love before, certainly not her father and her stepmother. When she tells Siegmund that he must prepare to die and the young man responds that he would kill Sieglinde rather than go to death without her, Brünnhilde decides to disobey Wotan and help Siegmund after all. Surely, in his heart this is what Wotan would really want anyway, she believes. But in the pitch of battle Wotan appears and causes Siegmund's sword to break in two. The boy is killed. Brünnhilde rushes Sieglinde off to safety. Fricka, the protector of marriage, is avenged.

No music moves me more than the last half hour of act 3 from *Die Walküre*. Wotan, almost insanely furious with Brünnhilde, tells her that as punishment she will lose her godly powers and be placed in a deep sleep atop a mountain. Whatever man awakens her she will have to marry. Wotan doesn't just mean that some galumphing guy will come along and that Brünnhilde will be forced to be his wife. He means that some galumphing guy will come along and Brünnhilde, once a warrior maiden and glorious god, will love him. Like a typically subservient wife, she will sit in the corner and spin, the butt of jokes from her husband's buddies.

Horrified, Brünnhilde pleads that she cannot be the bride of just any man. Let some fearful barrier be imposed around her so that only a hero deserving of a warrior maiden will dare to find her. Wotan, full of remorse about his own muddled life and aching with love for his daughter, relents. He has Loge surround the mountain with impenetrable fire and places Brünnhilde in a sleeping state. Wagner's compassionate and sadly resigned music in this long scene conveys everything about a father's regret over his failures as a family man, and about the impotency any powerful person feels in the face of eternal forces and inalterable decline. A ravishing descending chord progression depicts Brünnhilde sinking into sleep. Then magic fire music mingles with the motif of fate in the orchestra as Wotan sings his painful farewell to his beloved daughter and the godly life he sees slipping away.

The battle between Wotan and Alberich continues in the last two operas, but through their descendants. *Siegfried* is the story of the child of Siegmund and Sieglinde. Raised in the forest by Mime, the scheming brother of Alberich, who has his own designs on the ring, the motherless Siegfried is a natural man: strong, impulsive, unreflective, and unacquainted with fear. *Siegfried* is like the scherzo of a four-movement Wagnerian operatic symphony, that is, until the final scene, a rapturous love duet. Yet Siegfried has three consequential encounters along the way.

In the first, he kills Fafner the giant who, using the magic Tarnhelm, a golden hood that allows its wearer to assume any desired form, has turned himself into a ferocious dragon. Fafner sleepily guards the entrance to a cave where he has stashed the Nibelungen gold and Alberich's ring. Siegfried doesn't know what to do with the ring when he finds it but, intrigued, he keeps it.

In the next encounter Siegfried comes upon a sullen man in a gray cloak carrying a spear who calls himself the Wanderer. This is Wotan, now a weakened remnant of the god he was. Wotan tries to convince Siegfried to take the ring to the river, but the brash young man thrusts his sword and smashes the old man's spear. Hardly answering, the Wanderer just turns away and leaves. And that's the last appearance of Wotan in the *Ring*.

Eventually, though, as prophesied, Siegfried fights his way through the flaming mountain and discovers Brünnhilde. At first he thinks her a sleeping warrior. But when he removes her breastplate armor, he is stunned and confused. He's never seen a woman before and the sight of her fills the headstrong boy with fear. Suddenly he senses that all the certainties of his young life will be shaken, that he will be compelled to relinquish control. When Brünnhilde awakens, her godliness is gone and within her stir feelings of vulnerability that she has never known. As a token of his love Siegfried gives Brünnhilde the fateful ring.

The problem with *Siegfried* is the title role, which is nearly impossible to sing. You need someone with astounding stamina, floods of power, and, ideally, a youthful bloom to his voice. Moreover, by the time Siegfried finds Brünnhilde (usually, if it's an evening performance, around 11:20 p.m.), the poor tenor has been singing all night and the soprano singing Brünnhilde is fresh as a daisy. The biggest obstacle most opera companies face in presenting the *Ring* is not the scope of the work itself, but the challenge of finding a suitable Siegfried.

In *Götterdämmerung,* usually translated as *The Twilight of the Gods,* Alberich's bastard son, Hagen, becomes the instrument of his father's retribution against Wotan's descendants. Hagen has insinuated himself into a landed family, the Gibichungs, headed by Gunther and his sister, Gutrune. Hagen, who is their half-brother, has drawn the siblings into a labyrinthine plot to entice Siegfried to the castle and then spike his drink with a drug that will cause him to lose all memory of Brünnhilde and fall in love with Gutrune. It works. They even convince Siegfried to abduct a young maid on a mountain whom they tell him about (Brünnhilde, of course) and deliver her to Gunther as a suitable bride.

Though the outlines of the plot may sound convoluted, the opera is a powerful metaphor about the way families and tribes and whole nations pass on to the next generation legacies of hatred and festering resentments. By the end Siegfried and Brünnhilde, restored to reason, realize, though too late, what it really means to relinquish power for the sake of love. The *Ring* concludes with Brünnhilde's overwhelming "Immolation Scene." She places Siegfried's corpse on a funeral pyre, then rides her horse into its center. The fire spreads wildly until Valhalla and the gods are engulfed in apocalyptic flames. But the river overflows its banks, puts out the fire, and carries the ring back to the Rhinemaidens. The world order is restored. For better or worse, man will now have to get along without the gods.

Wagnerites have passionate feelings about the many complete recordings of the *Ring* that have been released over the years, including several historic sets taken from live performances that some devotees consider unsurpassable, like the 1953 *Ring* from the Bayreuth Festival conducted by Clemens Krauss and the imperfect but riveting 1950 *Ring* from La Scala in Milan conducted by Wilhelm Furtwängler.

Soprano Birgit Nilsson as Brünnhilde

For me, the very first complete *Ring* cycle that was recorded in a studio, the landmark Decca set conducted by Georg Solti, remains the best overall choice. The project began in 1958 in Vienna and took seven years to complete. Nothing so ambitious in classical music recording had ever been undertaken. In later years Solti conducted

Wagner with less whipped-up energy than he tends to in these recordings, begun when he was in his late forties. Still, his embracing conception of the entire work, the alluring warmth of the Vienna Philharmonic, the sense of dramatic tension, and the shimmering beauty he brings to these scores have seldom been matched.

The recording offers, for its time, for all times really, a dream cast. Ideally a *Ring* should have one Wotan. This recording has two but both are eminently distinguished: George London is a noble and virile Wotan in *Das Rheingold;* the great Hans Hotter is a commanding and pitiable Wotan in *Die Walküre* and *Siegfried.* The powerhouse dramatic soprano Birgit Nilsson, at her vocal and artistic peak, sings Brünnhilde. Gustav Neidlinger is a menacingly nasal Alberich. James King brings his heroic tenor to the role of Siegmund. Sieglinde, the soprano Régine Crespin, sings with melting richness and affecting vulnerability. Though Wolfgang Windgassen was approaching the end of his career when he recorded Siegfried in the final two operas, he summons power and charisma and conveys the character's impetuous youth. And in a lovely gesture, Decca asked Kirsten Flagstad, the great Brünnhilde of her day, to come out of what was essentially retirement in 1958 to sing the role of Fricka in *Das Rheingold* for this historic project. Christa Ludwig took over in *Die Walküre.* Decca's latest remastering of this historic *Ring* enhanced the presence and depth of the recorded sound.

The other complete performance to consider is Herbert von Karajan's set recorded for Deutsche Grammophon in the late 1960s. Whether by choice or necessity, Karajan employs two Wotans, two Brünnhildes, and two Siegfrieds. Following his penchant for inviting singers with less weighty voices to record dramatic roles in German and Italian opera, Karajan recruited the baritone Dietrich Fischer-Dieskau to sing Wotan in *Das Rheingold.* Fischer-Dieskau's baritone voice may strike some as rather light for the job, but he gives an insightful, literate, and vocally refined account. Thomas Stewart, an imposing and excellent Wotan, takes over in *Die Walküre.* Régine Crespin is the dusky-toned and elegant Brünnhilde in *Die Walküre,* and the earthy-voiced and authoritative Helga Dernesch takes over in *Siegfried* and *Götterdämmerung.* Jess Thomas brings his vocal prowess and energy to the title role of *Siegfried,* and Helge Brilioth brings a darker sound and more poignancy to the role in *Götterdämmerung*. Gundula Janowitz convinces you that Sieglinde is a role for a radiant lyric soprano. And Jon Vickers's intense, anguished, and galvanic portrayal of Siegmund may be the best on record. Karajan elicits a spacious, luminous, yet organically exciting performance from the mighty Berlin Philharmonic.

Either of these recordings should hook you on the *Ring*. Once hooked, you enter into Wagner time and these riveting operas seem not a bit longer than they need to be.

Decca (fourteen CDs) 455 555-2
(The four operas are also available individually)
Georg Solti (conductor), Vienna Philharmonic; Nilsson, Windgassen, London, Hotter, Neidlinger, Crespin, King, Flagstad, Ludwig

Deutsche Grammophon (fourteen CDs) 415 141-2 (*Das Rheingold*), 415 145-2 (*Die Walküre*), 415 150-2 (*Siegfried*), 415 155-2 (*Götterdämmerung*)
Herbert von Karajan (conductor), Berlin Philharmonic; Fischer-Dieskau, Stewart, Kelemen, Crespin, Dernesch, Vickers, Janowitz, Thomas, Brilioth

95. RICHARD WAGNER (1813–1883)

Tristan und Isolde

Richard Wagner, librettist

First performance: Munich, Nationaltheater, June 10, 1865

In 1984, the day after attending a deeply affecting performance of *Tristan und Isolde* at the Metropolitan Opera, I visited with the composer and critic Virgil Thomson, whom I knew well. "How was the show?" Thomson asked me. "Amazing," I said. "What an opera!"

"Yes, yes, indeed," Thomson replied. "And it's indestructible, you know. You can conduct it any way whatever. Fast or slow. You can push it or pull it. And it always lasts exactly the same amount of time."

Though Thomson was being wry, of course, he was on to something about the opera's immensity. *Tristan und Isolde* is one of a handful of genuinely landmark works in the history of music. Its greatness comes through even in less-than-great performances.

Seizing on the ancient legend of Tristan as a subject, Wagner saw in the story an ideal vehicle to explore romantic love as an overwhelming emotional state that transports us to a metaphysical realm beyond reality. The symbolism of Wagner's libretto is undeniably heavy-handed: the association of uncontrollable love with loss of will and death; the equation of intrusive reality with the light and the day, and of self-abnegating love with the dark and the night. Still, the mesmerizing power and beauty of Wagner's music transforms the opera's metaphysical mumbo-jumbo into viscerally involving drama. Though Wagner strove to create operas in which words and music were equals, in *Tristan* music dominates, sweeping the story along as it exposes the legend's psychological subtext. Wagner's harmonic language in this breakthrough work is so boldly chromatic, so unhinged from tonal moorings, that dissonance is emancipated. *Tristan* anticipates the radical atonality of Schoenberg.

In Wagner's version of the legend, set in the Middle Ages, Tristan is a knight, a faithful follower of his uncle, King Marke of Cornwall. The opera opens on board a ship. Tristan is transporting Isolde, a young Irish princess, to Cornwall where she is to become the wife of King Marke. Isolde is furious with Tristan and in the volatile scene called "Isolde's Narrative" we learn why. Not long ago Tristan, who had come to Ireland from Cornwall to collect taxes, killed Isolde's betrothed, Morold, in combat. Badly wounded himself, Tristan was nursed back to health by Isolde, a practitioner of herbal healing, who did not realize who he was. Once she did, she swore to take his life. But something in the young man's eyes softened her.

And now, abjectly obedient to his king, Tristan is bringing Isolde "like a chattel," she says, to be Marke's joyless bride. Yet, it's clear from her forlorn and agitated narrative that her hatred masks lingering yearnings. She asks Brangäne, her nurse, and an expert in magic and herbs, to prepare a death potion. When she and Tristan drink together, they will die together, she swears. But Brangäne, desperate for a way to stop her lady's rash plan, substitutes a love potion. In Wagner's version of the legend the love potion is clearly a kind of truth serum that unleashes hidden feelings, in this case dangerous and powerful feelings of ecstatic love.

The great love duet in act 2, when Isolde, now living with King Marke, meets illicitly at night with Tristan, begins with the mellifluously lyrical "O sink hernieder, Nacht der Liebe," the most gently undulant and harmonically grounded music in the entire opera—a rare moment of quiet bliss. But slowly the tonal center of the music grows unsteady and the duet builds in intensity phrase by phrase to an orgasmic climax that is stopped bluntly when Marke, crushed by the betrayal, arrives. This moment could be described as an operatic rendering of coitus interruptus.

To conduct this sprawling, three-act work with continuous ebb and flow while also indicating its shape and structure is a challenge met magnificently by Wilhelm Furtwängler in his classic 1952 recording for EMI, available in the Great Recordings of the Century series. Kirsten Flagstad sings Isolde. At the time of this recording Flagstad was a month shy of fifty-seven and had retired the role of Isolde from her repertory a year earlier. There are signs of wear in her singing: some unsteadiness in her top notes, a lack of bloom in the sound. Still, this recording captures the warmth and melancholic radiance of her voice. Every phrase matters. There is a world-weary gravity in Flagstad's young Irish princess that makes this intuitive portrayal unforgettable.

Tristan is the German tenor Ludwig Suthaus, forty-five at the time and in top form. Though he sings with plenty of heldentenor heft and ardency, the baritonal darkness in Suthaus's voice complements Flagstad's maturity. Blanche Thebom is an affecting Brangäne. Young Dietrich Fischer-Dieskau makes a robust and open-hearted Kurwenal.

And then there is Furtwängler, who seems more a channel for Wagner than a mere conductor. Furtwängler had a notoriously indistinct baton technique, complete with his so-called "curved" downbeat cues. But by sheer determination he communicated his powerful insights. And if he was hard to follow, this just kept musicians on alert. He draws luminous, spacious, yet inexorable playing from the Philharmonia Orchestra. And for 1952 the recording quality is exceptional.

Another choice, also distinguished, is the 1966 recording from the Bayreuth Festival with Karl Böhm conducting, Birgit Nilsson as Isolde, and Wolfgang Windgassen as Tristan. Nilsson brings her cool Nordic sound, powerful voice, and incisive delivery to this landmark portrayal, and Windgassen sings with heroic fervor and honesty. Christa Ludwig as Brangäne and Eberhard Wächter as Kurwenal are also excellent. Böhm leads a shimmering and organic account of the score.

Herbert von Karajan's 1972 recording with the Berlin Philharmonic is also superb and features the great Helga Dernesch as Isolde and a more mature Christa Ludwig as Brangäne. Best of all, Jon Vickers sings Tristan, a clarion, powerful, impetuous, and involving portrayal.

There are about four hours and fifteen minutes of music in *Tristan und Isolde*. As Thomson suggested, the opera may always last the same amount of time. But time stops when you listen to this staggering masterpiece.

EMI Classics (four CDs) 5 67626 2
Wilhelm Furtwängler (conductor), Chorus of the Royal Opera House, Covent Garden, Philharmonia Orchestra; Flagstad, Suthaus, Thebom, Fischer-Dieskau

Deutsche Grammophon (four CDs) 419 889-2
Karl Böhm (conductor), Chorus and Orchestra of the Bayreuth Festival 1966; Nilsson, Windgassen, Ludwig, Talvela, Wächter

EMI Classics (four CDs) 7 69319 2
Herbert von Karajan (conductor), Chorus of the Berlin Opera, Berlin Philharmonic; Dernesch, Vickers, Ludwig, Berry, Ridderbusch

96. RICHARD WAGNER (1813–1883)

Die Meistersinger von Nürnberg

Richard Wagner, librettist

First performance: Munich, Nationaltheater, June 22, 1868

Die Meistersinger von Nürnberg may be the most humane, tender, and generous of operas. It's about a modest medieval community that values music and poetry above all else. The mastersingers of the title are simple craftsmen: a goldsmith, a furrier, a baker, a soap maker, a tinsmith, a stocking weaver, and so on. Each contributes something essential to the town. But they have also all gained admission into the select guild of mastersingers. They have studied the traditions and learned how to fashion their own verses and melodies into songs that impress and inspire their townsfolk. And the most revered mastersinger of all is the self-effacing cobbler and childless widower Hans Sachs.

It's sometimes said that there are only two stories in all of fiction. The first is: boy meets girl, boy loses girl, or some variation thereof. The second is: a stranger comes to town. *Die Meistersinger* offers a wondrous melding of the two. The stranger who comes to town is Walther von Stolzing, a knight from Franconia, a young man in search of something though he's not sure what. He has noticed a girl from the town, Eva, the winsome daughter of Veit Pogner, a goldsmith and a mastersinger. When Walther sees her praying in church one day he decides to speak. But Pogner has promised Eva, his only child, as a bride to the winner of the town's imminent song contest. The girl will not be forced to marry against her will. But if she refuses the winner she will not be allowed to marry at all.

It's Walther's desire to win Eva, more than his love of song, that first entices him to enter the contest. But he soon gets hooked by the songwriting art. He is an aristocrat, of course, whom the mastersingers view with suspicion. Moreover, they are baffled and, finally, affronted by his free-wheeling approach to songwriting. Walther's harshest critic is Sixtus Beckmesser, the middle-aged town clerk, a fastidious upholder of the rules of songwriting, who has his eye on the prize and on Eva. By the end of the opera Beckmesser gets his comeuppance for scheming and cheating in an attempt to win the contest and claim Eva, who finds him obsequious and awful. Still, *Die Meistersinger* is a warmly comic yet profound parable about the dynamic tension that has always existed between revered tradition and pathbreaking genius.

With *Tristan und Isolde* and about two-thirds of the *Ring* behind him, Wagner was at the absolute summit of his creative powers when he composed *Die Meistersinger*. Yet, in many ways the opera looks back to music's past, with its evocations of songs, dances, marches, hymns, set-piece arias, and full-choral ensembles. Wagner even pokes some innocent fun at sturdy sixteenth-century counterpoint, which he evokes throughout the score. Yet the looking-back comes from a keen nostalgia that Wagner, touched by the story, allowed himself to express.

Whole stretches of the vocal writing set the libretto's chatty dialogue to music that comes close to conversational recitative. But the orchestra, serving as an astute and sympathetic commentator on the stage action, ennobles the characters, softening their occasional bouts of jealousy and pettiness. Wagner never composed more miraculous music. Writing about the work, his favorite Wagner opera, in a 1945 review for the *Herald Tribune,* Virgil Thomson wryly commented: Wagner "without his erotico-metaphysical paraphernalia is a better composer than with it. He pays more attention to holding interest by musical means, wastes less time predicting doom, describing weather, soul states, and ecstatic experiences."

Yet, *Die Meistersinger* has never shaken off charges from many critics that the story is anti-Semitic. When he wrote it Wagner was swept up in the conservative federalist tenets of Constantin Franz, who believed that Bavaria should remain neutral in the war between Prussia and Austria, that Bavarian culture was a precious thing in danger of being sullied by foreign (meaning Jewish) elements. *Die Meistersinger* ends with an uncharacteristically stern homily from the good Hans Sachs, warning that Germany is threatened by false foreign rulers, but that the German spirit will endure so long as German art is protected. You can imagine Hitler weeping at performances of *Die Meistersinger.*

Yet, for me Wagner's humanity trumps his convoluted politics. You cannot attend a good performance of this opera without responding to Wagner's humane portrayals of these disarmingly real and affecting characters.

Though *Die Meistersinger* has fared well on recordings, among relatively modern versions, two stand out. Eugen Jochum conducted a stirring, articulate, and radiant performance on a 1976 recording with the chorus and orchestra of the Deutschen Oper Berlin and a dream cast headed by Dietrich Fischer-Dieskau as Hans Sachs. In the opera house Fischer-Dieskau may have lacked some of the vocal heft this role ideally wants. But he brings wisdom, insight, richness, and immediacy to a moving and vocally distinguished portrayal. Catarina Ligendza is a sweet-voiced and plucky Eva. Plácido Domingo, in an early venture into Wagner, sings Walther, and his distinctively Latinate sound only enhances the sense of the knight as an outsider who confounds yet intrigues the people of Nürnberg.

The other choice, recorded live in 1995 at Orchestra Hall in Chicago, offers Sir Georg Solti conducting the Chicago Symphony Orchestra and Chorus in a special concert performance. The cast is superb, with José van Dam, one of the great artists of our time, as Sachs, the luminous soprano Karita Mattila as Eva, the ardent Wagnerian tenor Ben Heppner as Walther, and the young René Pape as Pogner. But the reason to own this recording is Solti's conducting, in which a dynamism evocative of his earlier Wagner performances is leavened by a mellowness that could only have come with age. And the Chicago Symphony plays gloriously.

Deutsche Grammophon (four CDs) 415 278-2
Eugen Jochum (conductor), Chorus and Orchestra of the Deutschen Oper Berlin; Fischer-Dieskau, Domingo, Ligendza, Lagger, Hermann

Decca (four CDs) 470 800-2
Georg Solti (conductor), Chicago Symphony Orchestra and Chorus; van Dam, Heppner, Mattila, Pape, Opie

97. RICHARD WAGNER (1813–1883)

Parsifal

Richard Wagner, librettist

First performance: Bayreuth, Festspielhaus, July 26, 1882

In the summer of 1845 Richard Wagner, just turned thirty-two, read the story of Parsifal as told by the medieval German poet and songster Wolfram von Eschenbach. This version centers on an obtuse young man who becomes the leader of a band of knights who guard a magical relic. Other accounts of the Parsifal story make clear that the relic was the Holy Grail, the chalice from which Christ officiated at the Last Supper. Eschenbach's account lacks this specifically Christian content. It's just an adventure tale of quests, battles, and rituals of brotherhood.

Thirty-five years would pass before Wagner fashioned his version of the story into *Parsifal,* his enigmatic and complex final opera. Virtually every aspect of the opera has been a source of contention. It has been revered as a sublime sacred work and denounced as a sacrilegious travesty. *Parsifal* is still presented by opera houses around the world as a solemn secular acknowledgment of the Easter season. Yet many music historians argue that the opera's themes of gaining enlightenment through compassion and renunciation more closely stem from Wagner's sympathies for Buddhism and the philosophy of Schopenhauer. Some decry the work for espousing what they interpret as veiled notions of racial purity. Yet Nietzsche, who had venerated Wagner as the ultimate Übermensch, or Superman, considered *Parsifal* a traitorous creation. Wagner, he wrote in sneering essays, had "suddenly sunk down, helpless and broken before the Christian Cross."

To me the most affecting theme of this transfixing opera is neither enigmatic nor particularly complex. It's a universal theme about the often hapless ways that wisdom gets passed down from generation to generation, from sage to seeker. There are countless variations on this

Composer Richard Wagner

story. Think of Mozart's Tamino, a confused young seeker who learns truth from Sarastro, a wise man who, nevertheless, has made a hash out of his personal life. Think of the *Star Wars* movies. Headstrong young Luke Skywalker embarks on an ill-defined quest to obtain the Force, essentially wisdom, which he learns from the most unlikely sages: a wizened Jedi knight whose teachings are exasperatingly veiled; a befuddled-seeming Jedi dwarf; and, in the ultimate twist, the evil Darth Vader, who turns out to be Luke's fallen father.

In *Parsifal* the sage is Amfortas, the leader of the Knights of the Grail in what appears to be a remote region of northern Spain in medieval, or perhaps mythic, times. Amfortas is a man so shattered by his own sins of the flesh and spiritual shortcomings that he feels unworthy of enlightening anybody. Carried on a sickbed by his dispirited knights, Amfortas suffers from a wound in his side that will not heal. Yet his suffering seems to come more from guilt and despair. It's not through Amfortas's words that Parsifal, a young, clueless, and isolated wanderer, learns wisdom. Indeed, the old man never speaks to him directly. It's the good-hearted veteran knight Gurnemanz who tries to pound some sense into the "stupid boy," as he calls him, though he wonders whether Parsifal could perhaps be the innocent fool who, it has been prophesied, will learn compassion and bring healing to the brotherhood of knights.

To lend resonance to the legend and narrative complexity to the opera, Wagner introduces a pivotal new character: Kundry, an ageless, wild-eyed, tormented woman. Perpetually at war with herself, Kundry lives on the outskirts of the castle of the grail knights. She serves them with abject humility, and carries messages to crusaders in distant and dangerous places, always returning with healing balms for Amfortas's wound, balms that never work. Though Kundry longs for spiritual grace and release from her anguish through death, she has also yielded to sensual temptations as another means to escape herself. Kundry regularly disappears into the realm of the sorcerer Klingsor, who knows how to kindle her seductive passions. Klingsor forces Kundry to lure the knights into his den.

All this may sound terribly metaphysical. But Wagner lures the listener into his den with this astounding score, music of diaphanous beauty, transcendent spirituality, and, especially in the second act at Klingsor's castle, volatile intensity. Here Wagner's harmonically unhinged musical language points the way to the radical developments of the early twentieth century, especially the breakdown of tonality.

From its spacious, time-stands-still prelude to its sublime final chords, the score moves at a daringly slow, though subtly inexorable, pace. If many operas seem overly long, *Parsifal,* typically a six-hour evening with two generous intermissions, seems psychologically the length it must be. From its first stirrings you can sense Wagner saying: "Forget the outside world, you are on my watch now and we are living according to Wagnerian time."

Parsifal has fared well on recordings. Though Wagner buffs have strongly partisan feelings about the various accounts, there is general consensus over the live performance conducted by Hans Knapperts-busch at the 1962 Bayreuth Festival. *Parsifal* is the only opera Wagner wrote with the specific qualities of Bayreuth, the theater he designed himself, in mind. Wagner called the work a "sacred stage festival play," and referred to its 1882 premiere as a "consecration" of the house. Knappertsbusch's palpable belief in this score comes through in every tremulous, reverent, and wistfully beautiful moment of his calmly paced performance. The cast is superb, with the robust tenor Jess Thomas as Parsifal, the resonant bass-baritone George London as Amfortas, the magisterial bass-baritone Hans Hotter as Gurnemanz, and the sensual mezzo-soprano Irene Dalis as Kundry.

Some Knappertsbusch admirers prefer his live 1951 recording from the Bayreuth Festival with Wolfgang Windgassen as Parsifal, George London again as Amfortas, Martha Mödl as Kundry, and the voluminous bass Ludwig Weber as Gurnemanz, who gives a sturdy and poignant portrayal. The sound quality, while perfectly adequate, does not match that of the 1962 account.

Another favorite of mine is the 1980 recording with Herbert von Karajan conducting the Berlin Philharmonic and an admirable cast. The tenor Peter Hofmann suffered premature vocal burnout in his promising career, but as Parsifal he is captured here at his youthful best. José van Dam is a moving Amfortas, and the powerhouse bass Kurt Moll is an impassioned Gurnemanz. Karajan elicits an authoritative and radiant performance from the great Berlin Philharmonic and the clearly inspired cast.

James Levine also brings insights and alluring colors to his impressive recording with the forces of the Metropolitan Opera and Plácido Domingo in the title role. If I could own only one, I'd pick the classic 1962 Knappertsbusch recording. But like the seeker Parsifal, you will gain enlightenment from any of these splendid recordings.

Philips (four CDs) 289 464 756-2

Hans Knappertsbusch (conductor), Chorus and Orchestra of the Bayreuth Festival (1962); Thomas, London, Hotter, Dalis

Teldec (four CDs) CD 9031-76047-2

Hans Knappertsbusch (conductor), Chorus and Orchestra of the Bayreuth Festival (1951); Windgassen, London, Weber, Mödl

Deutsche Grammophon (four CDs) 413 347-2

Herbert von Karajan (conductor), Berlin Philharmonic and the Chorus of the Deutschen Oper Berlin; Hofmann, van Dam, Moll, Vejzovic

Deutsche Grammophon (four CDs) 437 501-2

James Levine (conductor), Metropolitan Opera Orchestra and Chorus; Domingo, Moll, Morris, Norman

98. KURT WEILL (1900–1950)

Aufstieg und Fall der Stadt Mahagonny (*Rise and Fall of the City of Mahagonny*)

Bertolt Brecht, librettist

First performance: Leipzig, Neues Theater, March 9, 1930

The classic 1956 recording of Kurt Weill and Bertolt Brecht's *Rise and Fall of the City of Mahagonny* makes an enthralling case for this daring 1930 work. But not as an opera. The pungent playing of the North German Radio Orchestra hooks you, though it sounds like the reduced ranks have been infiltrated with jazzy banjos and saxophones and some of the strings have been sent packing. Here Weill's score seems to evoke the music hall, the cabaret club, and only intermittently the opera house. Some voices among the cast have operatic heft, but the main character, Jenny Hill, one of the girls at the Mahagonny tavern and flophouse run by the widow Begbick, is sung by the incomparable Lotte Lenya, who first sang the role in Berlin in 1931. Lenya's raspy voice is earthy and insinuating, but not remotely operatic.

So when the Metropolitan Opera presented John Dexter's starkly powerful production of the work in the 1979–1980 season, I found the whole experience an epiphany. Suddenly *Mahagonny* seemed not just an opera but a towering operatic masterpiece. Without beefing up the instrumentation the conductor James Levine drew resonantly orchestral sonorities from the Met orchestra. From the fervor of the singing of the Met chorus you would have thought its members were swept up in a performance of the Verdi Requiem. Made up to give her hollow cheeks and an emotionally spent face, the petite soprano Teresa Stratas was a riveting and gritty Jenny. Yet, her voice somehow also had the vocal culture of a major opera singer. And the heroic tenor Richard Cassilly, an acclaimed Tristan and Otello, gave what may have been the performance of his career as the gullible Jim Mahoney, who has arrived after seven cold, hard, and dispiriting years cutting timber in Alaska with some money to spend.

Actually, Brecht was not pleased with the operatic trappings *Mahagonny* took on once Weill's music was joined to the text. At the time Brecht was immersed in Marxist thought and general theories about the social utility of art. He wanted *Mahagonny* to shock and offend audiences, which it certainly did at its riot-provoking Leipzig premiere. The story is a bleak satire about a pleasure city, the "city of nets," founded by rapacious schemers and lowlifes who, fleeing bankruptcy and the forces of the law, realize that "you get gold more easily from men than from rivers." So they found a city with promises of abundant gin and whisky, girls for the asking, and seven days a week of leisure pursuits. The work was overwhelmingly viewed at the time as a biting Leftist critique of capitalist America, and the text encourages this take with its playful evocation of exotic locales like Alaska, Pensacola, and, in the score's best-known song, "O Moon of Alabama." But Brecht insisted that Mahagonny was meant to be "in every sense international."

Brecht grew to be extremely suspicious of the power of music to soften the soul, to smooth the rough edges of any sharp polemical point with aural pleasure. If anything, Weill was moving in the opposite direction at the time. Though in his earlier collaborations with Brecht on songs and stage works his music was spiked with astringent dissonance and raw colorings, in *Mahagonny* he tries to compose an intricately detailed score with an overarching musical structure. Brecht was soon debunking the work in his political writings.

I'd argue that Weill was ahead of his time. As other dogmatic works from that era grow more dated by the decade, *Mahagonny* seems increasingly timeless. Weill's music lends Brecht's text an affecting ambivalence. For example, in the scene when Jenny asks Jake Schmidt, Jimmy's friend, how much money he has to spend on a girl, and Jake answers thirty dollars, Jenny sings a cool, wry, yet tough little song accompanied by reedy winds and quietly palpitating strings. "Think it over," she says, "what can you buy for thirty dollars! Ten pairs of stockings and nothing more." Weill's music brings a poignancy to the exchange that must have driven Brecht crazy. But it makes the characters real and the polemical point easier to take.

In the final scene, Jimmy is marched to the scaffold. His crime? Murder? Theft? Assault? No. He has no money to pay his bills, a capital offense in the city of Mahagonny. Citizens join in a procession with placards reading: "For the unjust distribution of worldly goods!" "For the just distribution of other-worldly goods!" And so on. The whole scene might have been little more than silly agitprop had Weill not humanized the characters with bleakly powerful and harmonically subtle music.

So, *Mahagonny* is an opera. But I still recommend the 1956 recording with Lenya and a superb cast including Heinz Sauerbaum as Jimmy and Fritz Göllnitz as Jake, with Wilhelm Brückner-Rüggeberg conducting, especially since it was reissued in 2003 on a two-disc Sony Classical set. One problem, though: this budget-priced recording does not include a libretto. You might want to pick up the English translation by W. H. Auden and Chester Kallman, a brilliant performing edition. They translate "Netzestadt" (German for "City of Nets") as "Suckerville." An ingenious solution.

Sony Classical (two CDs) SM2K 91184
Wilhelm Brückner-Rüggeberg (conductor), North German Radio Chorus and Orchestra; Lenya, Sauerbaum, Litz, Mund, Göllnitz

99. JUDITH WEIR (b. 1954)

A Night at the Chinese Opera

Judith Weir, librettist, based on a drama by Chi Chun-hsiang

First performance: Cheltenham, Everyman Theatre, July 8, 1987

In recent decades, most composers writing operas, successful on not, have thought big and chosen ambitious, realistic, and well-known subjects adapted from major novels (*The Great Gatsby*), iconic plays (*A Streetcar Named Desire*), memoirs turned into popular films (*Dead Man Walking*), or current events (*Harvey Milk*). Other composers, finding this traditional approach to opera too stale, too grandiose, have tried to come up with unconventional approaches and aim for something brash, impish, and distinctly contemporary.

Such was the goal of the Scottish composer Judith Weir in her first full-length stage work, *A Night at the Chinese Opera*, commissioned by the Kent Opera and given its premiere in 1987 at the Cheltenham Festival. The work was deemed a vibrantly theatrical triumph; Weir was hailed by many as the most provocative voice in British opera since Britten.

By the time she had settled on her subject Weir was so involved in the material that she wrote her own libretto. Her literary skills proved as deft as her musical voice was original.

At first she thought of simply setting a late-thirteenth-century Chinese play, *The Chao Family Orphan* by Chi Chun-hsiang, which tells of a loyal subject of the emperor who is falsely accused of treason by an evil general. The man commits suicide. But his child winds up being adopted by the false accuser, unbeknownst to adopter and adoptee. When the child grows up he learns the truth and exacts revenge.

Weir had the clever idea of using an operatic setting of *The Chao Family Orphan* as a play within a play. The outer play, set in the thirteenth century, tells of a real man named Chao when China was under the domination of Mongolia and ruled by Kublai Khan. Chao, an engineer, is commissioned to tame a wild environment and build a canal. By chance he learns that his father had once begun work on the same project and left behind a map and draft of his plans. Among the slaves conscripted into constructing the canal is a troupe of three actors. Act 2 of *A Night at the Chinese Opera* is a performance of *The Chao Family Orphan* that the actors, playing multiple roles, present for the entertainment of their fellow laborers.

Watching the play, the real Chao is struck by its parallels with his life. Before the play ends, though, an earthquake hits, forcing the actors to stop and giving Chao time to ponder what he has seen. In act 3 he ascends a mountain and examines his father's drafts, which reveal the grim story of his father's death and the true identity of his adopted father. He plots to murder the military general, but is captured and executed. Then, the players present the conclusion of *The Chao Family Orphan*, a happy ending in which the general is vanquished and justice reinstated.

Though the story touches on themes of family secrets, identity, national heritage, economic inequity, and military oppression, Weir leaves these themes to resonate, or not, on their own. Instead she concentrates on giving her audience a wickedly fun time, though, as the critic Rodney Milnes writes in his program note to the NMC recording, Weir's humor is drenched in irony; it's the humor of "the raised eyebrow rather than the falling trousers." Like Rossini and Mozart before her, Milnes adds, Weir understands that the "only way to say something really serious is through comedy."

Yet, this description does not convey the pungency of Weir's music, the grit of her theatrical vision, the wondrous strangeness of her opera. To steep herself in the Chinese musical tradition Weir studied notations from the period and listened to recordings, though it was never her intention to evoke authentic Chinese music. The opera is scored for a reduced Western orchestra of flutes, violas, basses, percussion, and occasional reeds.

Still, the exercise of exploring Chinese musical culture jolted her already vibrant and eclectic musical voice. Listen to the opening orchestra flourish, which suggests a vaguely Chinese fanfare. But the chords, the harmonies, the actual notes are more riveting than the harmonic languages in most scores written today by brainy and uncompromising modernists. Also, with a confidence that was doubly impressive coming from a neophyte opera composer, Weir continually varies her style of text-setting. There is spoken dialogue, spoken dialogue accompanied by music, half-sung vocal lines, skittish vocal flights, and, now and then, a tellingly placed long lyrical utterance.

There is only one recording, from a live performance at the Glasgow Royal Concert Hall in 1999 (presented in conjunction with BBC Radio 3's *Sounding the Century* program). Fortunately it's a brilliant recording, featuring the Scottish Chamber Orchestra conducted by Andrew Parrott and a winning roster of actors and singers.

NMC Recordings (two CDs) NMC D060
Andrew Parrott (conductor), Scottish Chamber Orchestra; Gwion Thomas, Adey Grummet, Timothy Robinson, Michael Chance

100. HUGO WEISGALL (1912–1997)

Six Characters in Search of an Author

Denis Johnston, librettist, after the play by Pirandello

First performance: New York, City Opera, April 26, 1959

The New York City Opera boldly celebrated its fiftieth anniversary in 1993 by presenting the premieres of three works on three consecutive nights. And what was the hit of the series? Not the trendy work, Ezra Laderman's stylistically muddled *Marilyn*, about the last years of Marilyn Monroe's life. And not Lukas Foss's charming but slight children's opera, *Griffelkin*.

It was Hugo Weisgall's biblical opera *Esther*, a craggy, dense, and bracing score, saturated with dissonance, uncompromising and completely riveting. The audience sat rapt, then cheered Weisgall, eighty-one at the time, ecstatically.

That premiere was heartening. Opera companies, fearful that

audiences will resist challenging works, have too often played it safe by commissioning operas on popular subjects with accessible scores. Here, for once, audiences were excited by the work of a formidable composer. The opera's intellectual authenticity and theatrical impact just broke down any resistance. Inexplicably, *Esther* disappeared after this premiere and has not yet been revived, not even by the City Opera. There is no commercial recording. Though regarded within the profession as a major figure, Weisgall died at eighty-four in 1997, fearing for the future of his ten full-length operas.

So, it's good to have the New World recording of an earlier but equally gripping Weisgall opera, *Six Characters in Search of an Author,* based on the Luigi Pirandello play. Commissioned by the Alice M. Ditson Fund at Columbia University, the work was given its premiere by the New York City Opera in 1959 and was repeated successfully the following season. All too typically, it languished until 1990 when the Lyric Opera Center, a training company with the Lyric Opera of Chicago, revived it. The New World recording was taken from live performances of the Chicago production.

The son of a cantor, Weisgall was born in Bohemia in 1912 and immigrated as a child to the United States, where he received thorough conservatory training while also earning a Ph.D. from Johns Hopkins for a dissertation on primitivism in seventeenth-century German poetry. Not surprisingly, given this background, Weisgall chose substantive literary sources for his operas: Shakespeare, Racine, Strindberg, Mishima, Yeats. But to his credit he was never intimidated by the loftiness of his sources, as his rejiggered operatic adaptation of Pirandello's remarkable 1921 play makes clear.

The play shatters the boundaries between illusion and reality by boldly manipulating the play-within-a-play setup. A company of actors is rehearsing *Mixing It Up,* a new play that none of them likes by this pretentious modernist named Pirandello. As they work, six strangers walk onstage from out of nowhere: a father, a mother in mourning dress, a surly adult son, a volatile stepdaughter, and two silent sullen young children. They are, they say, characters from a play left unfinished by its author and are searching for someone to complete their story.

In creating an operatic version of the play Weisgall and his librettist, Denis Johnston, an Irish playwright, turned the actors into singers who were rehearsing an overly complex new opera, *The Temptation of Saint Anthony*, by a composer named Hugo Weisgall. The six strangers are characters from an incomplete opera.

Weisgall's brilliant and haunting music, though never strictly bound to twelve-tone techniques, is imbued with European expressionism. The harmonic language of pungent atonality and thick chromaticism is leavened when called for with wistful diatonic harmonies. While not conventionally melodic, Weisgall's melodic writing, closely allied with the text and the dramatic intention, can be ruminative, conversational, skittish, jagged, or elegiac. In act 1, for example, the stepdaughter sings a melancholic soliloquy about her life as an audition piece for the director. How can this ravishing aria not have achieved independent life as a recital piece?

The Lyric Opera Center performance, tautly paced and conducted by Lee Schaenen, boasts a gifted cast of younger singers who sound palpably involved with their characters. It's fun to hear as fledglings some artists who have gone on to notable careers, like the soprano Elisabeth Futral (The Coloratura), the tenor Bruce Fowler (The Tenore Buffo), the baritone Robert Orth (The Father), and the mezzo-soprano Nancy Maultsby (The Mother).

The success of some audacious and complex new operas in recent years—Poul Ruders's *The Handmaid's Tale*, Kaija Saariaho's *L'Amour de Loin*, Thomas Adès's *The Tempest*—gives me hope that a new generation of operagoers are ready for musical drama that doesn't ask them to turn off their brains. I hope Weisgall's operas will be among the new repertory. And, take it from this critic, when an opera company finally revives *Esther*, that will be a big story in the opera world.

New World Records (two CDs) 8-454-2
Lee Schaenen (conductor), Lyric Opera Center for American Artists, Members of the Lyric Opera of Chicago Orchestra; Orth, Byrne, Maultsby, Fowler, Futral

The Essential Twenty

For newcomers to opera who feel daunted by the prospect of choosing among a hundred recommended operas, I offer a whittled-down list of twenty works that will get some absolute staples into your hands but also give you a sense of the exciting diversity within the genre.

Beethoven: *Fidelio*

Bellini: *Norma*

Berg: *Wozzeck*

Bizet: *Carmen*

Britten: *Peter Grimes*

Donizetti: *Lucia di Lammermoor*

Gluck: *Orfeo ed Euridice*

Handel: *Giulio Cesare in Egitto*

Janáček: *Jenůfa*

Mozart: *Le Nozze di Figaro*

Mozart: *Don Giovanni*

Puccini: *La Bohème*

Puccini: *Tosca*

Rossini: *Il Barbiere di Siviglia*

Strauss: *Elektra*

Strauss: *Der Rosenkavalier*

Stravinsky: *The Rake's Progress*

Verdi: *Rigoletto*

Verdi: *Otello*

Wagner: *Tristan und Isolde*

Selected Bibliography: Find Out More about Opera

In discussing the historical backgrounds of the selected operas in this book I was aided by several reference works that I also recommend to readers as sources of additional information. *The New Grove Dictionary of Opera,* in four volumes (London: Macmillan Press Limited, 1992; edited by Stanley Sadie), is the gold standard in the field. The entries on the individual operas typically provide comprehensive and trustworthy discussions of each work, including a plot synopsis and musical/dramatic analysis. Particularly fine are the articles by William Ashbrook on the Donizetti operas, Barry Millington on the Wagner operas, David Murray on the Strauss operas, and Julian Rushton on the Mozart operas. For the background, evolution, and sources of many Russian operas Richard Taruskin's entries seem definitive. I also found quite perceptive the shorter articles by the critic Paul Griffiths on Bartók's *Bluebeard's Castle* and Ligeti's *Le Grand Macabre.* Roger Parker's lengthy article on the life and career of Verdi with an overview of his works is excellent.

In cases where there is some question as to the number of librettists who collaborated on a particular opera or the locale and date of the first performance I have deferred to the information in *Grove.*

Other books I found immensely helpful, which I also recommend for additional information, include:

Benjamin Britten: A Biography by Humphrey Carpenter (New York: Charles Scribner's Sons, 1992)—the best book on this British giant.

Mozart's Letters, Mozart's Life by Robert Spaethling (New York: W. W. Norton & Company, 2000)—a perceptive examination of the composer that deftly intertwines excerpts from his letters with Spaethling's commentary.

Janáček's Operas: A Documentary Account by John Tyrrell (Princeton, N.J.: Princeton University Press, 1992)—another book that helpfully brings together letters, historical documents, and commentary.

The Complete Operas of Richard Strauss by Charles Osborne (New York: DaCapo Press, 1991)—a readable and informative overview of the Strauss operas, especially good on the evolution of the works.

The Callas Legacy: The Complete Guide to Her Recordings by John Ardoin (New York: Charles Scribner's Sons, 1991)—an exhaustive chronological discussion of the great soprano's discography by an acknowledged expert, who was also Callas's good friend.

Illustration Credits

Grateful acknowledgment is made to the following for permission to use copyrighted photographs:

Copyright © *The New York Times:* Luciano Pavarotti (photo by G. Paul Burnett), György Ligeti, Valery Gergiev (photo by Chris Lee), Carlo Bergonzi, Maria Callas, Renata Tebaldi
Metropolitan Opera: Joan Sutherland (photo by James Heffernan)
Estate of Louis Melançon: Jon Vickers, Leontyne Price, Birgit Nilsson
Copyright © Neil Libbert/Network Photographers: Peter Pears
Courtesy of Boosey & Hawkes: Benjamin Britten
Copyright © Marianne Barcellona: Plácido Domingo
Copyright © Art Shay/PhotoSource: Mirella Freni
© Robert M. Lightfoot III: Georg Solti
© Contrast: Wolfgang Amadeus Mozart
© Bettmann Archive: Giacomo Puccini, Giuseppe Verdi
Sony Records/Courtesy of Columbia Records: Igor Stravinsky
Courtesy of Jim Kallett: Richard Wagner

Index

Belasco, David, 168
Bellini, Vincenzo, xii, xvii, 9–15
Belsky, Vladimir Nikolayevich, 182
Beňačková, Gabriela, 61, 97
Bentley, Paul, 194, 195
Berg, Alban, 16–21, 47
Berganza, Teresa, 28, 187, 190
Berger, Erna, 243
Bergonzi, Carlo, 161, 162f, 170, 259
Berio, Luciano, 173
Berlin Opera, 18
Berlin Philharmonic, 52, 162, 283, 286, 293
Berlin RIAS Symphony Orchestra, 122
Berlioz, Hector, 22–25, 76
Bernanos, Georges, 144
Bernhardt, Sarah, 164, 205
Bernstein, Leonard, 28, 213–24
Berry, Walter, 5, 8, 133, 214, 220
Bertati, Giovanni, 126
Berton, Liliane, 146
Betrothal in a Monastery (Prokofiev),
    151–53
Billy Budd (Britten), 35–37
Bizet, Georges, 25–29
Björling, Jussi, 158, 163, 170, 174
Blackwell, Harolyn, 66
Blankenheim, Toni, 21
Blau, Edouard, 103
Bluebeard's Castle (Bartók), 3–5
Bohème, La (Puccini), xi, 67, 159–63, 173
Böhm, Karl, 18, 21, 122, 131, 220, 286
Boito, Arrigo, 249, 250, 260, 261, 264,
    265
Bolshoi Opera, 227
Bolshoi Theater, 155
Bonynge, Richard, 15, 55, 56, 58, 143, 174,
    191, 193, 243
Booth, Philip, 237
Boris Godunov (Mussorgsky), 134–37
Borodina, Olga, 136, 139, 155, 227, 230
"Borough, The" (Crabbe), 29
Boston Baroque, 76
Boston Symphony Orchestra, 210
Bostridge, Ian, 40, 119, 178, 224
Boulez, Pierre, 20, 52, 53, 198
Bourgeois gentilhomme, Le (Molière), 215
Brecht, Bertolt, 294, 295, 296
Bretzner, Christoph Friedrich, 120, 121
Bride of Lammermoor, The (Scott), 57
Brilioth, Helge, 282
Britten, Benjamin, xvii, 29–32, 32f, 33–37,
    38–42, 43–46, 148, 178
Brooklyn Academy of Music, 98
Brückner-Rüggeberg, Wilhelm, 296
Brunelle, Philip, 50
Büchner, Georg, 16–17, 19
Budapest Opera, 5
Budden, Julian, 156
Bumbry, Grace, 259, 272
Burden, William, 75
Burgtheater, 121
Busenello, Gian Francesco, 110, 111

Busoni, Ferruccio, xvii, 46–48
Bussoni, Giacomo Francesco, 80
Bychkov, Semyon, 227

Caballé, Montserrat, 175, 255
Callas, Maria, xii, xiv, 10–12, 13–15, 58,
    68–69, 166, 167f, 170–71, 187, 243,
    245–46, 252
Calzabigi, Ranieri de', 70, 71
Cammarano, Salvatore, 56, 244
Capecchi, Renato, 190
Capece, Carlo Sigismondo, 84
Čapek, Karel, 97
Cappuccilli, 15, 240, 250
Cariou, Len, 202, 204
Carmen (Bizet), xv, 25–29
Carnegie Hall, 18, 234
Carré, Michel, 76, 141
Carreras, José, 250
Caruso, Enrico, 245
Cassilly, Richard, 63, 295
Ceccato, Aldo, 248
Cellini, Renato, 243
Cenerentola, La (Cindrella) (Rossini),
    188–91
Cerha, Friedrich, 19, 20, 21
Cesari, Renato, 161
Chailly, Riccardo, 190
Chamber Orchestra of Europe, 128, 131
Chao Family Orphan, The (Chi Chun-
    hsiang), 297–98
Cheltenham Festival, 297
Cherniakov, Dmitri, 184
Chernomortsev, Viktor, 151
Chernov, Vladimir, 230
Chi Chun-hsiang, 297–98
Chicago Symphony Orchestra and Chorus,
    289
Chorley, Henry Fothergill, 12–13
Chorus of the Netherlands Opera, 198
Chance, Michael, 112
Christie, William, 85–86, 88
Clarey, Cynthia, 66
Clark, Graham, 103
Clark, Patricia, 193
Claycomb, Laura, 103
Cole, Vinson, 75
Colette, 179, 180
Collard, Jeanine, 181
Collier, Marie, 210
Columbia University, 29, 115, 236, 300
Comeaux, Elisabeth, 50
Concert d'Astrée, Le, 178
Contes d'Hoffmann, Les (The Tales of
    Hoffman) (Offenbach), 141–44
Copland, Aaron, 48–50
Corbelli, Alessandro, 190
Corelli, Franco, 12, 68, 77–78
Corena, Fernando, 128
Così fan tutte (Mozart), 115, 129–31
Cossa, Dominic, 56
Cossotto, Fiorenza, 170, 245, 252

About the Author

ANTHONY TOMMASINI is the chief classical music critic of *The New York Times,* the author of the award-winning *Virgil Thomson: Composer on the Aisle,* and a pianist. He graduated with a bachelor of arts degree from Yale University in 1970, and later earned a master of music degree from Yale School of Music, and a doctor of musical arts degree from Boston University. His teachers have included the pianists Donald Currier and Leonard Shure. As a pianist, he recorded two Northeastern Records compact discs of Thomson's music, titled *Portraits and Self-Portraits* and *Mostly About Love: Songs and Vocal Works.* As a journalist he has also written about theater, dance, jazz, rap, books, and AIDS. He lives in Manhattan.